How We Are

How to Live
1. How We Are

VINCENT DEARY

ALLEN LANE
an imprint of
PENGUIN BOOKS

ALLEN LANE

Published by the Penguin Group
Penguin Books Ltd, 80 Strand, London WC2R ORL, England
Penguin Group (USA) Inc., 375 Hudson Street, New York, New York 10014, USA.
Penguin Group (Canada), 90 Eglinton Avenue East, Suite 700, Toronto, Ontario, Canada M4P 2Y3
(a division of Pearson Canada Inc.)
Penguin Ireland, 25 St Stephen's Green, Dublin 2, Ireland (a division of Penguin Books Ltd)
Penguin Group (Australia), 707 Collins Street, Melbourne, Victoria 3008, Australia
(a division of Pearson Australia Group Pty Ltd)
Penguin Books India Pvt Ltd, 11 Community Centre, Panchsheel Park, New Delhi – 110 017, India
Penguin Group (NZ), 67 Apollo Drive, Rosedale, Auckland 0632, New Zealand
(a division of Pearson New Zealand Ltd)
Penguin Books (South Africa) (Pty) Ltd, Block D, Rosebank Office Park,
181 Jan Smuts Avenue, Parktown North, Gauteng 2193, South Africa

Penguin Books Ltd, Registered Offices: 80 Strand, London WC2R ORL, England

www.penguin.com

First published 2014
001

Copyright © How to Live Ltd, 2014

The moral right of the author has been asserted

Grateful acknowledgement is given to the following for permission to reproduce images:
Freaks (1932), MGM / The Kobal Collection; *Ghostbusters* (1984), Columbia / The Kobal
Collection; *The Truman Show* (1998), Paramount / The Kobal Collection / Melinda Sue Gordon;
illustration by Eric Winter for *Jack and the Beanstalk*, copyright © Ladybird Books Ltd, 1965;
Portrait of James Macmillan by Calum Colvin, 1996, National Galleries of Scotland,
copyright © Calum Colvin, reproduced by kind permission of Calum Colvin.

Set in 12/14.75 pt Dante MT Std
Typeset by Jouve (UK), Milton Keynes
Printed in Great Britain by Clays Ltd, St Ives plc

ISBN: 978–0–241–00538–5

www.greenpenguin.co.uk

You keep saming when you ought to be changing.

Lee Hazlewood, 'These Boots Are Made for Walkin''

Contents

List of Figures

Introduction

We live in small worlds. At the beginning of most movies we are shown a status quo, more fully a *status quo ante bellum*, the state of things before the war. We are shown a routine and comfortable life, a small world, one that is soon to end. In screenwriting parlance, this normal, soon-to-be-over world is known as Act One, and the 'inciting incident' is the event that precipitates the move into Act Two, into the war of change and adjustment. And, usually, we prefer to maintain ourselves in the status quo, in comfort and predictable ease. It takes a lot to get us out of that – a compelling call, an overwhelming imperative. Or maybe we were pushed. But sometimes it happens. Things change. The movie-makers like to end Act One fairly quickly and get stuck into the spectacle of change and adjustment. That's where the drama is, that's what we pay to see.

In life, as in this book, the balance is different. Our Act Ones, our normal lives, tend to last for longer. We like it that way. We are creatures of habit and we live in worlds small enough for us to come to know their ways and to establish familiar ways within them. Unless we are uneasy, unless something disturbs us from within or without, we tend to work to keep things the way they are. That is the subject of this book's Act One – Saming – how we creatures of habit work to establish and maintain our ways of life.

These ways of life, these routines, are not just habits of thinking and doing the same things in the same way, although of course that is part of it. But our habits are not only established internally, in muscles and nerves. As birds feather nests, so we also embed our ways of life in the places where we do our living. We beat paths through our environments and we surround ourselves with others, our tribes, who act as mirrors to remind us who we are and what we do. These, then, are the elements of our small worlds: the habits, routines, people, places and things that we have become accustomed to and comfortable with. That's the terrain of Part One of this book, that's where the journey starts. If you wanted to be scientific, and we will be at points, but not dauntingly so, we could call this part *homeostasis*. But let's think in movies. As in a movie, Act One of this book shows us how this world is before anything happens, before the disturbance or unease of an inciting incident forces us to begin the difficult work of deliberation and adjustment.

Then, inevitably, something interrupts our routine lives, some 'News from Elsewhere'. The war begins. The end of our small worlds can take many forms: more likely the gaining or losing of a job or a relationship than the mass geo-political catastrophes of the movies, but end they will. And so with some ingrained physiological inertia and reluctance, we leave normal and begin the uphill struggle of change, Act Two, the second half of this book.

Act Two – Changing – always begins with the difficult first moves of adjustment, those clumsy early days and first nights of becoming accustomed to a new way of being. It really is hard at first, that's why we resist it. Beginnings, and ends, are terrible times. Now we are in the process of *allostasis*, of trying to re-achieve stability in the face of change, to reach a new set-point of comfort and familiarity, to get back to normal. Heightened arousal and attention are the hallmarks of these times of transition. They always accompany our attempts to adjust to the rhythm of the new, putting us under constant internal pressure to get back to normal, a new normal, as quickly as possible. During such difficult times it is often easier to fall back on the consolation of old habits, even though these will not get the job of change done. And it is here we glimpse the roots of much of our suffering. We are sometimes too keen to reach the end of the process of change, or not to begin it at all, or to avoid it whilst in it; we trot out our old responses when something new is called for, we keep saming when we ought to be changing. This is the ground we will cover in Act Two, following the arc of the drama

of change through to Act Three, the establishment of the new normal, the new small world.

It's a daunting prospect. There is a whole book ahead of me – of us.
For my journey, like a climber off to scale a mountain, or a general
off to battle, I prepared a detailed campaign. Even for this part I
made some notes. I knew early on that I wanted to draw attention
to the act of dedication that is necessary to initiate and sustain
something as fundamentally improbable as the writing of a book.
Only recently the notion came to me of swimming upstream,
against the tide of decay and degradation, the slow and subtle ebb-
ing away of order; the way that every day in every way you and I are
getting worse, losing ground, memory, teeth, and the battle just to
stay as we are, let alone get better. And this is all about getting better. I could even call it 'Getting Better'. That would do. People,
things, do get better. It's unlikely, against nature and in the teeth of
the second law of thermodynamics – the inevitability of disorder –
but just occasionally, things improve. I believe that.

As a therapist, I have seen it, worked with it, seen people move
upstream, struggle uphill. The physics of these metaphors is spot
on – to work against the prevailing forces of habit, inertia and gradual decay, you really need to put in some effort. And that's not easy,
not right at the start. The first steps are all effort and no reward.
Something else needs to keep you going until reward kicks in, until
the road begins to rise to meet you. A cussed mixture of faith in the
process, hope for change and a devotion to a purpose not dictated
by the prevailing conditions. In sum, dedication. It's hard at first.*

So why bother? What makes us change? Well, sometimes we
have to, and sometimes we just see that things could be better than
they are. We get a glimpse or have a vision of a future that is not just
a continuation of the present. And if that vision is compelling
enough, then desire kicks in, the yearning for things to be other
than they are. You're off to a good start there, with the vision and

---

* 'Dedication – because it's hard at first.' Can you hear the marketing campaign?

the desire. With them comes a quickening of energy, the beginnings of an urgency, the impulse to change. That's quite a trio now – vision, desire and urgency – quite a team. But even then you could let it lie. Let the impulse die, the desire fade, the perception dim. They will stop bothering you, eventually, if you ignore them. How much choice we have there is a subject that we can come to, but for the moment let's just say it feels like there are little moments when everything is in place and all we need to do is *act*. Do something about it. 'Well, if that's how you feel, why don't you do something about it?' You know those moments – we've all had them or seen them on television. A moment of decision. 'OK, I will.' And you do, you *will*. You manifest your will in an action, and things change. Maybe not much at first, but definitively. Things have changed. Something has passed from potential to actual; you've started something new, brought something into the world. It's magical and relatively rare. Beginnings are terrible times, and so are ends.

On my campaign map (see Figure 1), I can see the road stretch in front of me: a thrilling and daunting prospect. There are ten chapters to cross in this book alone, and then, dimmer, more distant, two more books ahead of that.* May I not falter. I am dedicating myself to this project on transformation in the hope that it might be a transformative project. I am dedicating myself to the perception that, however unlikely, however against nature, improvement happens, people get better. I mean better at living, at being who they are, at handling life with grace, humour and courage. Some people handle life admirably. And other people really don't. Some get stuck in hideous deforming places and postures and become ever more unbearable versions of themselves. This is not arbitrary – people become stuck or remain fluid and graceful because of the kind of beasts we humans are, and how we handle saming and changing.

* Don't worry, each one is self-contained; you don't have to sign up for the whole trip.

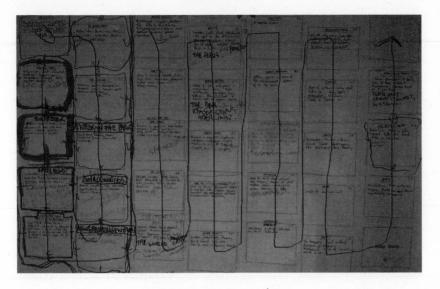

Figure 1. Campaign Map

Professionally and personally, I have had a ringside seat at the theatre of change and I'm beginning to get an idea how it's done – what it is that gets people stuck and unstuck. And we do know a lot about this; there are centuries of writing on the technologies of change, from the most ancient ethical and spiritual writings up to the most modern schools of therapy. Parallel to this run the descriptions of the human condition, from ancient souls, through early modern ids and egos to the brand new neural networks of neuro-science: descriptions of the beast the 'stuckness' and the change happens to. And I think I can bring all that together, seamlessly and clearly. That's the vision. I think I can synthesize that into a coherent version of what a human being is like, how it works and in working gets worse and better, gets stuck or manages to free itself. I think it might help, that's the desire. And I know I want to do this for me, to take stock, midway in my life's journey, to see what wisdom I have acquired, and to use it to direct my future course, before it's too late. That's the urgency. To recap the story so far and move on more deliberately; drift less, get better. I am dedicating myself to this book.

5

And I am dedicating this book to Lenny, Sara, Sarah and Ben and Jamie, James, Andrea, Marc, Charlotte, Ish, Lilian, Isobelle and Hughie, Elayne, Stevie and Ian, to Abhi and Vicky.

But first, before Act One begins, a brief prelude – 'The Beaten Path'. The making of ways is the central theme of this book: how our established paths define us, how we get stuck in them, how we struggle to make new ones. Throughout this book, we shall mostly keep the focus at the individual level, and will talk about people going through the kind of saming and changing that you and I do. In this opening prelude, we pan our camera out a little to see how the process of making ways underlies most of life.

Chapter 1

The Beaten Path

A kind of overture, in which themes from the whole book are touched on. In particular, we focus on the process of making *ways of life* through acts of repetition. This process is considered at the individual level, in such mundane acts as learning to drive, and on the grander scale in the formation of culture and the process of evolution. Finally, we consider how the process of making ways may be fundamental to our sense of self.

How is a road beaten down through the virgin snow? One person walks ahead, sweating, swearing, and barely moving his feet . . .
Five or six people follow shoulder to shoulder along the narrow, wavering track of the first man.

Varlam Shalamov*

Strange reciprocity:
The circumstance we cause
In time gives rise to us . . .

Philip Larkin†

I. Urban planners and landscape architects describe a phenomenon they call 'natural desire lines' or simply desire lines. The new park near my old house had a striking example. The park's planners had designed gracious curving paths, which walked the walkers around the borders of the newly planted lawns, through avenues of young shrubs and fledgling trees. The public were being instructed, guided on an improving and scenic detour. From the main road there was one path that led through the park to the entrance of a large supermarket. The park had, in fact, been built by the supermarket owners, placed between it and the road to mask this new and unsightly growth of commerce. This path was curved like a long archery bow, cutting a grey and gentle swathe

---

* Varlam Shalamov, *Kolyma Tales* (1980; Penguin Books, 1994).
† Philip Larkin, 'The Daily Things We Do', written February 1979, *Collected Poems* (Faber & Faber, 1988).

through the young and vibrant grass, taking the public on a stroll on their way to and from the store, encouraging them to stop and smell the roses. Which of course we didn't. Loaded with desire one way and bags the other, we chose expediency over prescribed detour. We voted with our feet. Gradually a line was worn through the grass, connecting the ends of the curve like the string of an archery bow. With use, this line gained definition, lost its green. Soon it was a solid beaten path, a taut and muscular line inscribed by desire and necessity. In fact you could say that this path was the record of a public decision and not only a record but a new suggestion, a new instruction, a new way of solving the problem of getting to and from the shops which was at odds with the official prescription.

II. So desire can inscribe itself on the landscape, make a big mark. No one planned it and no one sanctioned it, but still this mark upon the world happened. Massed desire expressed itself. There is, in a way, nothing remarkable about this process. All the paths that lead from here to there, all the places they connect, all are formations of desire. The political question would be whose desire – *cui bono?* – who stands to benefit from this particular formation? In the case of the park, the path is notable precisely because it's such an anarchic gesture, though at the same time it also speaks of a herd urgency to rush to the pasture of commerce. Sheep also make desire lines to their troughs. The official avenues and park walkways of our premeditated built world stand as a polar, political opposite to this crude herd formation. But consider this desire-line urban myth, a fable of urban planning best practice: an American college campus has been newly built. Its buildings are scattered over a wide area, so paths will have to be built between them. Rather than prescribe or attempt to predict the ways the public will want to go, the designers decide to record them first. They sow the campus with new lawns, without pathways and let the students loose. Over the next year, the pathways of natural desire and necessity are worn down. Only then are they paved, their anarchic spontaneity memorialized in stone. And maybe this is closer to how the world was made, a strange reciprocity between the forces of natural human desire and those in charge of controlling and containing its expression, giving it form. In the infancy of any culture there will have been first steps in which desire and necessity will have sketched its rudimentary form onto the landscape. This form in turn directs subsequent desire as a riverbed does water. The worn ruts become ever more substantial and compelling, and the movements of the collective more coherent as a result. Deliberate human agency – the decision actually to build the path, or rather to endorse the path of common use – need not enter the process until fairly late.

III. What is at work here is a dialectic of force and form. The raw force of human compulsions, the lacks and needs that make us move – hunger, anger, sex, comfort, curiosity – are translated into movements and actions. These movements and actions are not arbitrary – some are more effective at satisfying our needs than others. A random sample: certain trade routes are more profitable; the river is more easily accessed at a certain point for travelling or fishing; there is a 'best' route to a neighbouring village. So certain movements and action will be repeated more than others, and will in their repetition become established and routine. These routines, these rudimentary formations of desire, will begin to leave marks, expressing themselves as paths or even as stories about the best way to build them. These marks – these semi-permanent forms, these tangible manifestations of desire – are what we call culture.

IV. In *La Rabbia* (*The Rage*), and in his films in general, the Italian poet and film-maker Pier Paolo Pasolini was constantly trying to discover how the earth looked before it was overlaid with the markings of desire. This is like wanting to see the dawn's new snow beneath the over-trodden slush of lunchtime. This question runs through Pasolini's work: what would *we* look like were we not overrun by culture, by what he calls in *La Rabbia*, 'the old, bleeding roads of the earth'? He made a short film about his search for the locations for *The Gospel According to St Matthew*, the latter being a luminously simple telling of the gospel narrative. In it, we watch him and a priest visit the Church of Christ in Jerusalem. He is struck by how the magnificence of the temple stands in relation to the humble rock on which it was founded; how the grandiose architectonics of Christendom have been established upon a foundation of humility and simplicity. It is 1964 and Pasolini, a Marxist and an atheist, had been arrested for a film he made only a couple of years earlier, about a poor man, a film extra, dying on a cross on a film set depicting the Crucifixion. The Catholic Church had not liked this equating of the sub-proletariat with Christ, and had Pasolini charged with blasphemy. So he was wary. In his contemplation of this new cinematic life of Christ, he decided to consult a Vatican expert about his intentions before he began filming. His question for the Vatican was this: could he dismantle the edifice of Christendom and show the humble rock on which it was built? Or at least try? Can I do this, he asks the priest, as they stand by the temple, can I tear down the temple, can I show the luminous, simple, humble truth *before* it is overrun, over-built with all this grandiosity? Yes, says the priest, you can. You have the authority.

V. Like that other visionary poet, Rimbaud, Pasolini was suspicious of our thoughtless inheritance of the desire lines that we walk every day – these old, bleeding roads of the earth. The future is not conjured from nothing. The future is the past renovated, its paths thickened, embellished, reinscribed with a firm and then a firmer hand. The present is a kind of memorial of the past, both a living monument preserving its memory and a dead weight obscuring it. The present both preserves and effaces. Parents know this, as does anyone who has watched a growing thing. Each new version eclipses the one before: the child at five obscures the child at four, the adolescent effaces the toddler, but also preserves an essence we believe we see unfolding and maturing before us. The face more definite, the gestures more assured, the voice stronger. The present as the past once more with feeling.

VI. The pagan temple, then the church and now the hall for yoga and meditation: our spiritual communions have tended to take place in the same locations, on the same patches of hallowed earth. As with God, so with Mammon. The money tends to stay put. Witness how the mercantile areas of cities are ceaselessly renovated. The most recent advances in infrastructure and design are rushed to money like tributes to a monarch, with the advance of technologies fired by the desire to appease and facilitate the life of money. But while these parts of the civic body, these city areas, may be the most absolutely modern and shiny and new, they are also some of the oldest and most established. Indeed, it is the very age of their establishment that ensures their smooth running. The paths of money are well worn and constantly tended. 'Beneath the pavements, the beach!' ran the old French situationist slogan, reminding us, as Pasolini and Rimbaud did, that there was a *before* of all this building, all this enculturation, which we went through as a people and as individuals. Beneath the pavement is a well-established road; beneath that a track; beneath the track a path; and beneath that path a worn rut. Beneath the pavement a desire to move written in earth.

VII. Interesting to watch the new technologies at work. Consider the way a whole new network of paths has been established by the internet, and the way the old desires are re-emblazoned on this new land. Gossip and sex, money and violence, desire and desire for communion, all the old urges wearing down new electrical pathways.

VIII. It takes a lot to efface the traces of desire. Think of the gay districts of the major cities. These were once the cruising grounds of furtive criminals, the camouflaged haunts of outlaws. But they persisted for years at the same locations until, for now, the law assented to legitimize this particular desire and it became gradually visible. Now you can buy gay maps. How many lives would those maps have altered not so many years ago, when hardly anyone knew that such exotic lands existed? Think of all the coded, still-secret geographies, the subterranean, marginal or illegal currents that must traverse our lands. From drugs to free-masonry, from Elvis fans to swingers and doggers, every desire will have its map, leaving its marks for those who can read them, find them. It takes real destruction to efface the traces of desire. The Earth has habits too.

IX. I'm going to be learning to drive soon. I imagine the parts of my body that will become dedicated to driving as a field of virgin snow, a landscape as yet unmarked with desire. It will involve effort, willed and conscious effort at first. First steps always do. There are sequences of actions to be learned, routines combin-ing and coordinating gross and fine muscular movements with a whole new set of sensory and judgemental processes. I'll have to think a lot at first, to deliberate. My movements will be very con-scious and clunky, klutzy; as long as they are deliberate, they will be bad. Only when the inner paths have been trodden and re-trodden, again and again – pure repetition – only through this effort, willed and deliberate and conscious and muscular, sweat-ing and swearing and painful and clumsy repetition, only after this, only then will I become good, when it begins to get effort-less, thoughtless, unconscious, automatic. I can't wait.

X. 'A walk in the park' is a synonym for ease because the park knows how to walk. It does it for us. A good park anticipates our desire. Anticipated desire is the key to leisure. People have been paid and good money has been spent on figuring out what we are going to want to do. They care so that we don't have to. The good hotel, the theme park, the penny arcade, the pub, the cinema – all of them relieve our consciousness of the burden of worrying about what to do next. Think of those early difficult days with a new

thing – a computer or a mobile phone, a guitar or a car, or a relationship in which you now feel comfortable. Learning the right
moves, what they mean, how to, when to, what not to, where to,
repeating and rehearsing, experimenting and getting it wrong:
'Poise and grace and assurance were not qualities inbred in me, but
were things to be acquired, painfully perhaps, and slowly, costing
me many bitter moments.'* We want to rush past our bitter
moments, to a place of facility and ease, we want to be old at this
new thing, but rushing won't do it. Only time and repetition bring
ease. Then it's second nature, a walk in the park.

XI. *Second Nature*. A telling phrase – so what's *first*, what comes naturally? A lot. It seems the snow is not so virgin after all, a whole
host of routines are fitted as standard. The old and bleeding roads
of the earth are emblazoned upon you. The vast and folded architecture of your brain and nerves are waiting for the world and
have a strong presentiment of exactly how the world is going to
be – waiting for space, expecting time, ready for language, antici-
pating movement and other people, prepared for sex and violence,
fear and loathing. As the parks and cities are public records of
millennia of problem-solving, of desire facilitated to the point of
ease, so you are the repository of millions of years of very hard
thinking about this world. You know the world already as your
lungs know air and your kidneys water. Its weight and shape have
determined your height and form, its light has demanded your
eyes, its noises called for ears, its food and water shaped your
mouth, your teeth and guts, its earth and roots and branches formed
your grasping hands. You, the newest, shortest route between
desire and fulfilment, are more intricately traversed by patterns
and pathways than the entire world. Imagine the first attempts at
hunger, matter desperately maintaining its structure through
stealing other matter, the elemental stirrings, the prehistory of

* The nameless heroine of Daphne du Maurier's *Rebecca*, struggling to be at
home amongst the upper classes.

hunger. Clumsy, primitive molecular structures managing, just, to cannibalize the earth, to maintain and repeat themselves. Imagine hunger's first steps, desire's primal movements, life's beginning. Look how good it's got at it. Look how good we are at eating now, at maintaining and reproducing the integrity of a staggeringly complex structure, without even thinking about it. You just know. You were made for this world, by this world, of this world. You are the record, the embodiment of life's ceaseless desiring, written in tiny molecular hand, transcribed and translated into flesh, from dust and water. Knowledge of a billion years of living in this world is folded up inside you, *is* you. You are the latest model, the most recent experiment in living.

XII. The world runs in our blood. The hunger within us is a billion years old. There are glimpses of this ancient in us. We have little intuitions of it when we hear phrases like the 'reptilian brain', or when we read how we are only a vehicle for our genes that have been around for a billion years. Meaningful parts of us really are millions of years old. Science tries to point out what is only fact, but must also struggle to make us *feel* that weight of years that it took to reach a point when a couple of buckets of water and a bag of earth became this you, here now, so blithely reading, turning pages, this earth made flesh, this flesh alive with vision and reason, this reasonable meat conjured from dust. It took that amount of effort over that amount of time to reach the point where there is some clay that can 'see' and 'feel' and 'know' and 'think'. And that it does all this with such a lack of effort. This ease, the smoothness of the mechanism now, our hands moving to the places we want them to go before we have even thought to ask, they just know how. It took a long time, a lot of learning, more than just one lifetime, to get *that* good. How old is life? That's how long it took for you to learn how to read and turn this page.

XIII. The first stirrings of life, the first *response*, the first repetition of an elementary gesture directed at the world in desire, the first hunger to persist. The first steps on the path of life. Can you imagine?

Darkness and concealment are the dominant characteristic of the primordial time. All life first becomes and develops in the night; for this reason, the ancients called night the fertile mother of things and indeed, together with chaos, the oldest of beings.*

XIV. *Looking Back*. Melanie Klein, the psychoanalyst, tried to imagine our beginning harder than most, tried to picture the start of our selves, the prehistory of 'I'. She filled it with monsters. Neither self nor not-self, just – shit rage tits fear cock milk envy – an unholy conglomeration of parts and forces, like those foetus-like tumuors made of teeth and hair. For Jacques Lacan, another psychoanalyst, there is a body in pieces, dismembered limbs struggling to form a whole. Now the scientists trying to scry how much the baby knows, how much of the world is already folded up within us, waiting to unfurl, talk in terms of face recognition, object constancy, language recognition; still in terms of parts and forces, bits and pieces, with no idea of their binding, of what it's like to be that incoherent mass of stuff we all once were. Looking back, we don't see ourselves begin there, for we seem to start much later. Our first memories are of things out there, worldly happenings taking place in a world of circumstance, to this 'I' here, to this little self. Our real beginnings are veiled in darkness. Below the coherent order of the rational world, before the light of reason and reasonableness which illumines the world wherever we care to glance, beneath this familiar world, lies what? The scientists and analysts can only hint, guess or romanticize, but they seem to agree on this: that beneath the present coherence lies a time of chaos. Our sense of continuity, this coherence we rarely have cause to question, let alone notice, had to be formed, order had to be imposed, coherence grown, sense made. There was no

* F. W. J. Schelling, *The Ages of the World* (1811–15; Columbia University Press, 1967).

'I' to do it, because the 'I' was the result. At some point the 'I' that is you and me began to form the living breathing world that we now inhabit, at some point this world began to form an 'I'. This strange reciprocity gave rise to us. What tumultuous energies must we have struggled to harness and tame, with what hideous strength did we bind and form those primal forces that also *were* us, hauling ourselves by the bootstraps up and out of the maelstrom into the beginnings of coherence and order? Into beginning. How do we begin? Where do we start?

XV. The beginning is always obscure. The first steps are effaced by all the subsequent ones, with the whisper of our beginning persisting but indiscernible beneath the clamour of our present being. But we can say something about it. Tie it up – and back to where we began – with desire lines. Those primal forces that made up the climate of our individual pre-dawn life, when the 'I' was without form and void, those forces achieved form through a consistent repetition, through establishing and maintaining routines. The word 'routine' derives from 'route', itself deriving from *'rupta via'*, meaning a road forged by force, a forced and beaten path.

XVI. Keep doing the same thing and eventually it makes a way, establishes a form with consistency, shape and coherence. A path is made and 'I' begins. From the impersonal forces, from the 'It', an 'I' begins to form. In learning to drive, walk, see or talk, in our very being, we are a massive interpenetrating collection of paths and routines worn by repetition; we are each a landscape, shaped by recurring patterns of force and formed by desire.

ACT ONE

SAMING

Chapter 2

The Automatic

In which we see that we are largely Creatures of Habit, and that the basis of habit is memory. Memory is shown to be not so much a library but more a repository of ready-to-run routines that enable our daily living. Next, we see that even the more apparently library-like part of memory is impressionistic and closely related to imagination. This ability to remember and imagine is shown to be crucial to our sense of who we are. Finally, having shown that consciousness has very little to do with daily life, we address the issue of what consciousness might be for.

PART ONE

The Knack

THE ORACLE: There are programs running all over the place.
The ones doing their job, doing what they were meant to do,
are invisible.

The Matrix Reloaded (2003)

PRESIDENT BARTLET: The most costly disruptions always happen
when something we took for granted stops working for a moment.

The West Wing, Series 3, Episode 9

The Truth about Killing. It turns out that we didn't do a lot of
killing in the first two world wars. A lot of people died, but not
many killed. We just couldn't do it, not when it came down to it,
not when we came face-to-face and hand-to-hand with the other life
that we were meant to extinguish. We just couldn't, not most of us.
The statistic is the usual one, illustrating the economist Vilfredo
Pareto's principle of the vital few, also known as the 80–20 law.
Twenty per cent of people own 80 per cent of the wealth; 20 per
cent of the population take 80 per cent of the sick time; 20 per cent
of the criminals are responsible for 80 per cent of the crime. There's
always a determined minority hogging the lion's share of any common property. The same was true of killing – most of us just weren't
ready for the close-up. Killing at a distance – that we can all do. Put
us in a room pushing a button which causes someone to quietly die

in another room, that's easy. But forcing the life out of another face-to-face person? Not most of us. And this became a problem for modern warfare. This became a problem for science. How do we make killers of men?

The House of Mirth. In her novel, Edith Wharton describes the life of a lady sinking slowly down the social ladder. It's a real tragedy, which does not, as such, concern us. One of the key markers of her decline is the way in which the social machinery of her world becomes ever more apparent. In the following quote, Lily, our tragic heroine, has been reduced to living in a boarding house:

> She lay late in bed, refusing the coffee and fried eggs which the friendly Irish servants thrust through her door, and hating the intimate domestic noises of the house and the cries and rumblings of the street. Her week of idleness had brought home to her with exaggerated force those small aggravations of the boarding-house world, and she yearned for that other luxurious world, whose machinery is so carefully concealed that one scene flows into another without perceptible agency.*

Something that Lily had taken for granted has stopped working and so has become apparent. The imperceptible agency, the invisible hand of servitude that sustains the elegant theatre of high society, has become noticeable in its absence. When the machinery is there and working, when the technical support of upper-class life is working properly, the mark of its efficiency is that in working it effaces the sign of its presence. Life just happens, as it was meant to, as if it were natural. Just as it is with society, so it is with you. The more natural the appearance, the more transparent and elegant the gestures, the more we can be sure that there is an elaborate invisible mechanism upon which money has been spent and effort expended. As we learned in the last chapter, nature took a long time, a lot of

---

* Edith Wharton, *The House of Mirth* (Charles Scribner & Sons, 1905).

effort and a lot of blood to become *that good* at life. The bigger the budget, the less likely you are to notice the work behind the scenes.

The House of Death. It was the military historian S. L. A. Marshall who first suggested that there was a problem with killing; that in the Second World War only 20 per cent of the soldiers did the work. The figure has been disputed since, but the debate led the American military to employ behavioural scientists to increase this 'fire ratio'. A Channel 4 documentary of 2004, *The Truth About Killing*, also took us behind the scenes of this science of 'killology' and its attempts to make killers of men. So, when the behavioural scientists were employed by the government to make their boys into better killers, where did they go? Behind the scenes, to look at the technical support of the action of killing. It wasn't so very difficult, making killers. The behavioural science expert summed it up in two words – 'repetition and realism'. The trick, as Sylvia Plath noted in her poem 'Lady Lazarus' – the knack of killing – is to do it so it feels real. So now our soldiers are trained in as close to real combat situations as the technical support of the military-industrial complex can muster. And can they muster! They shoot each other with guns which stop short of killing but which produce wounds and pain, and fear of those, enough to make you run like hell. They feel real. They use them in scenarios that look and feel and taste like war. These are big-budget productions, constantly rerun. These soldiers-in-the-making run the killing routine again and again and again.

It was interesting hearing these soldiers interviewed in the documentary talk about their first time. They snuck along, their backs tight against walls, scuttling across open spaces, dodging sniper fire, doing that thing of kicking down doors in smoking buildings and going in with their guns in both hands, scanning with eyes and hands and weapons working as one, becoming one big cocked gun as they cased all the corners of the room, doing that thing as close to real as they could muster and 'killing' whoever they could before they were 'killed' themselves. These first times really cost, were all attention, work and effort. Heart pounding extra-fast, adrenaline-fired nerves and muscles straining at their limits, high-gear brain and body working overtime, every part of them on alert and paying close attention, ready to fight or flee. Ready to kill. It was interesting to compare this to what the soldiers said who had done this enough times to forget the number, who had trodden and re-trodden this path. All those handsome young marines were talking about killing as if it were now *second nature* to them, which is precisely what it was. 'You think about it afterwards, you just do it automatically at the time.'

Sure, their hearts beat a little faster and their brains and bodies stepped up a gear or two. But without perceptible agency, gearing up precisely as much as they needed to get the job done. They did it on Automatic. The technical support for killing had been cultivated and established. Now the army can produce killers to order. There was some wry reflection from the training experts on how you could train people to do anything, given enough repetition and adequate realism.

Know-how. We often think of memory as a kind of dry old library of rarely consulted images, or dusty shelves of unwatched home videos. And there is an archival aspect to memory, which we will come to in Part Two of this chapter, but most of memory is more like the ongoing education and training of the hired help, the technical support, the imperceptible agency of, well, you. This memory is not about events, but about *procedures*, about 'how to X' when X is any action or process that you can now do without much thought, which is most things. What happened in the production of those human killing machines is what has happened to you countless times. At the beginning there will have been that klutzy, clunky and effortful stage. New paths needed beating, through muscles and nerves, beating and then beating again, into patterns of thought, feeling and action. Repeated and refined, these muscles and nerves, these feelings and thoughts and actions, will have worked themselves into a routine, one that will run with increasingly less need for conscious prompting. The heart won't beat so fast anymore. Whether making a cup of tea or killing someone, the action has become a no-brainer. When the world was new to you – and once it was so new it must have hurt – you paid attention, you really had to sit up and take notice. Now you are such an old hand at the world that you actually pay very little attention. You know how – or part of you does. The invisible agency. This is memory, or a major component of memory called procedural memory. It has the knack of things.

The Notion of Smoking. I was talking to a woman from the west coast of Scotland about giving up smoking. 'Ah huvnae smoked in years,' said she, no pride or shame, just fact. Having struggled with this one myself for some time, I am always curious as to people's exit strategy, how they got off the wheel. 'Ah just lost the notion of it,' she said.

I first remember hearing this use of 'notion' from my mother. She was telling me about 'having a notion of' the film star Montgomery Clift. It's the Scottish version of having a crush, of fancying someone, or of someone taking your fancy. All these phrases suggest that an external thing has left a mark in our inner world of forms and representations; that something out there has blazed a trail, beaten a path, established a routine within us. To have a notion of a cigarette, as a Scot could do, or to fancy one, as the rest of you might, is to have more than just the know-how of smoking. You also yearn to, for the pleasure centre of your brain is tingling with anticipation, because it already knows and feels what it would feel like to be doing it. You have a lack that smoking would complete, and you remember how that completeness feels. The tendons and muscles of your fingers and lips are primed, your wrist and hand are ready; your ribcage and lungs are beginning to take the shape, to assume the position, of smoking. And as smoking sees, so smoking looks. To have the notion of smoking is also to have a perceptual bias. A smoker entering a public space for the first time will scan a room very differently from a non-smoker. They will see a very different public space. Images of smoking will have a different charge. There will be a whole skein of associations, of memories and images dedicated to smoking. Smoking will have wrapped itself around everyday activities: eating and drinking, sex and sensuality, waking and wakefulness, sleep and slothfulness, boredom and irritation. Every state and action will have developed some kind of relationship with smoking. This may be one of intensification, in pleasure; of appeasement, in anxiety; of annulment, in torpor; of beguilement, in boredom. To have the notion of smoking is also to know how to use it to change the present, to calibrate or to alter the current mood.

And this leaves marks, not just on your teeth and in your lungs. Like a pianist or a cyclist or a dancer, the repeated actions of the smoker will have physically sculpted them, inscribed themselves on their muscles and nerves and in their repertoire of automatic gestures. The notion of smoking is a *complex*, a concatenation, a convocation of parts, an articulation of concepts, percepts, moods, behaviours, gestures, muscles, nerves and chemicals, recognitions, anticipations, memories and desires. Given these different parts, it is unlikely that there is, within the body, a single location of this notion. Rather, it is distributed throughout the person, and also throughout their external world, in the props and the paraphernalia, the people and the places, of smoking. 'Smoking' is a distributed notion then, residing in furniture, in dopamine receptors, in the local shop, in the muscles of the fingers, the hand and eye and the movies. What holds this distributed network together? Obviously the person of the smoker, but more specifically it coheres in the beaten paths, the desire lines, worn by use, within them. The poet John Ashbery puts it like this, talking of how belief and memory 'gets worn into the mind like a crease in a road map that has been folded up the wrong way too many times'.

Imagine your will is like water, running through a landscape. Where will it run? Down the paths of least resistance – the beaten ones, the deepest, smoothest and oldest. Left to its own devices, your will will run like water through the worn runnels and folds of constant use. Let us call this enactment, this performance of a notion, a *routine*. Routines. We all have them, thousands upon

Figure 2. Portrait of James MacMillan by Calum Colvin

thousands of routines, dormant notions just waiting for our desire or circumstance to activate them.

Notional Portraits. There is a picture by the artist Calum Colvin of the musician James MacMillan. From a distance the picture looks like a rather crude sketch of a face, like one of those deliberately artless paintings artists sometimes do, when they want to appear like kids. Closer still and you see it's not a painting but a photograph of a room. A room on which a face has been painted. The musician's lips, the left corner of his lips, are on the seat of the chair; the next section of them is on the wall behind the desk and the chair; the centre of his lips is on the leg of the table; the right-hand side is on the wall again. At the angle from which the photograph is taken, the line of the lips is entirely coherent and consistent – they are lips – but there is no single surface onto which they are emblazoned. So it is with the entire portrait, for the subject of the painting isn't really there at all. If you were in that room, or if you were to look at that room from any angle other than the one of the photograph, the face would no longer be there, or rather it would not be apparent. This says something about perspective and illusion, sure, but it also reveals how our notions, our dormant routines, are distributed.

Imagine, or remember, the slow and tidal process of forgetting and remembering we call grief. Think how long they take, the big griefs, the ones where the lost figure has really left a mark. It looks to me as though it takes about two years to get through that process, to arrive at the other side to some kind of new equilibrium, a new normal. The first year, the year of the phantom limb, is the year of putting down the cup on the table that's not there, the year of habitual calls which no longer receive their habitual responses. A tough year, a year of realizing what has become tangled up with that person, of quite how extensive our notion of them is, and quite how much they are part of our routines. Grief that year is a constant surprise that waits in the most mundane and unexpected of places. By the end of that year, you begin to get it, you begin to check yourself before you put the cup down. And then comes the year of learning to do things differently, the year of beginning to build new notions and routines. This is the year of going on and of doing without.

My friend Maureen tells me of a characteristically deliberate enactment of this. She had lost a love, a love which happened in, and so shaped and coloured, the streets of Belfast. She summoned a friend from overseas, and with that friend Maureen spent two weeks reclaiming the city. They revisited the places where the notion of love was strongest, and there they enacted new routines, she and her friend, not so much in an act of negation, but in an act of addition, allowing those streets to be the place where more than one thing had happened, allowing new things to happen and thereby laying the foundations of a new normal.

Like the musician's portrait, the person who has become a real part of your life is not located in one part of you, and can never be neatly excised. To really lose the notion of them . . . Well, how would you? You couldn't lose the picture without destroying the room. In time, however, the furniture will be rearranged and will come to represent other people and places. But the old shapes linger, haunt the room. If you look from a certain angle, you can still see them there. But you move on, your perspective shifts. New friends walk beside you through the streets of Belfast. You practise and perform new routines until, eventually, you can't quite remember how the room used to look or how the streets used to feel when walked in the days of love. That is perhaps the saddest loss of all, and why we want to linger for a while at the end of grief. We don't want to lose the notion.

And . . . There is no real forgetting. Everything leaves a mark, whether you remember it, whether you can bring it to mind or not. There is no subtraction in mind. Only *and*. You won't forget the dead parent, the old lover, the absent friend. If miracle or circumstance brought them back before you, your response would be as automatic as the hand to the cup or the fingers to the pen. These reactions were just temporarily obscured by a host of 'ands'. Grieving is not forgetting. It is in the addition that the healing lies, the sufficient accumulation of new experience to balance the weight of the old, to give you new routines, new things to do, and other notions, other things to think about it.

I imagine us to be a kind of quantum room, capable of representing multiple portraits simultaneously. The one you see is dependent on where you are currently standing, on who you are currently with or considering. There are certain lines everyone will say before they die. There are only so many lines. 'I hadn't seen him for years, but we just picked up from where we left off, as if it was only last week.' Chances are that some time you'll speak a variant of that. With certain people there is a groove, a mutual groove, which runs itself. If, like me, you are very/overly sensitive to the energy expenditure involved in interpersonal exchange, you will particularly value these interpersonal free rides, these downhill slides, where notion calls to notion, routine follows routine and the whole show runs itself.

Think of those soldiers, those killing machines. How for them killing eventually became effortless. Those are the kinds of friends you want, where your heartbeat only raises to just the perfect pitch of anticipatory excitement, where all that awful effort of the beginning of things is over, the paths beaten and the shovels shelved. Look out for those kind. They are hard to find, and difficult to lose.

Drunkard's Walk. You are walking across a room. Get up now and walk to the next room and do something that you do daily, like make yourself a cup of tea. Do one of your routines.

You probably won't, for no one ever follows an author's instructions, but say you did. What were you thinking of as you did it (say you did)? Were you thinking about walking and making tea, were you consciously rehearsing your routine? Unlikely. You may have noticed, or looking now you may notice, an odd uncoupling of which the human mind is capable between what it is doing and what it is thinking. This may be our defining attribute as a species, that the system of representation, the signs that we use to represent the world to ourselves, have become uncoupled from any ongoing business. They have a life, a mind of their own. Or, to put it another way, you rarely need to pay attention to what you are doing.

In the interests of research, I just went to the local shop to buy some milk, which I needed for the tea we are all supposed to be making. Routine stuff. I was paying, given the nature of this section, more attention than usual to my attention. It really wasn't involved in the activity at all. My attention wandered, like an under-trained and over-eager dog, or a child, or someone who has been given the day off and doesn't know what to do with it. It meandered around the act of walking to the shop, making the occasional intervention – walk more upright, hold your stomach in – then wandered off again into how it would write about this and all sorts of other nonsense – a rambling drunk on a long leash. It paid a little more attention when it entered the shop and started choosing items. Some mulling went on, some imagining of meals and the possibilities for consumption, some idea of what it would like to eat and how it might prepare it – images of that, stories about this. But I didn't rethink my tastes. Having been to this shop before, I didn't think about where to go in the shop, nor did I even think overly long about choices that were pretty much the ones I always make. The most attention-heavy part was at the counter, at the checkout. Here let us distinguish two things. There was the self-consciousness of standing there with a queue behind me, of taking up people's time and of figuring in their awareness. There was that. And then there was the attention to the actual task in hand: the counting out of change, trying to get the sum right, interacting with the checkout boy. This was the only truly deliberate part of the whole buying-milk-at-the-shops affair, deliberate in the sense of deliberated, thought out. Though even then it had time for 'I wonder if I'll get that wrong' and 'Do I look like a fool doing this?' and 'I'm counting this money rather stylishly'. And had there been less self-consciousness, there would have been less task-attention necessary, for even this was fairly automatic. I didn't have to learn how to count or to socialize again. But it was at this point in the milk affair when there was most coupling between the inner and the outer, when there was focus, concentration and a little effort, in the crucible of the checkout.

Then it was over. At ease, as you were. Off out of the shop again, with some lingering rumination on the walk home, but the drunk was off again, leching and wandering and throwing up all kinds of stuff. All I really had to do in order to get some milk from the shop was to point myself in the right direction with that intention. Given that, I could pretty much switch off, like the drunk who somehow gets home at night, with no recollection afterwards of how he managed it. Well, he didn't manage, if by 'he' we mean that part of us we count as consciousness. The Automatic took over. The Automatic knows how to walk, talk and get from any familiar A to B. It really doesn't need us. Indeed, as with my self-consciousness at the checkout, we interfere.

I write this having just decided to employ more fingers than I normally do to type, and I wish that I had not. A process that once worked perfectly well – with two fingers buzzing around the keyboard in a blur of inspiration, just knowing where to go as the words rose up, a process that was once as transparent and as easy as speaking – has now become aware of itself and demands attention. Not only am I thinking, or rather not only *is there thinking* about this stuff that you are reading (and that's a whole other story, one we'll try to tell, this thinking that-just-happens, that comes from some-where/nowhere), but there is also now another layer, another energetic, muscular and attentional demand. I now need to think about where my fingers go, which fingers to use and when. I'm *try-ing*. It's *tiring*. I wish I had never started. Indeed, the faster I type the more the old 'inefficient' way of typing is reasserting itself. The more there is a demand for transcription, the more the way I know best, my old routine – the Automatic – is taking over. With this pro-cess I want to be drunk again. I want to point myself in the right direction and find, magically, that I am home. I don't want to think about how to get there. Me, my conscious attention, is just getting in the way.

Life is Cheap

The brain is constantly trying to automate processes, thereby dispel-ling them from consciousness; in this way its work will be completed faster, more effectively and at a lower metabolic level. Conscious-ness, on the other hand, is slow, subject to error and 'expensive'.

Gerhard Roth, neuroscientist*

Faith. 'In order therefore that there may be a place for faith, all the things that are believed must be hidden away,' wrote Luther. Now imagine if there was no place for faith, and we are here slightly appropriating and extending Luther's notion of faith to include

* Gerhard Roth, 'The Quest to Find Consciousness', *Scientific American*, special edition, *Mind* 14 1 (2004): 33–40.

anything we put our trust in or rely on. Imagine, in my walk to the shop, if I had had no faith in the processes sustaining the walk. Imagine if I had had to think about how to walk, had to plan and execute every step deliberately. There was a stage, long ago, when that was the case, when we had to try walking quite deliberately. But now I put my faith in my ability to walk. I trust and rely on it, for the how-it-is-done is long since hidden away. The more self-conscious amongst you may recall times when walking has become unnaturally conscious, when you are aware of walking in the sight of others and imagining all sorts about what they may be thinking of you. You may have been close to being paralysed by that gaze, but still, fundamentally, you remembered and no matter how conscious the process became, you could still do it. Or imagine if I had had to think about breathing, on the way to the shop. Again, many of us have briefly been there, particularly in childhood, when we became convinced that only conscious effort would sustain our breathing. If you have no recollection of what a bad idea that is – conscious breathing – I suggest that you try it just before falling asleep. Or rather, not falling asleep, because you won't. No, breathing is really better hidden away.

Talking. Imagine having to try and talk. Imagine, like learning a new language, that you had to consult memories of vocabulary and grammar, had to put sentences together deliberately, as if you were building a wall brick by brick. Imagine my checkout at the shop then. I may have been self-conscious but I just knew that if I pointed the *words* in the right direction, if I had the intention of communicating: something-about-hoping-that's-the-right-amount-of-change-with-a-hint-of-diffident-cheerfulness-that-implies-you-know-it's-the-right-amount-but-you-want-to-draw-attention-to-the-fact-that-you've-given-them-a-load-of-useful-small-change-and-shouldn't-they-reciprocate-with-just-a-little-warm-acknowledgement-that-your-effort-was-also-for-them; I knew that if I pointed myself in that intentional direction, the words would follow, would flow, would automatically rise to the occasion – which, as they usually do, they did. Unless of course we experience that crippling self-consciousness again, in which case our words may stumble, our intention misfire a little, but we don't forget our language, we merely fluff the speech.

In the next section, we will see how we don't remember in the kind of detail that we think we do. We store the gist of things and, when we need to, we construct a memory from the gist. Speaking is like this. When we speak, we have in mind the gist of what we want to say, and then we just step off the cliff. Generally, it pretty much works out and we land on our feet. I couldn't give you a first-hand account of it for the life of me, nor could I tell you how I formed those sentences – no more than I could tell you how I *saw* the boy at the checkout. We know that neurologically you can break seeing down into a thousand parts and stages, locate and track its movements in the brain, but if I became aware of any of those mechanisms, then they would immediately cease to work. Imagine, for a moment – or try to – that you could deconstruct seeing from the inside, that you could 'see' at first only the cells processing the vertical lines, then the horizontal ones, then the moving horizontals, the moving verticals, the stationary diagonals, etc. So fundamental is seeing that it is almost all hidden away. Like an engine, a smooth-running engine, you would only notice the mechanism at work if it began to falter.

Take this one step further – too far perhaps – and imagine that you had to think how to think. It's here that we get a glimpse of the Automatic, which is always at work, producing you. No matter how self-conscious you become, there is a mass of ground and grounding below which you cannot see or dig because you are always already standing on it. As the Oracle says in *The Matrix*, describing the programmes that produce the world she and Keanu Reeves appear to be sitting comfortably in: 'there are programs running all over the place. The ones doing their job, doing what they were meant to do, are invisible.' As President Bartlett notes in *The West Wing*, only when they stop working for a moment, or for good – in age, in stroke, in Alzheimer's, in illness – only then does what was once transparent become apparent. Only then do we glimpse the extent of the acts of faith by which we live.

PART TWO

The Gist

Much of what happened will become assimilated as slight changes to circuit patterns that already exist. This is why the details grow blurred in our minds, leaving behind only a gist. We can still prod our brains to yield anticipatory images based on this gist, but it will have to recruit a generalized best guess about how such an event might have looked and felt.

John McCrone*

Indeed, it seems undeniable that we have memories and that we make plans . . .

Shaun Gallagher†

50 First Dates. An odd subject for a romantic comedy. In this film, a woman – Drew Barrymore – has had a head injury and can no longer transfer information from her short-term to her long-term memory. She still understands her present experience. She recognizes and responds to familiar stuff, based on all the old stored routines. But she no longer modifies, tweaks and adapts. She has new experiences, but no longer retains them. A man – Adam Sandler – falls in love with her and, most days, so too does she with

---

* John McCrone, 'Reasons to forget', *Times Literary Supplement*, 30 January 2004.
† Shaun Gallagher, 'Philosophical Conceptions of the Self: Implications for Cognitive Science', *Trends in Cognitive Sciences*, 4/1 (January 2000).

him. However, each morning he is a stranger to her again, and he needs to make her fall in love with him all over again. Nothing garners or accumulates from day to day. There is no learning and growing because every day starts at zero again.

How, then, can a relationship form? If experience leaves no trace, surely a relationship can never do what relationships do: form, develop, grow. Two points on both of which the film is surprisingly accurate. First, there *is* an emotional trace. In an old, unethical experiment a scientist shakes hand with a short-term memory impaired lady every day. She never remembers him. One day he has a pin in his hand. She shakes his hand. Next day, she still doesn't remember him, but she won't shake his hand. It is these kind of experiments that have allowed us to see that memory is not a single system. In Part One of this chapter we have seen 'The Knack', the 'know-how' at work. This is part of what the scientists now call 'non-declarative memory', which is an interesting way to name it, revealing that we are used to thinking of memory as something that we can declare at will. But much of it is not. The way the lady pulled back her hand, that she remembers how to do. The fact that this man's hand is dangerous, that she 'remembers'. Procedural and emotional memories are not things we can declare, or even know that we know, but nevertheless they leave their traces in how we respond to the present. In the film, this begins to happen, for there is a hint that she begins to associate him with good things, with nice feelings.

Second point. They begin to build the Drew Barrymore character a memory, from paper and ink and tape and every prop they can think of. This is also what happens in real memory disorders. An artificial memory is constructed in which storage devices, props and automated prompts take the place of the missing pieces. Bleepers go off at key times, followed by text messages – 'check your mail', 'brush your teeth', 'call your mum', etc. Conspicuous lists and cue cards are pinned on walls, logs of who the person is and what has happened recently are committed to photo, tape and print. Of course, all this compensation for a pathology only exaggerates what we all do anyway, for we all use a whole set of props to remind us to do stuff, who's who, what's what, when and where and how to be. Having delegated our remembering to various devices, all we need do then is remember where we've put them and when to consult them. This artificial memory is a version of what we do automatically, a clunky but not inaccurate version of the real thing. We all forget most of our experience – after a few days much of the detail is gone. What we retain are the essentials, the gist. What Drew and Adam commit to their ongoing log of events, as they go from their dates through to marriage and on to having children together, what she has to watch and read again every morning is the gist. She feels good about this man, she trusts him, she is his wife, they have a child, they are currently living on a boat, she's lost her memory because of an accident, everything is all right, everything is going to be fine.

Every day she does what we never have to do, or rather she does what we do implicitly and automatically. Every morning she has to read and re-consult a record of her life, learn who she now is, who that strange man in her bed is and how she feels about him being there, how she feels about her life. He makes a video for her to watch every morning. 'Everything is going to be all right' is how the video starts, stating the emotional gist of things. Every day, like a diabetic with insulin, or a thyroid patient with thyroxin, she has to absorb an artificially produced essence of what she can no longer produce herself. We don't have to do that. Like her, we will probably forget most of what we have done, but what stops us feeling as though we have lost our past is that we have produced and kept the gist, the essence. We remember that we liked this or that person, that they make us laugh and feel good. We remember who and where and what we are. We do not have to consult an inner record to approach our loved ones trustingly; rather, we are now formed as trusting-towards-them. A beaten path, a tendency to approach them with trust has been shaped. In the same way that you have the knack, the *know-how* of your daily acts, so you have the gist of your life, you *know what* matters about it. Assuming that you do.

Public Library. This *know-what* is the declarative part of memory, the part we think of as memory, the more conscious element that we can easily translate into speech and language. And this translation, this speaking out also highlights the social aspects of memory. Our relationships are shaped by the mutual forming and recalling of memories. They are the ties that bind us to another person. 'We have history', 'we go way back', 'we've been through a lot, you and I'. These are generally estimates of the weight of a relationship, its seriousness and worth measured in time spent, in memories made together and later to be recalled together. We are mildly obsessed with the loss of this kind of memory, the memory of facts and events, for we intuit that to forget too much is to forget who you are. So we become a little compulsive about hoarding our memories. More accurately we feel the need to rehearse our memories, as if they can be kept fresh only by frequent airing. And our feeling is right, for unrecollected memories tend to fade. Those who worry that the loss of memories of the past may lead to its tragic repetition in the future, those who preserve the memory of historical trauma by recalling it in the present, attest to this belief that memory, unless repeated, fades away. This shared, social memory seems almost like an organic life-form with which we have been entrusted. Ignore it and it will die, like a plant or a child. Or like a ritual. There is an element of ritual in shared recall, a binding of communities, groups, clubs or relationships by acknowledging and keeping alive the story of their formation and growth. If that past is not kept alive, it dies, and if it dies the things it binds will also perish. The common past we keep alive is both the ground of our shared bond and its fruit, both the cause and effect of relationship. Consider how the Jewish people have maintained their community identity over years of geographical dispersion by keeping memories alive in the form of traditions. Tradition is the shared memory of a people. As those with dementia lose everything that makes them them, so would a people lose their common mind if they lost their tradition. That's why the rituals of the Jewish religion contain so many prescriptions for the transmission and repetition of key texts and memories, to make sure that little is lost, that it is kept alive.

Chinese Whispers. So, memory as a library, as photo album and video tape, as an organic and shared responsibility that needs to be tended to remain alive, something that could otherwise die and be lost forever. All of these metaphors attest to a certain faith in the fidelity of memory, a belief that we are, singly and collectively, recording machines in which facts and events are faithfully transcribed. And this is true for a time, but for a few days at most. For a few days only you retain a more or less precise record of events. If you want to keep it any longer than that, if you want a record of the minute-by-minute fact and event, you are not equipped to do it on your own, and you will need, like Drew Barrymore, external help in the form of props: diaries, lists, real photo albums and actual videotapes. They remember so you don't have to. This has made people worry, with reason, about the times when memory really matters, such as in witness testimony.

In Andrew Jarecki's 2003 Academy Award-nominated documentary, *Capturing the Friedmans*, we are presented with an apparently simple story of a father and son who, in the late 1980s, were convicted and imprisoned for child sex abuse. The abuse had happened in the Friedmans' home, where the father had run a small computer class. During these classes father and son had horrifically abused their pupils. Or so the story seems at first. As more witnesses are interviewed and more videotapes are shown – for in this family the father, mother and three sons had obsessively videotaped themselves both before and during these events – something about the past begins to unravel, something apparently solid begins to shift and melt. There are a couple of striking incidents. One man, his face in confidential shadow, tells of a rape by the father and son, a punishment rape. As the interviewer probes, this memory begins to look a little improbable, but the interviewee clearly holds it to be true. Returning to him later, we hear how he went into therapy one day and 'came out with the memory in my head'. The memory was born that day, years after the event it was a memory of. Then we hear the Friedman son and his lawyer both recall the trial, years later, each giving utterly incompatible versions of why they had agreed to a guilty plea. No surprise, perhaps, that lawyers and convicted criminals might lie, but something else seemed to be at work in them, a degree of passionate conviction in their version, and this passion ran through every other interviewee – the police, the parents, the Friedmans, the press, the lawyers and the judge. The emotional impetus, the force behind the act of recall, the beliefs and convictions acting in the present, in the moment of recall, were actively shaping the past, actively forming the moments recalled to fit those convictions. This was not merely a matter of past experience shaping current convictions, this was a dialogue between past and present, a negotiation between beliefs, emotions and memory in which none were really distinguishable, where each shaped the other.

It was the archival part of our memory, our episodic and bio-graphical memory, which was on trial in the Friedman case. Most of us expect an archival accuracy from this kind of memory. What the Friedmans showed was that this memory is prone to the Chinese Whispers effect. We now know that memory is remarkably plastic and malleable. Each time a memory is 'consulted' and brought to mind, it is altered, added to, embellished. The more it is repeated, like Chinese Whispers, the more it has the potential for distortion. And in the Friedman case we see that it is not only repetition that leads to distortion. There was, in each individual, something like a direction, a bias, a gradient, a prevailing force pushing the memories to distort in a particular way, so that with each recall the images were edited closer and closer to their conviction of how things really were. Thus we see a policewoman recalling with passion and disgust how she broke into a house overflowing with shameless stacks of child pornography, while actual photographs from the time show a small pile, carefully concealed behind the piano. Both father and son were convicted, but the facts of the case remain in dispute to this day. What elevated the documentary above mere true-crime drama was precisely its emphasis on what the film critic Roger Ebert called the 'elusiveness of facts'. 'Who do you believe?' was the tagline of the film, and the question goes beyond the veracity of the individuals involved to the reliability of memory itself. For memory is *not* an accurate archive. It can't be, because:

> I would need a virtually infinite look-up system that would be extremely costly in time and space as well as physically impossible. Instead my brain reworks my memories into a more general fabric of inclinations to act and feel in certain ways in response to certain stimulus conditions.*

Remember this the next time you are arguing with those you love over the shape of the past. The act of recall is never neutral, and the emotions prompting the recall will shape the events recalled, mixing memory with desire.

Last Tuesday. How many parts to your nervous system, how many possible arrangements and connections? More than the stars in the sky. Where in those parts do we find last Tuesday, and how is that information stored? 'Information', writes the information theorist Hans Christian von Baeyer, 'is the transfer of form from one medium to another.'† We currently have little idea how external experience comes to be coded in the human medium, how the form of last Tuesday has re-formed us. How is Tuesday's breakfast kept in your brain and how is the rain that fell that afternoon transcribed? We don't really know. We have an idea where that experience may be encoded, but not how. We can point to locations in the brain that light up when we remember, on photographs of brain activity, but beyond that we have no real clue.

Do you remember last Tuesday afternoon? If you are doing it

---

* J. A. Hobson, *Dreaming: A Very Short Introduction* (Oxford University Press, 2005).
† Hans Christian von Baeyer, *Information: The New Language of Science* (Harvard University Press, 2004).

now, don't believe everything you see. The images you have of it are like a dramatic re-enactment, a reconstruction with special effects, based on the gist. Some extremely economical shorthand version of Tuesday has been scribbled down in your brain. You know there was rain, from which you sheltered beneath a main street shop front, while you looked at the park benches on the far side of the road. Your brain has made some notes: Tuesday, rain, Edinburgh, park benches, shop front, glass and chrome. If you wish to call that afternoon to mind, that shorthand note will be used by your brain to reconstruct a version. There will be best-guess benches, rain from the props department and generic pavements, if you decide to remember the pavements, but as soon as you do there will be pavements, best-guess pavements. If you don't try to remember, if the pavement doesn't come to mind, there will not be one. Like a movie in which they only build the scenery that will be seen by the camera. One turn of the camera to the left and you see the rigging and the scaffolding and the empty sound stage, but that doesn't matter, because your camera won't turn that way. And your memory is much smarter than a movie crew. It's a magic crew, a crew of magic pixies trained for a million years and moving at close to light speed. As soon as you try to remember a bit of the memory, wherever you look in the memory, they will build you one, as if wherever the camera randomly scans on an empty sound stage, there is suddenly scenery, hastily cobbled together from the props department. That's how memory works.

After a day or two, you retain only the gist of Tuesday and the rest is imagination. You can see this process at work, or so we think, in brain scans. The recent experience leaves a trace in the more conscious part of your brain, in the part that pays attention. That trace is like a little path in the snow of the neurons. That transient shape haunts the brain for a little time, that particular pathway is easily run again, still 'jangles', as one scientist put it. But not for long. Attention needs to stay fresh to every moment, so the memory gets shifted into temporary storage, still relatively intact, for a few days at most. And it is then that the gist is extracted from it. The gist is all you need. With it, you can construct the memory again should you need it. The downside of this is the unreliability and malleability of memory. The upside is the enormous saving of space and time, and the flexibility of a system that can, given a few hints, reconstruct almost any scenario.

Next Tuesday. From those cameras that photograph your brain, we know that the parts of your brain that light up when you try and remember are the same parts that will light up when you are trying to imagine what *next* Tuesday might be like. Memory and imagination are closely linked. One reconstructs based on the gist; the other builds on whatever desire or dread is fuelling your image of the future. Both are essentially creative activities; where they differ is not in form but in their source of inspiration.

And this gives us the ability to time-travel. In all of evolution this only seems to have happened once. We have, however notional and fabricated, both a last Tuesday and a next Tuesday. We can visit them both. And we can visit many other times we have lived through, and we can plan and imagine, in vivid, useful detail, many times to come. 'Indeed, it seems undeniable that we have memories and that we make plans'; that we can time-travel. And this makes all the difference.

My friend Lenny, documenting the progress of a relationship that he sees as perpetually teetering on the verge of extinction, is exquisitely aware of its defining moments, its narrative progression to what he imagines must be an end. There are particular acts he notices. Often fuelled by tiredness, alcohol and a sense of incipient abandonment, in one or the other partner, there is a lashing and an acting out, almost an attempt to enact the end which he imagines is imminent. In the morning there is rueful acknowledgement and apology. 'Well, my dear,' he will say to his partner, 'how many more disfiguring incidents before we call it a day?'

Defining moments, disfiguring incidents. Act Two, the part of this book dealing with change, will track the progress of defining moments, those times when our autobiography takes a definitive turn, and we become more this or less that. And this is what we have that other animals, so far as we can tell, do not, this archive of becoming, this ability to revisit and relive our defining moments, and to weave them into a narrative about who we are, and why we are who we are. This kind of memory – episodic or biographical – is the basis of not only our sense of self but also of our most intimate bonds. When we stay up all night and share our life-story with our nascent lovers, we will not recount to them a list of presidents, kings or battle dates, nor the way the benches looked in Edinburgh last Tuesday, nor will we show off our cricket swing or walking skills. We will share our moments of becoming, the defining and disfiguring and inciting incidents, the dramatic highlights, the key players and recurring themes in the unfolding story of us. And then we'll tell them about our hopes and plans. We'll share our past and future. Indeed, it seems undeniable that we have memories and that we make plans.

We know – from the brain-damaged stars of memory research – that those who lack this kind of memory also lack the ability to imagine a future. For them there is, in a sense, nothing for the future to happen to. Time travel needs a self, and the self needs to travel in time. This formation of a story of the self, and a sense of that story developing through time, through incidents, encounters and events, in continuity, that's the human trick, the one the other animals can't do. What they lack and what we treasure is the *know-who* of a self emerging from past and extending into a future. It may be just as fabricated, partial and biased as last Tuesday's pavements, the Friedmans' witness testimony or next Tuesday's weather, but it is nevertheless who we think we are. Above all else, memory gives us the gist of ourselves.

PART THREE

Pause for Thought

The Unconscious isn't a theatre, but a factory, a productive machine.

Gilles Deleuze and Félix Guattari*

Think Fast. You know the trick: someone throws a ball, an orange or a baby at you and as they throw they exclaim 'Think Fast', and you do. You do the fastest thinking you are capable of, which is the kind you only notice once it's over. You think with your muscles and nerves and eyes and the balls of your feet. Your body thinks and, as long as you don't get in the way, everything will be fine. And that's the game of 'Think Fast'. The very injunction encourages the kind of conscious thinking that will get in the way of automatic action. It says 'think about this catch', whereas the catch will only happen if you don't. To think fast, you need to stop thinking. The dual processes involved here are the Automatic versus the Deliberate.

Deleuze and Guattari, the two French philosophers heading up this section, prefigured by several decades the position that cognitive scientists have recently reached. The unconscious, they said, is not a Freudian theatre of repressed desire and Greek tragedy, but a factory, an automated assembly line, an armoury of semi-autonomous agents. Or, as cognitive scientist and philosopher Daniel Dennett puts it, a pandemonium, a host of automated routines and notions that largely run the show. We can also call it the

* Gilles Deleuze and Félix Guattari, *Anti-Oedipus* (1972; English trans. Viking Penguin, 1977).

Automatic, the gist and the knack of all you know. It knows so you don't have to, so you can think fast.

Here's an analogy. Imagine two film producers. Producer One is a bad delegator. He is always telling the director how to direct, the actors how to act. He's questioning the angles of the camerawoman, he's insisting he helps in setting up the tracking shots; indeed, he's on his hands and knees now, building the track. He's mixing the sound himself and editing the final cut. There he is coaching the lead actor's accent. Now he's cooking the meal for a cast of thousands, for each of whom he feels individually responsible. He's sweeping up at the end of the day.

Now for Producer Two. She has employed the best director. The director has hired the best casting agent. The casting agent has employed the best actors. The catering is top-notch. No expense has been spared in securing the services of a top sound team. The camerawoman is legendary for the understated, unobtrusive beauty of her framing of the shots.

So, which producer would you rather be? It's OK, you are the second one. Your team is well established, and as producer of the *You* show, you can pretty much let them get on with it. Three signs of a good producer? Delegation, delegation and delegation.

Short Delay. Indeed, as Producer Two, you are often the last to know when important decisions are made. That is, if we identify 'you' with conscious, deliberate thought. That conscious you is always a little behind the game. Some researchers claim the lag is up to ten seconds, whilst the older, more conservative research has it at about half a second. But however long the lag, lag there is, between the decision being initiated, issuing from the factory floor, and you becoming aware of it. Again we see it by peeking as best we can into the brain. The actual decision has already been made by the agents and routines that make up the Automatic, and then consciousness gives it the nod, mistaking its assent for agency. The cup of tea, the decision to go and make it, happened half a second, maybe even ten, before 'you' decided. Which really only becomes spooky if you decide that the Automatic isn't 'you' and that there is some great divide between the conscious you and It, the factory that produces you. Whereas it couldn't be more you. It's everything you've ever thought, every place you have ever been, every action you have ever practised or mastered, every dream and wish and hope, every encounter, every place, every face and feeling, everything you know. Or the gist and knack of it all. You, It, the Automatic, are informed by all your personal past and by all the evolution that went before that. Your collection of parts is now arranged in particular forma- tions, with your autonomous agents and routines formed by and according to that history. It makes a good deal of sense to let that do the thinking, to automate that. It knows best.

Where Am I? We have mentioned agents and agency a few times now. An agent is someone, or something, that acts on our behalf: a person or thing that does. And agency – to have or exercise agency is to be the source, the cause of the doing. If conscious thought is not the real agent of our action, then who or what is?

There are semi-autonomous agents in cyberspace now. These cyber-agents acquire knowledge of the kind of stuff we like. We inform them, shape them, and they go off and look for stuff that looks like our likes, and bring it back to us, inform us about it. We inform them and they inform us. They are a form of delegated will, which works on our behalf. But there is nothing so very new here, it's just that these particular agents happen to be outside our bodies. But every day we delegate our will to ever more agents. We just tend not to notice because we tend not to think of ourselves this way. We identify with the executive producer, not the grunts on the shop floor. But let's revisit my trip to the shops. Where did that come from? Who made the decision to do that?

My writing had reached a natural break. The thought came to my head that I could go for milk, and there I was, rising to get my coat. I didn't originate the thought, so much as I responded to it. More accurately, there was a response to it. It's difficult (try it), to account for your actions without resorting to an originating 'I'. But if I try (there we go again), all along the way, responsibility for that little break can be traced to more and more delegated agents. Consciousness wasn't much more involved than it was in doing the actual walking to the shop. Let's try.

At that time 'I' was a series of agents or routines, involved in writing and thinking this. As we said before, I cannot in any way that makes sense have *caused* these thoughts. Thoughts there were, however, and a set of habits for transcribing them. This set of routines and agents, this often lazy and reluctant labour force, is usually willing to call a break at the least provocation. Occasionally 'I' try and supervene on that impulse to stop, to give up at the first hurdle or alternative urge. Or rather, ditching the ghostly 'I', another series of routines comes into operation – older and more guilty routines – producing thoughts and images of earthly hell, a wasted life and a squandered talent. With those big guns they try to compel the workforce to continue. But the workforce are just waiting for those Calvinist bastards to weaken a little, and an urge for tea will do nicely, and lo! the tools are down. Working with this lot, of late, is a new agent, an attempt at a routine of just getting up every day and writing regardless. It's a young and impressionable routine and more often than not the old crew have it down the café by lunch.

Looking for the authentic, originating impulse, the originating agency, within all of this is an endless chase down a hall of mirrors. Each time, in each decision, there are only more agents, more old and new routines, and my decision seems to be some algebraic summation of their collective activity. They decide and I say yes. I go along. I nod and agree, assent to the decision made by this parliament of dunces, these mindless agents. But there, I am using 'I', as if there was a separate I of assent. It's hard not to, so for the moment let's leave 'I' there, no longer as an original agent, but more like the monarch in a democracy: I nod and I wave but the decision was already made. Main skill of the monarch: smile and wave, smile and wave, smile and wave.

Live, on the Air. Deliberate, conscious thought is the very least and last of you. A late arrival at the evolutionary party, a tiny mote atop the massive mountain of automatic life, of knack and gist. And we should ask, as we do of the monarchy in a democracy, what is it for? What is conscious thought for?

When live radio shows are broadcast, particularly a live phone-in, the producers usually build in a delay. It's not quite live. Usually it's only a few seconds, enough so that if anyone decides to do the aural equivalent of flashing or throwing eggs at politicians, they can be excised from public broadcast and the show can continue un-sued. The delay will only be used in exceptional circumstances, when something is about to go off the rails. Cognitive scientists talk about consciousness serving a similar function, having a similar kind of power, the power of veto. For sure, the decisions are all made by the parliament of dunces, but consciousness, like the queen, can, in exceptional circumstances, say 'No'. Which makes sense until you wonder – which processes, which routines constitute this veto, this monarch? Surely that veto is in turn an impulse arising from the depths of the Automatic, yet another decision made earlier, which we can assent to or not. And if we do say 'no', where did that 'no' come from . . . and so on. The myth that haunts us here is the myth of a pure, free consciousness, above and separate from all the machinery that produces it, looking down on the work of its minions and largely assenting to their work, and occasionally stepping in with a royal, *deus ex machina* 'NO!' It's not like that.

Between the impulse and the act, there is a gap. A gap in which imagination can picture outcomes, in which alternative impulses can compete, in which, for instance, morality (such as yours is) has time to encounter impulse (such as yours are) before it commits to act. There is time to think. And when you are most consciously deliberating, just now and again, when you are genuinely poised over the whole question of what to do next, watch those routines interact and compete for supremacy, for access to that final common pathway they all want access to – enactment. And try, if you can, to watch that moment where action commences, where a final decision is made. The nearest I can picture it is like being a host, in most of its senses, from genteel (host of a party) to spooky (host to a possessing spirit). In these moments when we are hosts to the decision-making process, we are holding open a space for notions, routines and agents to meet, encounter and network, to deliberate – a get-together of a group who somehow manage to accomplish a common task. As host, or even more accurately, as the venue, you merely provide, you *are*, the material conditions where this team-work happens.

Mind the Gap. During that pause, our ability to remember and imagine comes into its own. Without the recourse to the gist of all our past, of who we are, without the ability to use that same faculty to imagine and construct future possibilities, there would be no space or time to think – no deliberation.

> With full gaze the animal sees the open.
> Only our eyes, as if reversed, are like snares,
> set around it, block the freedom of its going*

This is the poet Rainer Maria Rilke, comparing the thoughtless 'pure' gaze of the animal to the human's gaze, in which

> Never, not for a single day
> do we have pure space in which the flowers
> are always unfolding

For we live always in a partial world, of second thoughts and doubts, of versions and revisions of the present moment, which is, of course, never completely present. As Rilke puts it:

> so we live,
> forever saying farewell.

---

* Rainer Maria Rilke, 'The Eighth Elegy', *Duino Elegies: with English Translations by C. F. MacIntyre* (University of California Press, 1961).

For Rilke, the animal's unmediated pure and present acting, the immediacy of its response, is a freedom which we humans can never attain. It is certainly a freedom *from*: freedom from doubt, from deliberation. But our delay, our smear of consciousness that is simultaneously always ahead of itself and always trying to catch up with itself, that time for thinking is precisely what gives us the freedom *to*: to deliberate, to predict, to project a future and decide.

Or, rather, that pause provides the space in which deliberation can occur, where recall, prediction, projection and decision can happen. These processes are no less automatic, but they happen in the space of awareness. This space, to finish on one last analogy, is rather like the Greek forum, where multiple voices can be heard and brought into some kind of reconciliation, some consensus. Notice, no monarch in this analogy. There is no ultimate authority in us, rather we are a republican self. On the whole, with almost all the laws of the city already passed, this space for debate is unnecessary or minimal. The city will run itself, automatically. But occasionally something new will come along, which will give us pause for thought. And it is here that conscious deliberation comes into its own. Something new enters the picture, some 'News from Elsewhere' disrupts our normal service and causes us to question what is called for now. Before very long normal service will resume, with the old agents doing something differently, with a few new routines running, or some old ones terminated, but it is pretty much back to business as usual.

But for a moment there was a pause, and it is there that being human happens.

Chapter 3

House Rules

The Automatic is not confined by the borders of our skin. In this chapter we look inside our rooms and see how we use them to remember, think and act for us. We look at how our lives are lived in common rooms, shared spaces of established habit. As environmentally embedded habit greatly augments the life of the individual, so we see that the collective Automatic is what allows society to happen.

PART ONE

A Room of Our Own

Rebecca v. The Shining. Remember our beaten paths, the ways we wore within ourselves in becoming who we are. These paths are not only beaten in our nerves and memories, our muscles and gestures and habits of thought. We also beat them through our environment. As much as any collection of neurons, the rooms we live and work in remember who we are. The spreading of the load of ourselves into the environment is the subject of a new wave of psychological research and theory, sometimes known as 4E cognition. These four Es are embodied, embedded, extended and enacted. Each E emphasizes the extent to which thinking takes place outside the brain, in a body which is in turn situated within an environment which is an active participant in cognitive work. Or, as Richard Menary, philosopher of the mind, puts it:

> the construction of cognitive tools and artefacts in the cognitive niche, scaffold and support human cognition.*

Foxes have holes and birds have nests, but the Son of Man has a 'cognitive niche', an environment made with and for thought. This idea is the central theme of Daphne du Maurier's novel *Rebecca*. The young, nameless ingénue who is the book's heroine is haunted by the continued presence of Rebecca, the late wife of Maxim de Winter. When our nameless heroine becomes the new Mrs de Winter, she moves into her husband's house, Manderley. Like the Outlook

---

* R. Menary (ed.), *The Extended Mind* (MIT Press, 2010).

Hotel in Stephen King's supernatural horror story, *The Shining*,[*] Manderley is a handsome and famous building with a long history of social events and parties, and a host of expectations attached to it. Like the Outlook, Manderley has a past which, the new wife finds, expects itself to be repeated, a set of routines that are eager to continue running. And, again like the Outlook Hotel, Manderley has a presiding spirit; it is haunted by a presence that attempts to possess the new resident, and almost succeeds in physically destroying her and morally corrupting her. That spirit is Rebecca, the dazzling and charismatic first wife of Maxim de Winter. In both *Rebecca* and *The Shining*, the haunting ends with the conflagration of the host building. However, there is one key difference between these texts. *Rebecca* is not a horror story, nor a ghost story, nor is it even remotely supernatural. *Rebecca* is unique, to my knowledge, in being a novel about a secular, worldly haunting. Below, in a section narrated by the new Mrs de Winter, we see the profane version of how the dead continue to manifest:

> He [Maxim] did not belong to me at all, he belonged to Rebecca. He still thought about Rebecca. He would never love me because of Rebecca. She was in the house still, as Mrs Danvers had said; she was in that room in the west wing, she was in the library, in the morning-room, in the gallery above the hall. Even in the little flower-room, where her mackintosh still hung. And in the garden, and in the woods, and down in the stone cottage on the beach. Her footsteps sounded in the corridors, her scent lingered on the stairs. The servants obeyed her orders still, the food we ate was the food she liked. Her favourite flowers filled the rooms. Her clothes were in the wardrobe in her room . . . her nightdress on her bed. Rebecca was still mistress of Manderley.[†]

[*] Stephen King, *The Shining* (Doubleday, 1977).
[†] Daphne du Maurier, *Rebecca* (Gollancz, 1938).

As the quote above shows, Rebecca persists not as a singular focused and persecutory entity, but is embedded and extended through people, places and things. She has sculpted the gardens and paths that the new wife walks through, she has chosen all the furniture that she sits on, the dinner menus and the recipes are hers, the servants – particularly the sepulchral Mrs Danvers – still follow her instructions and work to routines established by her. Saturated by Rebecca, the house continues to run to her rules, rhythms and rituals.

In *Rebecca* there is what we might call a haunting from the ground up. In the normal ghost story, the spirit gradually enters normal life and begins to shape events, to manifest as interruptions to normal routine. Eventually the spirit distorts normality enough to create the conditions in which it can manifest in possession, or in quasi-material form. That's what happens in *The Shining*. The spirit manifests by gradually obsessing Jack, the new caretaker, with the Outlook's past, and by degrees possessing him. Unsettling and spooky things begin to happen to him, and to his wife and child. Normal reality in the empty, snow-bound hotel gradually becomes infused with the supernatural and horrific. It is slowly and master-fully done. Almost the exact opposite happens in *Rebecca*. The new wife arrives in a situation in which every part of the environment she moves in, every person she meets, every move she makes – how, when and where she has coffee; how, when and where she reads and answers her letters; how she deals with guests, dresses, sits, eats, walks – have all been prescribed by Rebecca. All *encode* Rebecca; embody, extend and enact her, continually manifesting her embedded presence. As difficult as this state of affairs is for the new Mrs de Winter, think how easy this would have made life for Rebecca. Having beaten paths all around her, how much easier the work of her daily life would have been, how much lighter the cognitive load. Like us, Rebecca lived in an environment that manifested her past decisions, and embedded and enacted her will automatically. This is another, external Automatic, an extension and embedding of the Automatic of Chapter 2, but an Automatic nevertheless; a repository of previously made decisions and of established routines, all of which enact us.

We live in rooms haunted by ourselves.

Holy Ghosts

... by names and images are all powers awakened and reawakened.

Aleister Crowley

Aleister Crowley, Dion Fortune, and other English occultists of the early twentieth century had a lot of time for the Catholic Church. Why? Because they knew real magic when they saw it. Occult magical practice – or a particular branch of it involving invocation – is essentially a prop-based practice. For instance, if you want to invoke the martial war-like energy of Mars, you surround yourself with appropriately Martial props – red clothing, swords, the number five, red crystals, the appropriate God or Angelic name, astringent incenses, etc. Having thus created 'a vehicle for manifestation', the occultist then expects the rituals and the props, the *form*, to invoke the spirit, the *force*, which will then inhabit the form. Form invokes force. The occultists saw exactly the same kind of practice at work in the Catholic Church, in its routines and rituals, in the choreographed movements, the incense, the robes, the consecrated tools and props, the altar, in the sheer theatricality of it all. By these means the Catholic Church attempts to invoke the divine presence, to set up the conditions for its manifestation. Similarly, the Jewish temple and its rituals can be seen as a building created specifically to be haunted by the presence of God – the Shekinah – 'the haunting presence of Yahweh in the Temple of Jerusalem'.*

This magical/religious tradition stands in contrast to the mystical/charismatic one. You can see the latter tradition at work in

* Rudolf Otto, *The Idea of the Holy* (Oxford University Press, 1923), p. 132.

evangelical churches. Here the Holy Spirit possesses the congregation. Some speak in tongues; others pass out, slain by the Spirit. The Spirit comes, descends upon the flesh, shapes, contorts and transforms it, claims it. These church services are notable for an absence of ritual and a deliberate cultivation of spontaneity. In these evangelical services, the Spirit descends unpredictably, breaking into and disrupting the normal reality of the room, determining the drama.

It's *Rebecca* versus *The Shining* again. In the Catholic tradition, the spiritual analogue of *Rebecca*, form invokes force, rituals and repetitions invoke the Spirit. In the other tradition, in the evangelical church and in *The Shining*, the spirit enters willy-nilly and starts to shape whatever it finds. We find the same distinction at work within different schools of acting. Some actors work from the outside in. They collect the props, the gestures, the words, the clothes, the facial hair, the shoes, and they build a character piece by piece, from the ground up. They build a form to invoke the spirit. Others work from the inside out. The Method men and women find the emotion first – the spirit – and they let that shape the form of the character.

So what? Why do all these priests and actors matter? What have they to say about us, our routines and their maintenance? Something essential. What *Rebecca* illustrates with such convincing force is that our routines, our habits and *our selves* are not confined to our bodies. Rebecca lived on as a real force, invoked by the form of her earthly props and routines; she was continually manifested in and by the house and its rules, its gardens and landscape, in the expectations and habits of the people that she knew. *Rebecca* shows us that these things continue to embody and invoke 'the essence', the real presence of a person, as effectively as any lingering ghostly soul. Similarly, priests and actors both remind us of the power of set and setting, of the centrality of props in embodying our identity. Shamans and showmen know the value of props.

Props Matter

Patients with such damage [to the frontal lobes of the brain, responsible for deliberate action] may exhibit . . . 'utilization behavior', a tendency to perform actions using objects or props that are instigated (often inappropriately) by the mere presence of those objects or props . . . One patient given three pairs of eyeglasses donned them in sequence and ended up wearing all three. It is as though, in these individuals . . . the idea of the act that is suggested by the object is enough to instigate the action.

Daniel Wegner[*]

Substance abusers usually become both behavioural and chemical addicts. They condition to cues connected with their drug taking, becoming turned on not only by smoking, drinking or injecting the substance itself, but also by the routine of preparing and administering it, and by other external cues concerning people, places and things associated with it.

Isaac Marks[†]

I am walking one night through Leicester Square in London. This is the Square where the big movies premiere, where you can sometimes see stars. There is also in the square the entrance to one of those nightclubs celebrities go to. As I walk, I notice a crowd has formed. Barriers have been erected, those temporary fences installed to separate the famous from the not, and on the not-side there is not so much a crowd as a border, four or five people deep, lining the fence that delineates the walkway from where the celebrity-carrier will pull up to the entrance to the club. Someone is coming. I hang about, hoping to see a star. So does everyone else. Bored but

---

[*] Daniel Wegner, *The Illusion of Conscious Will* (MIT Press, 2002).
[†] Isaac Marks, 'Behavioural (Non-chemical) Addictions', *British Journal of Addiction*, 85/11, (November 1990), 1389–94.

curious, I ask someone, who are we waiting to see? They are not sure. I ask someone else, they too are not sure, and have only gathered because they saw everyone else gather. I ask again and receive a similar reply every time. Eventually I ask a policeman. No one is expected that evening, he says. The barriers had been put up either too early or as a result of misinformation – even he wasn't sure – but as soon as the barriers were there, a crowd began to collect, and throughout that evening it continued to thicken.

My Room. Rooms suggest; props invoke. There is a well-observed phenomenon amongst older people with mild memory loss. If they are moved into a new environment, for example if they are put into a care home, they quite often undergo an apparently rapid decline in mental functioning. What is happening here is that their cues, their props and prompts, have gone. Their embodied routines have been abolished, the system of people, places and things which had hitherto guided their lives. With the beaten paths of habit removed, they no longer know which way to turn.

Look around my study. Before I started this project, I had spent two months arranging the room, collecting and ordering the books, papers and articles into one space. I mapped the shape of this book onto a wall chart. Before that I had spent several years writing notes in notebooks and dictating ideas into a Dictaphone and then transcribing them. Having decided on the form of each chapter, I created an index card file for each one, and on index cards I cross-referenced the chapters to the relevant notes and transcriptions, which I had also spent time indexing. I filled a filing cabinet with files, one for each chapter, each one containing articles and images that resonated with the chapter. In short, I spent several years getting this book out of my mind, and then two months spreading it all over this little room. Like a possessing spirit, I took over the room and shaped it, wrote all over it, intricately formed it. Like Rebecca, I now haunt this room.

Having thus formed the room, the operation went into reverse. The room will now write the book. This inanimate structure, this collection of notes, papers, cards and files, embodies this book and will invoke it, much like the rituals in the church, the junkie's works or the barriers in Leicester Square. The room *remembers* the book, so I don't have to. Part shrine, part cognitive prosthesis. Remove me from all of this and I would have to think long and hard about how to proceed. Like the old person in the care home, I wouldn't know where to go next.

We saw in the last chapter how memory is not confined to our minds. Drew Barrymore's character, in the film *50 First Dates*, had a memory, and thus an identity, artificially constructed for her from videos and notebooks. So I have here a mental prosthesis, a thing that thinks and remembers for me. I need it because, like you all, I can't really think for myself – not much. My working memory can only deal with a few bits of information at any one time. My ability to contain and develop a prolonged idea will run out quickly, as the end of the idea forgets its beginning. Like a word written in the night by a moving light, the glow sustains itself for just a few letters. If I want to write more, I will have to record it, I will have to contract out the job of memory to my environment. By contracting this work out – by compressing, say, two years of thinking about structure and content into a wall chart – I can amplify my cognitive capacity enormously. All I need to do is remember how to get to my room.

Look at the length of this riff on rooms and props. By writing down my arguments, by using this laptop prop in this study room, I can sustain and develop these thoughts for much longer than I could unaided. This is one of the enormous advantages of language and writing, one of our most useful props. I have been able to develop an argument, such as it is, not because my mind is prodigious, but because I have learned to use language, writing and external props to do my thinking. These tools and props are as much part of my thinking process as any thought 'in here'. Indeed, the 'in here'/'out there' thing seems almost irrelevant. My thinking is all over this room. My thinking happens in the negotiations between the various props and memory banks, external and internal devices and working spaces, articles, brain parts and filing cards. My thinking needs the props. It happens with them. As does yours.

Give any of us long enough in a space and we will upload to it, imprinting large portions of our thinking and our feelings onto our space. We will write our own house rules. It's particularly clear in work spaces, spaces where we want to do or to produce something. Work doesn't tend to happen in empty or unstructured rooms. We see on TV the effect that 'de-cluttering' has on people in makeover shows. We know how tidying the desk will make us think and feel sharper, or how a messy room can make us feel overwhelmed and fatigued. Senile or not, most of us depend on our environments to do a lot of our thinking for us. Without this room, I'm just a guy with a notion for a book. Equally, without me this room is, well, just weird. If you came and sat here, you would probably feel as comfortable as the new Mrs de Winter did in Manderley. Together, the room and I can do stuff that alone would be impossible. Rooms think.

The Language Room

In general, evolved creatures will neither store nor process information in costly ways when they can use the structure of the environment and their operations upon it as a convenient stand-in for the information-processing operations concerned. That is, know only as much as you need to know to get the job done.

Andy Clark, *Being There**

One does not *first* entertain a thought, and *then* write it down: rather the thinking is the writing.

Carruthers, quoted in Andy Clark, *Being There*

* Andy Clark, *Being There: Putting Brain, Body and World Together Again* (MIT Press, 1997).

Cognitive scientists talk about environmentally augmented thinking as 'scaffolded', attempting to convey the sense that there is no hard margin in thinking, no inside and outside; that when you are working on something, there is a flow of information and you are only one location in that flow. This writing, now, is happening as the thinking moves from wall chart to index card, to page 189 of philosopher of mind Andy Clark's book on extended cognition, to my notes on institutions, to thoughts of Bentham and Burke, to this laptop recording and remembering this evolving argument. From eye to hand to brain to machine to this. This thinking is happening in and with this room. There is even music from another room, a deliberately placed little nag, an emotional crutch placed to contain all the other background nags. Philip Larkin used to smoke while writing for a similar reason; his cigarette represented the necessary distraction for the task to be completed. This thinking, then, is taking up my whole living space. It is dependent on a whole host of prosthetics, cognitive prosthetics, the ultimate one being language.

It almost makes no sense to think of it so, but try and think of thinking without the institution of language. Andy Clark calls language 'the ultimate artefact'. The imposition of a shared language on our human nervous system augments our cognitive capacity to such an extent that it is not entirely clear how or if we could think without it. The ability to encode our knowledge in symbols, be they external or internal, and then to be able to manipulate these symbols, means that our ideas can 'die in our stead'. We don't need to go through costly and dangerous manipulations of the environment to figure out what the outcome might be, as we can use representations which we can manipulate to predict likely outcomes. We can control and coordinate our behaviour, with lists and inner and outer prompts. We can communicate our ideas to others, and plan and coordinate large and complex group activities. And, perhaps most importantly for our uniquely human faculties, suggests Clark, we can have thoughts about our thoughts. A thought captured in language then becomes like any other object in the world, something we can think about. This is indeed something that the animals can't do, for language gives us the ability to self-reflect, to consider the present thoughts in our head, to distil the past into propositions and conclusions and use them to interpret the present and predict the future, to time travel (see Chapter 2, Part Three). Language and representation is what allows us to pause for thought, to act well or badly, to deliberate, to be human. Indeed, Daniel Dennett goes so far as to suggest that it is the imposition of culture and language on our brains that gives rise to consciousness and to our sense of self. For if language and symbols are what allow us to think, to deliberate and reflect in the here and now, they are also what allow us to put together a thing called a self, and for that self to become another thing that we can think about.

Our passage through the world leaves an impression, a record written in language and symbols. Over time, in these memories and records, we have written the biography of us. And not just, of course, in internal symbols, but in our rooms and the things we accumulate within them.

Through all of these, *in* all of these, we accumulate a biography and write a story about ourselves. Rooms remember who we are.

PART TWO

Common Rooms

A *World without Props*. If, like Rebecca, we have indeed distributed ourselves through our environments, then to damage these props could have as profound an effect on us as damage done directly to our person.

Or, to put it another way, our person resides as much in our props as it does in our body. We have looked at how I might be relatively senile if I was removed from this book-room, but let's extend this and go to the heart of the argument. Take *all our props* away and what are we left with, how are we then? For sure, some inner cognitive record stays. If I am fairly cognitively robust, I'll retain enough of the gist of me to reconstruct a new environment. If I am older or slower, this process will take some time, throwing me for quite a while. If I am already at the beginning of a cognitive decline, it will hasten my fall. And to some degree – think of the temporary disorientations of moving house – it will really matter. I will change. Let us take this even further and begin to think about our collective props. In imagining the collective world without its props, we begin to see that props are more than a personal record, more than just a story of 'I', for they also tell the story of *us*.

Imagine a society without all the props. For me, an image springs to mind of a snail or tortoise without its shell, something hideously vulnerable and incomplete, something that isn't going anywhere. Hollywood sometimes tries to picture this, though rarely with as much dour conviction as the Austrian film-maker and philosopher Michael Haneke. In his film *Time of the Wolf* (2003), he cuts straight to disaster's aftermath, leaving us to infer a preceding apocalypse. He paints the days after in the colours of documentary realism, and for much of the film there is no artificial light, only day- or fire-light. People gather in frightened herds where psychopaths vie for leadership. Men control the supply of food with power and violence. Women barter sex for food and protection. No one is happy.

Kevin Costner also tried to think about the world without props, in two films, *Waterworld* (1995) and *The Postman* (1997). Both films were universally derided, but *The Postman* received a philosophic rehabilitation when the philosopher Slavoj Žižek used it to illustrate something about society. Žižek's argument goes something like this. Like Haneke, Costner shows us a world after an unspecified apocalypse. Like Haneke, he presents us with a picture of frightened herds and ruling psychopaths. But he takes it one step further and attempts to show how society begins to re-stitch itself together. In doing so, he sheds some light on the texture of the social fabric. The agent of this reparative weaving, the first thread that creates the warp through which the new society will be woven, is a lie.

Costner, the unnamed hero of the drama, is on the run from one of the ruling psychopaths. Arriving at a new community, seeking shelter, he invents a story. He pretends that there has been a reconstitution of the central government. Since there is no communication between the scattered herds, there is no way for them to know if this is true or not, but he provides a kind of proof. This 'government', he claims, has reinstituted the postal service and he is its first postman. Of course he needs some props to play this part. Having found some old letters on the corpse of a postman, he has taken his clothes and letters to this nearest herd. This was really only a ploy to get food and shelter, but the letters are received with an unanticipated degree of gratitude. Replies are drafted and he is given them in trust, and so becomes trapped into the role that started as a lie. Now the actual postman, he rides to the neighbouring communities and delivers the new letters. More replies are drafted. The herds begin to communicate, to recombine. A larger Us starts to re-form. A network of volunteers joins Costner, as enthused as he was cynical, and in the name of the reconstituted government, which is still a lie, they maintain and expand the scope of the postal service. Gradually, as the threads of communication are repeated and thickened, the fabric of society is renewed and the tribes are reunited. What started as a lie, as a prop-based lie, becomes – through its enactment, through a bunch of people acting *as if* – true; it becomes embedded, embodied and extended.

These celluloid experiments in de-civilization point out the obvious: that without the props of civilization we revert to basic bestial behaviour. But Costner's film points out something subtler: that there is something fictional, something performative at the heart of our civilization.

Fictions. The father of utilitarianism and philosopher of law, Jeremy Bentham was one of the first to notice that a lot of our civilized behaviour was, strictly speaking, based on fictions and fictitious entities. Legal contracts were his point of departure. A contract is purely notional, just some words on paper, full of abstract notions like 'rights' and 'obligations', which, again strictly speaking, don't really exist, yet if we all behave as if the contract and the notions within it are true, then it becomes so. And this fictitious entity, this contract, if we all believe it, has a very real, definitive impact on the world. Adherence to it, or a failure to do so, will change the lives of those bound by it. For Bentham, then, a lot of life was about fictitious entities and fictions, fictitious entities being the objects – the legal contracts – and the fictions being the set of relationships between them and the people they affect, the stories that happen when we treat the fictitious entities as real. The result, as Costner points out, is civilization.

The novelist Terry Pratchett makes the same point in his story about the Hogfather. In Pratchett's alternative universe of Discworld, the Hogfather is Father Christmas. Like Costner and Bentham, Pratchett wants to point out the civilized necessity of believing in the fictional; like Žižek, he wants to point out that for reality to happen, a certain amount of fantasy is necessary to underpin it. The following dialogue takes place towards the end of the TV film version of the *Hogfather* (2006). The personification of

Death (a skeleton in a cloak holding a scythe, of course) and his granddaughter Susan are reflecting on the meaning and purpose of their successful saving of this alternative universe's Christmas. By taking over the role of the Hogfather for the night, Death has managed to sustain belief in that entity, for he has a deeper sense of what happens when humans stop believing in fictions:

SUSAN: You're saying humans need . . . fantasies to make life bearable?

DEATH: No. Humans need fantasy to be human. To be the place where the falling angel meets the rising ape.

SUSAN: Tooth fairies? Hogfathers?

DEATH: Yes. As practice. You have to start out learning to believe the little lies.

SUSAN: So we can believe the big ones?

DEATH: Yes. Justice. Mercy. Duty. That sort of thing.

SUSAN: They're not the same at all!

DEATH: Take the universe and grind it down to the finest powder and sieve it through with the finest sieve and then show me one atom of justice, one molecule of mercy. And yet you act as if there were some sort of rightness in the universe by which it may be judged.

SUSAN: Yes. But people have got to believe that or what's the point?

DEATH: My point exactly.*

Going back to tribes and their cohesion, take another example to drive home the point of the strictly fictional nature of our communal house rules, our notional props: in Exodus, pre-Sinai, we have a dislocated people, a dispersed bunch of nomads, denuded of all their civilizing props, like the herds in *Time of the Wolf* and *The Postman*. What makes them cohere, civilizes and brings them together as a people? Words. Some words scratched into stone in the form of

* Two-part television adaptation of *Terry Pratchett's Hogfather*, shown on Sky One, 17/18 December 2006.

Ten Commandments, the ultimate house rules. But these ten sentences are more than a set of arbitrary prescriptions. Gershom Scholem, student of Jewish mysticism, writes: 'The revelation on Mount Sinai, is, as everyone knows . . . a summons to the human community'.

Those ten sentences transformed the herd into a people, a *them* into an *us*. Things begin to build from there. These sentences form the warp through which civilization was woven. As these fictions were assented to and acted upon, so they accumulated mass and became embodied in communal behaviour – in people, places and things – just as in *The Postman*. In the same way that the individual will form, re-form and transform their environment to become an embodiment, a cognitive prosthesis, a record and a part of themselves, so the collective action will alter and form the human landscape – it *has* formed the human landscape – the collective space in which you and I are passing guests.

The Collective Automatic. It was the philosopher and political theorist Edmund Burke who in the eighteenth century first noted the evolving nature of our fictions, how they have grown over millennia to form the grand proscenium, the stage and the set of the institutions and collective practices in which we all play our parts. He saw them as massive structural biases in history, deep-seated societal habits and prejudices, compared to which individual will and whim was a minor fleeting force. They are the societal equivalent of the Automatic. As we have seen, we humans are designed to automate most of what we do. As we grow, we become repositories of idiosyncratic habits, conventions and prejudices which, past a certain age, rarely get re-thought. So, Burke argued, with society: the buildings and books, the law courts, churches and schools, the universities, the institutions and the armies of the law and of the military; their constitutions, codes and traditions; the thing called money, its ways and means; our codes of morals, conduct and manners; this whole armature of civilization, its sub- and super-structure, is our collective cognitive prosthesis, an external repository of accumulated memory, the scaffolding of our thinking about how to live together.

This is the armature, these the props, without which we would be snails without shells. This is why Burke was so wary of revolution, of planned, conscious change. If institutions are the collective wisdom of the people, the result and repository of thousands of years of thinking, he was loath to recognize that the whim of a particular generation should be heeded over the voice of the centuries. Whatever one makes of this as politics, his insight is keen. The real revolutionaries, those who wish to start from the bottom up, the Year Zero guys, they know the truth of this. They know that to change the Collective Automatic, you need to eradicate every root, every embodiment and extension of the wisdom of the centuries. This doesn't mean just getting rid of a few people at the top. It means abolishing the entire scaffolding, or root system, of civilization, which is pretty much everything. Real revolution looks like a natural disaster, where all the buildings, all the embodiments of knowledge, have been erased, all the props smashed, the rooms trashed. In losing our civilizing props, we lose our collective selves.

A Walk in the Park. To encounter and appreciate our collective wisdom, we do not need to lose it. Take a stroll through your local park. The park is, at the same time, the map and the territory of enjoyment. This public space is our shared memory of the solved problems of leisure. The better the park, the less we have to think what to do next. We place ourselves at the beginning of the path and it walks us, guides us through its sub-routines, its different games. Here for children, there for the scenic stroll, there for tennis, here to sit and enjoy the sun. The path leads, we follow. Many other sets of circumstances, many other social objects, play a similar game with us. The fairground and the playground are the archetypes of these. We want to be taken for a ride, to give over agency, to abdicate will, for a while, to something that will move us without our conscious intercession. That is what we want from leisure, it's what leisure *is* – the switching off of choice and doubt. We want environments, sometimes, where the thinking has already been done. It thinks so we don't have to. We want to abdicate our wills in leisure, we want to be temporary Taoists. The Taoists were early Chinese philosophers for whom the ideal way of life was *wu wei*, or non-action. Not in the sense of doing nothing, but rather in the sense that a plant grows towards the sun. The plant doesn't have to consider and try, it just naturally does the right thing. We might yearn for this effortless and implicit knowing of the right action in day-to-day life, but we don't expect it. On holiday we do. By spending money, by employing people and placing ourselves in their pre-packaged routines, we expect a minimum of fuss and bother. We want the thing that Lily loved about high society in *The House of Mirth*. We want one scene to shift to another without perceptible agency.

A walk in the park is a clever synonym for ease. Move a little on and up from leisure, away from the fun, and the rules don't change so much, only the feelings of the participants. It's obvious with christenings, weddings and funerals, the sacraments and markers of birth and death. We have, collectively, beaten paths, worn ruts to guide and channel the actions, feelings and thoughts of these occasions. There are roles for the characters, places for them to be, actions for them to perform. Ritual contains things, allows life to happen. This is no less true as you walk around the supermarket or when you visit the cinema or restaurant or when you sit down to work, when you assume your office, your place in society, the thing that you do to get the money. Our living occurs within a pre-established and overarching order, and our relationship to our place within that order is ambivalent.

There is an old story, one we retell a lot, where the socio-symbolic matrix, the system in which we are immersed, is the source of oppression and the hero's defining characteristics are rebellion and subversion. Usually, in this story, the system is overthrown, transformed or escaped. Occasionally, Big Brother-like, it wins. In this light we might see revolution as a refusal to walk the desire lines of posterity, as an attempt to forge and walk new ones. The rebellious spirit is pioneering, ground-breaking, romantic. Who wants to be a cog? But we are as complicit as we are coerced. Apart from the most basic mass behaviour – mob rule – the coordination of collective human being requires a set of prescribed routines, moves and roles, props and scripts. In all this pre-scription, oppression may be there, but there is also a massive amount of freedom: the freedom *from* having to think again and reinvent, and the freedom *to* be with one another in complex and difficult states. In our collection of props and practices lie the possibilities of liberation and leisure, the machinery for communication and communion.

Giant's Shoulders. The sociologist William Sumner had another term for this collective Automatic: 'folkways'. Trying to imagine them beginning, he writes:

> The operation by which folkways are produced consists in the frequent repetition of petty acts, often by great numbers acting in concert or, at least, acting in the same way when face to face with the same need . . . It produces habit in the individual and custom in the group.*

Custom in the group. What distinguishes us from the pride of lions is pinpointed here in the analogy between individual habit and group custom. As habits accumulate over the lifetime of the individual, refining and automating ever more domains of their life, so, too, customs grow in the body of the group and knowledge accretes. The later we are born, the more knowledge we inherit about how to live. This has also been called by cognitive scientists the 'cultural ratchet'. While each new generation of lions is back to a kind of Year Zero of lion life, back to solving the problems of how to live again, we have evolved the means of transmitting them from generation to generation, so that even if the next generation does nothing,

* William Sumner, *Folkways: A Study of the Sociological Importance of Usages, Manners, Customs, Mores and Morals* (Ginn and Co., 1906).

adds nothing to the mix, still they stand on the shoulders of their ancestors, privileged inheritors of millennia of custom, born lucky.

The individual space of human cognition is small. Unaided human cognition is a luminous but brief trace, constantly erasing itself as it progresses, like the vapour trail of a jet. Compare the expert acrobat to the beginner. Through pain, effort and the repetition of countless little acts, the expert has automated a host of routines and sub-routines so that his performance is fluid and smooth. Real spontaneity emerges from thousands of little rules so rigid they are no longer up for negotiation. So with the species, for without the accumulation of culture and the props handed down from generation to generation, without the body of custom and habit, each generation would have to start again, like an acrobat forgetting every morning what he learned the day before. And we have become better and better at the retention and transmission of information itself. We have learned how to learn: much of our technology is devoted to devices that ensure the fidelity of our storage and transmission of information. We are born with an overwhelming inheritance.

Set in Our Ways. So here you are, here we all are, semi-automated creatures in our tram-track worlds, running through the paths of least resistance, the paths well known, running the routines we know and love the best, the old favourites. We play by the house rules, our own, and the ones we have inherited. After a certain age the customs you follow, the habits and routines you have acquired, the props you have established, the set you have built and furnished, the roles you inhabit and what you look for the world to afford you, all of this will be subject to fairly superficial change. You will have spread your identity through your world, as Rebecca did through hers, and it will repeat it back to you. It will say 'I' for you. There won't be a major rewrite and that's fine, because that's the whole point of being this kind of creature in this kind of world – to reach a state of relative ease, where most of the groundwork has been done, and where we only need to pay attention to the threats to the status quo, or to the challenging, or to the new. That's what we do and how we are. We live in and by routine, until we are forced not to. But before we encounter the inciting incident, the thing that will disrupt our settled ways and end Act One, there is one more element of routine life that we must consider.

We do not inhabit these rooms alone; there are other people to think about. Let us consider them.

Chapter 4
Cosa Nostra

Following a brief announcement of the impending end of our small world (Act Two), this chapter considers the importance of other people in establishing and maintaining our habits and routines. We see the fundamental importance of our social networks in reflecting back to us a self that we find more or less bearable. We set the stage for the beginning of the end of Act One.

Coming Soon. The end of the world. It's out there and it has nothing to do with you – it does not concern you, not at all. Given your likes and dislikes, your attractions and repulsions, it wouldn't even register. You wouldn't know what to do with it, wouldn't even know it if it hit you, which it will, because it *is* coming. From the moment you were born, the end of your world was heading your way: inexorable, relentless, measured and patient. It's heading for you, taking its time, every day bringing it closer. Heading for you here, now blithe and established in your intact and complete and forever world. The small world where you know the score, you know what's up, what's happening; you know how things go, how they look, where the thrills and fears come from; you even know what the disaster, should it strike, might look like. You have it all figured out and your fears are just as vivid as your hopes. You think you have it all sewn up, surrounded as you are by something like a bubble, a shelter, onto which you project some pictures of this and that – a hope, a fear. And you imagine that anything that came to disrupt this small world would look like the horror, or the longing, in your head, the pictures you have projected onto the walls, the vivid expulsions, the violent expressions of your hopes and fears, And the worst, the nightmare, the repulsive, the awful, the unthinkable end, of course you've pictured that, scrawled it in shit and blood, in crude and primal images, graphic and abandoned in the horror corner – you think the worst will come from there, looking like that. But something entirely different is heading for you, like an ocean liner or steamroller, a leviathan of unstoppable momentum, an enormous and impersonal weight slowly hurtling its way toward you. It will never ever stop and it's almost here. Now you

Figure 3. Jim Carrey

can hear a noise *outside* the shelter. Now there is movement *outside* your bubble and do you know, this is the first time that space has opened for you, that until this moment you thought outside was just how it looked on the pictures on your wall? Big surprise a-coming . . .

But before our world ends, let us look at a key component, so far missing from our account. We have looked behind the scenes of our Automatic and the beaten paths within. We have traced the shape that our routines make in the world of props and places. We have seen that there is a societal Automatic no less compelling than our personal one. But there is another important repository of our selves, one other element inside our small worlds that we rely on to say 'I' for us. It's time to meet the neighbours. Then, I promise, the world will end. In fact, let's start there.

The Parable of the Mustard Seed. The woman had lost everything. She had seen her sons being force-fed their dead father before they too were hacked and burned to death. Turning, running to her mother's home, she found it consumed in flames, her mother tied and screaming from within. Then – nothing, ashes.

Wild-eyed, extraordinary, avoided, she roamed the countryside, wailing and tearing at herself, at her clothes and hair, beyond, way beyond understanding. Then she met the Buddha, and something about him must have calmed her, brought her down just enough to get her story across, or something like it, for the story, the horror was conveyed – angry, furious, wild, desperate and, ultimately, right out there at the very tip of her fury, at the end of this slew of violent and bloody emotion, there glowed a tiny glimmer, against all odds, of hope, a little bit of hope which must have made her angrier still. And what he, the Enlightened One, said to her was: 'Go into every house in the village and ask for a grain of mustard, a mustard seed, but only take one from those who have never suffered loss, who have never known grief. Do this.' Now, why would she want to do that? What was the Buddha's point?

The standard interpretation is that this is the Buddha once again trying to illustrate that all life is suffering – that First Noble Truth of Buddhism. As a told-you-so, this message may seem both callous and de trop. After all, the woman of the parable already knows that life is suffering, and telling her to ask everyone else how they feel will probably not help. As my friend Maureen says, when people try the there-is-always-someone-worse-off-than-yourself line on her, 'if I don't have any shoes, it doesn't help telling me that there are people with no legs'. It just annoys. So why send our lady of horror on a quest to verify that all life was suffering? Why send her round all her friends' and neighbours' houses?

Friends and neighbours, there is the rub. A more subtle telling, or interpreting, of the parable has the Buddha know all along that the mustard-seed quest was just a wild goose chase or, more accurately, a McGuffin of the sort commonly used in film and fiction, a plot device that kick-starts the story but is of no intrinsic value. Imagine our story's extraordinary protagonist as she returns to her village and one by one visits all her friends' and neighbours' houses. They take her in, and she tells them her story and about her

Buddha-initiated quest, and they listen and in turn tell her their own stories of loss and horror. On this journey the mustard seed soon ceases to matter – the McGuffin is usually irrelevant by the middle of Act Two – and the story becomes about the results of the *process*, about the going from door to door to neighbours and friends. As she does this – moving, talking, weeping, holding and being held – as she communicates and communes, so she begins to re-stitch her social ties, begins to re-weave her network. And now that there are for her the beginnings of a new community, there is also somewhere for her grief to go, to be contained and dispersed, a new small world in which she can begin to find and re-establish herself, know herself and be known for what she now is.

Yet we shouldn't be too Disney about this. There will be strong lines of repulsion and avoidance in this new network. It will not be the weave of old, for not all can bear our transformations, and those who can and can't will be hard to predict in advance. But there will be a new weave, as she moves from door to door, like a spider making the first threads of a new web. The Buddha's surreal request had set in motion the re-establishment of her social matrix.

The Matrix Established

ma·trix *n. pl.* ma·tri·ces or ma·trix·es
1. A situation or surrounding substance within which something else originates, develops, or is contained: 'Freedom of expression is the matrix, the indispensable condition, of nearly every form of freedom' (Benjamin N. Cardozo).
2. The womb. [*Lat.*; *Fr.* Mater, Mother.] See *ground substance*.

There are two forces at work in the establishment of society, of what has come to be our civilization. There is, if you will, a dialectic between force and form. For the anthropologists this process is most stark at the beginning and they imagine a picture something like this: there was a point in history near the beginning of this brief civilized epoch in which we now live, when an explicit tension arose between male and female drives. They talk in terms of reproductive costs. These of course are high for women, involving a long and intensive gestation, followed by a long period of infant protection and nurturing. For men there are only a few isolated mechanical humps. Low cost, no maintenance. Under these conditions, common sense and game theory dictates that women will cooperate to try and keep the reproductive costs down. They will share them. To try and limit male depredations, they will unite. Men, on the other hand, will want to disband these cooperative efforts, to try and access and inseminate as many women as possible, to produce as many offspring as they can. This is a primal, and not so unfamiliar, tension. The unity of the women begins to assert itself at a biological level. To keep men from picking off the few women in heat, the women's menstrual cycles begin to synchronize. In a kind of biological equivalent of 'I Am Spartacus', all are in the fertile pool at the same time. An uneasy truce is imagined, in this dream of our beginning, in which the women form bargains with the men, allowing sexual access to the reproductive pool in return for provisions.* An exchange of energies. If the men will use their energy to acquire food, and pass it on, the women can give this energy to raising the children, and to keeping the weave together. Between this drive to form, to cohere, and the drive to disintegrate, to disrupt – between force and form – our society begins. All hail the supernal mothers.

The Matrix Continued

ground substance
noun: a more or less homogeneous matrix that forms the background in which the specific differentiated elements of a system are suspended.

* Nothing changes.

Visiting a new city recently, a stranger in a strange land, forced through work to meet a new group of people, I found myself stuck at lunch, in the middle of the canteen table, with a disparate group of people brought together by professional happenstance. A stranger among strangers: all in search of a topic to bind their lunch. You could feel the cohesion starting to form. Someone attempts humour; this is welcomed and amplified by laughter; this warms the group and encourages others to try. The soon-to-be-not-so-popular lady makes an awkward attempt at humour, which comes off a little flat, that topic ends, a moment's silence, then someone picks up another thread, runs with it; someone picks that up, does a little number; and so the weave builds, the lunch is sustained within a matrix of commonality, however hastily fabricated. We ate as one, we shared, we communed, we got by. The group of strangers kept each other company as they fuelled their bodies. Over five days of our forced propinquity, the cohesion grew.

What on earth did we have in common, this group from different worlds, brought together by accident and circumstance? The weather. Every day, every conversation started with the weather. How was the weather in my city? How was the weather here? Weather was the highest common denominator, the proscenium arch under which our acts would be performed; the weather bound us all first and foremost, united us under common skies. And after weather came the people we all knew, the people we strangers had in common, the people, places and things all of us (or most of us) had seen. These people, these places and these things, their struggles and their dramas, all occurred on television, mostly on so-called reality TV. Television, over those five days, allowed this intimacy at a common distance to form. It provided a collective background of people, place and drama, a place to reveal our individual moralities, our affiliations, our likes and dislikes, our preferences and fancies, the way TV does for people meeting at a distance. The way that in the village, in the fixed communities of some halcyon pseudo-past, we presumably just talked about the actual characters and dramas of the neighbourhood. TV knitted, for a time, our disparate group together.

More than knitted, for against this matrix, this ground substance, there were common objects around which we could differ. Gradually our characters emerged, our specific and differentiated elements began to stand out against this ground substance. Pretty soon we had an idea, a notion of each other. We began to get a sense of who we liked and disliked, who we wouldn't mind doing more of this with, who we would laugh with, who we would argue with, who we just wouldn't be bothered with. Occasionally we spot someone who feels like they are of our tribe, a distant long-lost family member. That's a rare one, when a little tingle runs between you, a channel already opened, just waiting to be run. Miracle of the modern age, it provides the means of bringing together these people from far-flung corners and gives them a common ground on which to meet and find each other's measure.

If not TV, then films and celebrities, or the most recent disasters or sporting fixtures, our modern pantheons, our electronic weather. Once, perhaps, in another halcyon pseudo-past, the common talking point of accidentally affiliated strangers was the gods, or simply God. That was the ground substance, the matrix in which we, the elements, could differentiate, against which we could stand out and know the others. God was our common substance, like these real and virtual weathers now, the proscenium arch underneath which we all stood and against which we stood out. And this is indeed the etymology of gossip: God-Sib, God-Sibs, God-Siblings, brothers and sisters under God, united in a weave, a common world of communication and exchange, united because there was something we all stood in relation to, like knights around the round table, like those women with their children around the ancient fires, on common ground, united by a common gossip.

So at lunch that day, the gossip bound us, but also kept us apart, at a distance, for the gossip was not about ourselves, but about the modern pantheon: shiny, distant, safe, dramatic. This was not the gossip of intimates, not the gossip we would share with our friends, of ourselves and each other – actual characters, real dramas. But either way, there is a shared substance, an act of spoken communion that temporarily unites the strangers, or binds the close-knit group, in a common world of gossip. To imagine a small social world, a close-knit group, a definite and closed community is to imagine a particular world of shared gossip, a talking around and about a shared and common ground. This shared gossip, the ability to participate in it, to know who and what matters not only coheres the group; just as importantly, it allows you to spot outsiders.

Guess Who's Coming to Dinner? The arrival of the stranger, the walking news from elsewhere, is the starting point of many narratives. How the stranger is received varies from genre to genre, but for the moment I am thinking of a certain type where the community does not so much absorb the outsider as consume them, where the alien body is not assimilated but destroyed. I am thinking of horror: *The Wicker Man* (1973), *Straw Dogs* (1971), the scene at the opening of *An American Werewolf in London* (1981) where the strangers arrive at the pub called the Slaughtered Lamb and as they enter all talk stops dead; *The Texas Chain Saw Massacre* (1974); *The Hills Have Eyes* (1977); *Deliverance* (1972). In each of these movies our point of view is attached to the stranger; with them we arrive in a community which has undergone a form of moral speciation.

Genetic speciation happens thus. If a part of the herd is geographically isolated from the main body, it begins to alter. As the tide of the group recedes and leaves the isolated pool of individuals behind, they can only breed amongst themselves and, generation by generation, they grow apart, differentiate, to the extent that one day, should they meet their mother-herd, they would not recognize them as family. They evolve on their own, away from the community they used to be part of. This is how new species are produced – genetically. And morally, too, in these communities of horror. The hillbillies in *Deliverance*, who use strangers for sex and blood sports, have a way of life that has evolved in isolation and become a world of its own. Its resemblance to its moral predecessors was one of contrast, not affinity. So too with all the small worlds into which the stranger walks. These are communities where the lines and threads of gossip run purely internally, where an intranet weaves them as one body. All threads and ties to the outside world have perished or been severed, and their very isolation ensures their coherence. Any threads that run outside the group would act as drains on its identity, or routes of infection; they would threaten the small world. These breakaway communities must police their borders ruthlessly. The stranger arrives, a foreign body full of foreign news. Group membership cannot be negotiable, for that would infect the group and end the world. The stranger will not be used for information, but for energy; his or her substance will be consumed, used as sacrifice or food, sport or entertainment, or all of the above.

Of course this is true of all of us to a certain degree. These horror communities are only exaggerations of our general herding tendency to affiliate and differentiate, to form elective affinities and definite dislikes, to form bonds and borders on the bases of taste and common ground. To distinguish us and them. The playground groups and adult cliques are no less exclusive, it's just that the violence of exclusion is less extreme and, usually, more symbolic than physical. But any adult of long enough standing to have left their family of origin will have collected a motley crew of others who make up their new small social world.

London Transport, the governing body of the capital's transport infrastructure, used to have a surprisingly abstract definition of family. On the back of their family ticket, where up to two adults and two children could travel cheaply, they defined family like this: 'Family are those who stay together for the duration of the journey'. And this really captures something of how we feel about our motley crew. They are the people whom we have met and shared a journey with, people who have stuck with us along the way. It's now almost commonplace to refer to these people as a kind of family. In modern sociology they talk about the chosen or urban family. The

TV series *Friends* was probably a turning-point in our way of speaking in public about this. *You* are my family, friend affirms to friend, you are my moral kin, my likewise, my type, my tribe. I recognize myself in you, with you I stand on common ground, under a common sky, siblings under a shared god, a law unto ourselves, in a world of our own. We talk the same language. You get me. Friends. But not all of these self-selecting families are a cosy group of friends. Some families go looking for strangers. Charles Manson knew what he was doing when he called his community of horror 'The Family'.

Cosa Nostra

Cosa Nostra
noun: a crime syndicate in the United States; organized in families; believed to have important relations to the Sicilian Mafia (lit. 'Our Affair')

We will manage our world for ourselves because it is our world, *cosa nostra*. And so we have to stick together to guard against outside meddlers.

Don Corleone in Mario Puzo, *The Godfather* (1969)

The Family is a cell. A mono-nuclear organism with membranes only semi-permeable to the outside world, enough to allow nutrition and a little light in, but strong enough to maintain the integrity of the whole and the isolation of the parts within it. The family is a cell from which we will never entirely walk free, will never entirely get over or out of. The world of families is a world of autonomous cells, units isolated from the world and beyond scrutiny, units only loosely attached to other units, potential terror cells in which all the atrocities and horrors of the world are hatched and nurtured, planned and perpetrated.

The Family is the root of all evil. A therapist tells me of a client who came to him with the story of how her father, from an early age up until she left home, would come and 'hug' her in the morning, lie behind her and spoon, how she could feel his erection press against her and, looking up, how she could see her mother's eye pressed against the crack in the bedroom door. Almost every morning she was caught between her father's cock and her mother's gaze. The question she had for the therapist was this: 'Is that normal?'

The Family is a law unto itself. To imagine a family is to imagine a way of life. 'Is that normal?' That's the question, there's the rub: is that normal? Every family is a little island of speciation, a pool of deviance. Every family is normal in its own way. It's hard to imagine how we got like that, by what imperceptible series of steps we got to the point where those kinds of things were normal, were OK, where we had to ask a stranger's opinion to see if that's the case for everyone. How many times have we heard it, read it or said it: 'I just thought all families were like that, I just thought that's how things were done.' When we see those programmes, where parts of one family are transplanted into another's – *Wife Swap*, for example – what we are seeing is not a clash of individuals, but of forms of life, of ways of living. The rules are unique to every family, in a way that we will never know until we leave it, until we get to ask someone else: 'Was that normal?'

The Family is normal. The family is the first normal we will encounter. 'Home is heaven for beginners,' said the clergyman Charles H. Parkhurst. Or hell. 'The family is society in embryo. It is the place where the performance of moral duty is made easy by natural affection,' said the *I Ching*. Or not. 'Microcosm, Moral Boundaries & Practice, Division of Labour, Social Organization,' says a more faithful, neutral translation of the same verse, this time not specifying the valence or nature of the boundaries, divisions, organization, labour and practices at work in this factory for forming lives. It could go either way. No one from the inside will stop it, because it's as normal as the weather. No one outside will see, because the law stops at the borders of the family, it's no one else's business, it's a family affair, our affair, our world, *Cosa Nostra*. The family is organized crime.

The Family will explain everything. The family is the first explanatory framework that we will have. Like a religion and a science, like a primitive tribe, it will have a cosmology, a theology, an ontology, a morality, an aesthetic and a very strict admissions policy. It will let us know what is what and what is right and wrong and how things should be done and where and why we got it wrong again, at which point it will proclaim the cry of matriarchs and patriarchs from time immemorial: 'this is *not* how things are done in *this* family'. The family will let us know.

The Family hurts. The family is more important than any of its individual members, who will be sacrificed if necessary to maintain the integrity of the whole. If we do not fit the family mould, like Procrustes it will stretch or cut us out to fit. No one will stop it, for the family is the first unit of exclusion, the primal, proto-division, the template of all subsequent divisions into us and them. The family is our first experience of affiliation and affinity, of repulsion and exclusion; the family will keep the meddlers out and us in. The family is us.

The Family is you. The family will let you know who you are and what you are like; the family will tell you when you have let it down, or when you have done it proud. It will set your standards and let you know if you live up to them. The family is your first experience of seeing yourself reflected in the distorting mirror of the other's gaze, your first experience of having to explain yourself, account for yourself, your first experience of having to decide what kind of 'you' you are, and to think up reasons quickly, because the family wants to know who you think you are, and what you think you are doing. Your family will tell you. Your family will tell you who you are.

Once you're into this family, there's no getting out.*

* Tony from *The Sopranos*, Season 3.

Net Working

> In Ersilia, to establish the relationships that sustain the city's life, the inhabitants stretch strings from the corners of the houses, white or black or gray or black-and-white according to whether they mark a relationship of blood, of trade, authority, agency.
>
> Italo Calvino, *Invisible Cities**

Babies grin like loons at strangers, sheer fear fuelling their joy-contorted faces: 'Please, I'm cute, don't kill me'. The stranger has no ties, no connections within the community. Until we get to know them, it is best to placate them, contain them or kill them. When did you last welcome a stranger? There is probably a graph in some book of new affiliations, the line that measures their number and frequency tailing off as age increases. To be set in our ways is not only a matter of personal routines and habits, it is also about who we know.

Imagine all the people you know as an array of dots, a pristine field, at first, of unconnected elements. Look at page 95, you'll find them all there. Now, place yourself at the centre (naturally) and begin to connect the dots. As in Calvino's city, you could use different coloured lines. Use blue to denote those relationships based on liking and affiliation.† These will be the ones you chose yourself – the adult, urban *Friends*-type family, the family you made yourself. You probably like the 'you' you are with them. Use black to denote relationships of commerce, based on work, and grey for those based on mere enforced propinquity: colleagues and neighbours (look, we even have names for them). Already, perhaps, there are some double lines. Some work friends, some close neighbours. Make the lines thicker depending on the strength of the relationships, the intensity of dependency

---

* Italo Calvino, *Invisible Cities* (Einaudi, 1972; English trans. Secker & Warburg, 1977).

† Apparently Facebook now allows you to do something very like this.

or power, liking or loathing or need. Choose another colour for family of origin, for blood, choose red for them (what kind of 'you' are you with them?). Set yourself at the centre of this web, at the hub of your small world.

Now begin to draw the lines between the elements. Other than knowing you, who knows who within this array, how are they connected, by what blood, liking, loathing or indifference? Draw these lines between the members of your small world. Within your world there may be separate groups, like zones of speciation where the only connector between the groups is you. Worlds that won't collide until you have a really big party, get married or die. There may be isolated individuals in this array who have a line to you and no one else. You two really have a little world of your own, don't you? Do you treasure that? Are they your guilty secret? There may be two people to whom you are equally close, but who cannot stand each other. Funny one, that, because you feel like a similar 'you' with them, and so you would think they would have an affinity. But no. There may be lines between two people that are stronger than either of their lines to you. Are you a little envious of that perhaps?

With a God's-eye view, you could now re-centre the map, take the focus off you and continue to map the small worlds of every individual that has a place in yours. You will know some of your friends' small worlds fairly well. With some friends you virtually share a world. Others, the colleagues and the neighbours and the shopkeepers, will inhabit unknown territory. And you might have, in yours, one of those occasional stars of the social firmament, the connectors, those who straddle and shine in many worlds. But God alone knows what kind of worlds lie just one line away from you. From this we get the idea of *degrees of separation*, the idea that between you and any other person on the planet there are only about six moves to be made, from you to him to her to her to him and gotcha; between you and me, say, how many steps?

In a world of unconnected elements, a world where all the lines are zero, like a shoal of plankton, a floating array of isolated

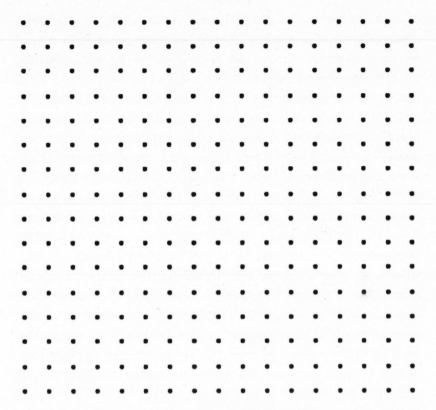

Figure 4. Your World Here

organisms in a mass, the distance between any one individual and any other is precisely that, a geometric distance measured in the distance or the time it takes to get from the one to the other. Our small worlds are different, not measured by distance. Our connections fold space, turn the blank and endless vista of other people into the small worlds in which we live.

Mad Men. The American TV series *Mad Men* portrays the world of the central protagonist Don Draper and his multiple belongings. The small world that we first gain access to as the series begins is that of Madison Avenue in the 1960s – the heart of the New York advertising industry, where he is one of the kingpins. This is a male-dominated world in which he is the dominant male, royally appointed in a palatial office, where other males vie for his favour or position, where the women are decoration and support. Next we see Don with his wife and two children, and a more complex identity begins to emerge. An unequal but affectionate relationship with a beautiful young wife, who is clearly ambivalent about her societally confined and conditioned role, who both challenges and relieves the pressure of being kingpin. But other unexpected affiliations emerge. Don has a lover, a free-spirited Manhattan bohemian, through whom he has an 'in' to a world of beatniks and artists, to whom he is the straight, the square, an object of derision and suspicion. And, as the first series unfolds further, we glimpse his family of origin, a world which he keeps firmly hidden from all the other worlds, for this Madison Avenue king is the son of a whore, orphaned and fostered to a working-class family, to whom he was always an intrusion and a source of shame. He has sundered all connection with that small world, and rejects the half-brother who appears, like an unwelcome stain, in his Madison Avenue kingdom; indeed, he pays him never to come back. This small world of his origins is only revealed to yet another secret liaison, a beautiful and smart Jewish heiress to whom this king is a charming chancer, to be kept at arm's length. Only with her does he feel both enough longing and vulnerability to reveal his roots.

You could map Don Draper's worlds on our grid. He sits at the intersection of many worlds, most of which will never meet. Indeed, his identity is shown to be precisely the sum of their influence and distance from each other, the 'I' that he is being a complex concatenation of the multiple belongings that he has. Like Don Draper, you could use this map and see yourself as nothing more than the place where these worlds meet, see yourself emerge as the product of the unique intersection of multiple social vectors, a star defined by its place in a social constellation, a place like no one else's, and you as the product of that place in the social matrix. You could use this grid to see that.

One of Us

> How does a sorority 'begin'? I could not guess. Parmenides' famous
> question *Why is there something, and not rather nothing?* did not seem
> to me, in this context, more profound.
>
> Joyce Carol Oates*

So, where are your belongings? Not your physical trappings, but
how would your network of belongings look? In which groups are
you one of us, and to which are you one of them? In Tod Brown-
ing's 1932 horror film, *Freaks*, Cleopatra, the beautiful, physically
unchallenged trapeze artist connives with her lover, the similarly
unchallenged strongman, to steal the fortune of Hans, one of the
sideshow freaks. She will marry him and poison him. Her first step

Figure 5. *Freaks*

* Joyce Carol Oates, *I'll Take You There* (HarperCollins, 2002).

is to try and be accepted into the company of freaks, to allay their suspicions. To do so, she must sit at a table and sup with them. Her disgust at doing so is barely concealed. They pass a cup between them, filled with champagne (the original script called for them to drool into it), a 'loving cup', the communion chalice. Like the mustard seed, like gossip, the actual object is secondary to the process it initiates of passing and sharing and imbibing a little of each other's common substance. As they pass it, they chant 'we accept her, we accept her, goo goo ga ga, goo goo ga ga, one of us, one of us, goo goo ga ga', an odd, chilling and fervent little rant that just pushes her beyond the brink of containment: 'Freaks, freaks, freaks, the lot of you!' Well, yes.

This failure to pass the portal, to enter the enclave of difference, alerts the group, if not her hapless lover Hans, to her essential otherness and her criminal intent. She is not 'one of us'. The spurned community has its revenge. With knives and violence they conspire to make her truly 'one of us' and carve a chicken-lady freak from her perfect flesh. Initiation rituals don't come much more formative than that.

Belonging costs. To become one of us, there will have to be, if not a deformation, then at the very least a sculpting, a selective shaping of the self to fit with the mores of the tribe or unit you want to belong to. To enter the world of the Jewish heiress, Don Draper was willing to pay the price of vulnerability and of self-revelation. Any group or partnership into which we enter will similarly demand something of us, at the very least and most generally an accounting for ourselves, a confession of who and why we are, some show-and-tell and loss of private self. This is the work we do to become intimate, to belong. As members of verbal communities we must become adept at this self-accounting, and must learn to speak whatever shibboleths the groups of our expedience and desire demand, and to exclude the parts of ourselves that wouldn't fit. And so, like Don Draper, we find that one world, one set of belongings, is generally not enough to contain us and define us. The parts that we marginalize in order to belong to one world will be central to our belonging in another. We will have a different set of selves in our different worlds, some more comfortable and some more costly.

And as it takes work to belong, so it takes work to include. Real work, love's work. There are very few people whom we say 'we' with, very few whom we include as 'us'. Richard Sennett, a sociologist and social theorist, suggests that ethics, interpersonal ethics, is based on a kind of creative mis-recognition, the ability to mistake 'one of them' for 'one of us', but without the usual entrance fee; the ability to see in the human stranger the common thread that links you to a community of human belonging. That charitable impulse is fitful and infrequent in all but the best of us, seeming to sustain itself only in those who have ceased to identify themselves with the personal ego that most of us use our tribes to maintain and cling to. These really inclusive ethical stars of the human firmament are rare and tend to have cast off any local set of belongings. Describing how we might attain this state, Krishnamurti, one of the spiritual stars of the last century, instructs us thus:

> For many lives and for all this life . . . I have struggled to be free – free of my friends, my books, my associations. You must struggle for the same freedom. There must be constant turmoil within you.*

Yet who wants constant turmoil? Most of us cling to our friends, to our books and our associations. We want this hall of mirrors, our tribes and families, to define us, to remind us who we are.

Mirror Me. Some neuroscientists have become excited by finding in the brain neurons that appear not only to fire when you are performing an action, or expressing an emotion, but also do the same when someone else is acting or expressing. These mirror neurons are thought by some to be a glimpse of where, biologically, the

* Quoted by Pupul Jayakar in her 1986 biography, *J. Krishnamurti, a Biography* (Arkana-Penguin, 1986).

other is in me, and where I am in them. Understandably these scientists have wondered if mirror neurons are the basis of empathy, the bio-bit of us that allows us to feel what the other feels, based solely on their expression and their enactment of that feeling. Maybe this is how we can cringe at another's embarrassment, and why we can cry and laugh with them. If we do. And perhaps the difficulty that some who lie on the autistic spectrum have with empathy – of imagining the other world of another's mind – is traceable to a failure to mirror, to the lack of a place for the other within the self.

Others argue that there is an over-literal excitement at the concept of mirror neurons. Closer to consensus, however, is the idea that our identities are from the beginning infused with our experience of other people, of our family and our peer group; that our identity is shaped not just by imitation, by mirroring those around us, but also by them being mirrors for us. 'The social brain' and 'the social mind' are relatively recent concepts in the field of psychology, which is waking up to the deeply communal nature of our self. There are enormous advantages to being able to read other people, to knowing what they are thinking and predicting what they might do. Having a well-honed ability to mirror them and to see the effect of yourself on them – to see yourself *in* them – means that you can predict, charm, frighten, control, placate, care for, survive and thrive.

Think of those around you now, that community of dots and lines which I suggested you sketch above. Think of the closest ones. More than likely they will be the people who 'get you', people who say the right thing, not in some anodyne act of placation but in a way which shows that they know about you. How good it feels to feel known. And more than likely you will 'get' them, for if this mirroring is mutual you will have a strong sense of them, and your knowing them is what they get from you. How close you are to them, even how much you like them, may in the end be very close to the amount that you like the 'you' you see in the mirror of their eyes. Generally, the inner circles of our small worlds will reflect a self that we like, or selves. We will maintain the bunch of peers who say 'I' for us in a way we understand, in a voice that we know and like.

Love-in. It is now possible to build a community from affiliation. Historically, affiliation tended to be something found by accident in your given locale, something discovered, or searched out and cultivated. Like the threads in Calvino's *Invisible Cities*, there would be invisible threads of kinships linking those of a kind. But imagine the tragedy of missing it! Of every day passing the door behind which lived a member of your tribe, one of you, and every day you failed to recognize each other. You would remain forever passers-by. Now, we can found our communities not on location but on *topics*. A Greek word by origin which means 'place' and more specifically *common place*, seeming to signal an early realization that we are close not just by our geographical standing in the actual world, but that we can also be neighbours in common themes, in gossip. So although we stand physically far apart, we can stand on common ground. Think of the Jewish community, dispersed for millennia, but united and defined by the common place of the Book and the Law.

Now, every one of your whims can find a common place, a network of affiliates and associates. Now, at the push of keys, you can – if you are in that minority of the world's population with access to the internet – find your online tribe.

We talked earlier about speciation, about how new species form. Speciation tends to be geographical, but, as we mentioned, there is also a kind of moral speciation, where human communities based on affiliation grow apart from the larger herd, run wild. They don't tend to create new biological species, yet new species *can* grow up around more than geographical isolation, or so some geneticists say. Speciation, based on grounds other than geography, is known as sympatric. The word means literally 'all from the same fatherland', and there indeed is the rub. It is not their being born into the same space which dictates their mating. Something else pulls them together. Richard Dawkins has suggested that a similar process may lie at the origin of *race*. His argument is that individual differences in *ideology*, in affiliation, might predate and be formative of racial differences. We are used to thinking of this the other way round, believing that different religions, languages and customs are the result of racial difference. But it could have *evolved* the other way. Imagine a motley crew of like-minds brought together by common values, united by the higher purpose of perceiving themselves as a meaningful unit. Like the Manson Family, like the *Deliverance* hillbillies, they policed their borders with shibboleths, knitting their coherence with common gossip and common values, deciding who was in and who was out. Perhaps these processes are the cause, not just the consequence, of the different human tribes?

Perhaps, but of course we want to be surrounded by like minds, and we feel ourselves deprived if we're not. It's what we look for. And now, every one of our desires can join a community. Now our every belief and every delusion can find a colluding team. Doubtless this has led to a diversification and reification – a making actual – of tribes; it has enabled the very possibility of many that would never otherwise have existed. In the old days we would have passed them on the street and never known we shared an inner secret fire. Now we have communities of desire.

Doing a Geographical

In the early ages of the world, we know, it was believed that each territory was inhabited and ruled by its own divinities, so that a man could cross the bordering heights and be out of the reach of his native gods, whose presence was confined to the streams and the groves and the hills among which he had lived from his birth.

George Eliot, *Silas Marner**

* George Eliot, *Silas Marner* (Blackwood & Sons, 1861).

Belonging costs. It can also kill. In the later stages of an addict's career, junkies who want to quit have to leave the streams and groves and hills where their God presided. The behaviourists talk about this phenomenon in terms of stimulus equivalence. We've talked about props before. When you show a junkie some piece of their gear, some prop, they will have a physiological reaction to it, just as they would to the drug. We all do it. Say 'spider' to an arachnophobe, or mention food to a hungry man, and they'll respond. There is a stimulus equivalence between the word and the thing; they elicit the same response and perform the same stimulation on the sensitized individual. Eventually, for the junkie, this network of signifying things gets tighter and tighter. The degree of separation between any part of the network and the junk gets less and less, until between them there is only one step: this god holds illimitable dominion over all; everything in this small world suggests junk. That's when they need to get out, or die trying.

It's the people, as well as the places and things that mirror and represent the problem. It's the people, as well as the rooms and props, muscles and neurons that act as reflector and repository of their identity. It's the people that the junkie has to leave. Sometimes, what gets reflected back is not what we want to see at all. I went swimming early today, as soon as the pool opened, hoping to avoid the usual squall and clamour of the child-clotted pool that happens by about 11 a.m. at the weekends. Instead of the infant squealers, there was a thick soup of ageing flesh, like mine, all like me trying to miss the fresh stuff that shows up later on. All were doggedly hogging their imaginary lanes, all performing that somehow very British pretence that no one else was actually there, heedlessly backstroking and side-swiping into each other. A pond of naked and colliding meat, graceless, disfigured by behavioural ugliness. Like me. I didn't stay. It was like the scene in the 1965 Polanski film *Repulsion*, where a deranged Catherine Deneuve is walking down a narrow corridor in her claustrophobic flat and arms emerge through the walls, caressing and molesting her. Sometimes our small worlds feel like this.

When the weave of your world becomes a knot then maybe it's time for the knife.

Noises Off. Eventually the junkie has to leave or die. Or, if not die, then dissolve slowly into the earth, to become part of the junkie-humus, the common ground that nurtures other junkies. The place will remain, but the desires will inhabit someone else. These worlds – the communities and tribes with their streams and groves and hills – will go on with or without any particular member. But sometimes a member, in order to live, to change, to grow, will have to leave. Before the walls start reaching out, before each part becomes equivalent to every other and the weave too dense. Sometimes the world has to end.

I moved from a big to a small city recently. I left the big metropolis, like a junkie doing a geographical, because sometimes the only way to stay alive, to change, to grow, is to move. Everything had become saturated with everything else, everything reminded me of an 'I' I no longer cared for. Character, said Aristotle, is habitual behaviour, and the big metropolis had become the setting and the support for a series of habits, for a character I no longer wished to prolong. So I did a geographical. When the social web becomes a confining net, then it's time to cut and run. Of course, I maintained some connections, while others became attenuated and withered. New ones formed. So I changed: as one world ended and another began, I changed. The degree of change could be measured by the number of ties I maintained, and the number of new ones I formed. To really go the distance, to really transform, I could have done something like this:

> *Sannyasa* is a state of being, a state of dying to the world and society. The *sannyasin* . . . ceases to be a member of society, and is outside its frame, having hardly any concern with social laws, rites, rituals, sacraments and so on. The *sannyasin* renounces caste, family, and adopts a new name signifying rebirth.*

* P. Jayakar, *J. Krishnamurti, a Biography* (Arkana-Penguin, 1986).

Symbolic suicide is another way to see this move, a phrase used by Slavoj Žižek, used here to express the idea that sometimes to end the self, to kill the 'I', all you need to do is to remove yourself from the network of associations that are currently defining you. I didn't, and few do, go that far. But the 'I' of one season ended, and another began.

These are the many ways our worlds can end. Desire or boredom can impel us out. On the whole, however, our impulse is to maintain. Our habits and routines are locked and fixed within ourselves and within a familiar world of people, places and things, rooms and props. Collectively, they let us know who we are: they remember so we don't have to. Few of us want deliberately to embark on the biographical disruption, the symbolic self-harm or full-scale symbolic suicide, the *sannyasa*, that would result from changing important parts of our world. For sure we might edit a little here – lose some characters, maybe even switch location – but the central themes tend not to be up for rewriting for extended stretches of time. We tend to want to stay within our common places, gossiping with our familiars about familiar things, where our world makes sense and where people know our name.

Nevertheless, change will come. It may start as a distant rumour, a noise from outside your small world, or an unexpected intrusion within it, an invasion, signalling the existence of another world. It might be a summons or a death sentence or a calling or an offer, a win or a loss, a catastrophe or an epiphany, or merely an accumulating chain of small events. Sooner or later, however, your current world will change, the present season will end.

No one said it was going to be easy.

Chapter 5

News from Elsewhere

In which Act One comes to an end. Life is shown to be a succession of more or less stable states – seasons – persisting for a stretch of time, but inevitably coming to an end. The ways of ending are shown to be various and need not be either dramatic or traumatic. We see that resistance is fundamental to the process of change, that as creatures of habit forced to adjust we will experience this resistance as the feelings, altered perceptions and new actions that are necessary to become other than we are.

George Gershwin died today, but I don't have to believe it if I don't want to.

John O'Hara*

But he will. The writer will believe it. We can only resist the inevitable for so long. But, oh, the poignancy of that little resistance. Like lying in, determinedly squeezing the last drops out of sleep. Like a child clinging to the railings of a park at dusk. I won't go home, I won't.

All may be impermanence and flux but that doesn't stop us holding on to whatever we've got. The writer, the Gershwin-death-resistor, knows that an era has come to an end, that he must wake up to a new and reconfigured world, but he is damned if he will, just yet. He has the information but he is not yet ready to meet it with belief. He is doing all the things that in grief you shouldn't do: denial, resistance, clinging to the old. I imagine Buddhists, Olympian athletes in the sport of moving on, sleek creatures of pure detachment slipping seamlessly from one event to the other, never gathering the material for loss, the stuff that builds the ever-ending eras of our mortal lives. When they have nothing, they have nothing to lose. I imagine them with some disdain because I don't believe in these Buddhists. I don't believe that even in their frictionless lives some things don't stick. A monk they like more or less. A particular cook and their meals. Preferences will accumulate unheeded, little patterns of comfort and unease, approach and avoidance. Even in the most unsuitable habitat, patterns and repetitions will become

* Gershwin died on 11 July 1937.

established for a while, a season. And to be fair to these straw Buddhists, they wouldn't disagree because it is our attachment to our desires and aversions that they would seek to lessen, not necessarily their occurrence. No attachment, so no grief. Well, sure, and no drama either. Nothing special, so nothing to lose. I wonder who gets there? I wonder what makes you want to? For there is something admirable in the way that John O'Hara is refusing to let Gershwin go, in this act not so much of denial as defiance: a noble, pointless stance against the end of an era, those temporary units of persistence whose succession shapes our human lives.

Seasons

O seasons, O châteaux
Where is the flawless soul?

Rimbaud*

Modern television, particularly the long-form American dramas – *Buffy the Vampire Slayer*, *Desperate Housewives*, *The Sopranos*, *Breaking Bad*, *Game of Thrones*, whatever is entrancing you now – are structured, written and shown in seasons. A season usually contains ten to twenty episodes, all under the aegis of a narrative arc. From the beginning to the end of a season, something large will play itself out. There will be a particular set of characters and there will be a predominant theme. An emotional colour will predominate, a thematic weather will prevail. Room here to play with the other sense of season as flavour, for there will be a taste, a unique savour to this stretch of time.

And so, too, with our own seasons. Stretches of times wherein certain people, places, things and routines become persistent, become what that time is about. Seasons – stretches of persistence and attachment to the persistent. Times in which we get to know particular locations, props and characters, in which we get to work

* Rimbaud, *A Season in Hell* (1873; Eng. trans. New Directions, 1961).

out and run our routines long enough for them to become our current Automatic, our present way of life. We have worked out the rules and play by them, or break them and know we are transgressing, for we have found and set the limits of our current small world. And so we grow *accustomed*, as this way of life becomes habitual. As we grow attached to people, places, things and routines, they tell us who we are for a time, a season.

Think about the beginning of something new. The first few days of a holiday. Something starts in those first few days and as it unfolds you begin to get the feel for the kind of time you are having. There will be defining moments, high watermarks of excellence or disaster will be set; the coalition of people, place and event will stamp its flavour on that stretch of time, on everything around and in that time. You begin to recognize what kind of holiday you are having, as it becomes *like* something. Soon you know what this episode, this brief season, is about. So, recently, what kind of time have you been having, what is your current season like?

Unlike television, movies are about transition. Movies are about the end of one season and the attempt to start another. They track that difficult in-between time, the one we are generally loath to begin and quick-as-we-can to end, for we are uncomfortable with that uncertain stretch between one stable state and another, the move from one normal to the next. If you look at our average lives, they are, like the lives of our species, a spectacle of punctuated equilibrium. There tend to be long periods of stable states, extended spells of predictable weather and routine. But then, from within or without the borders of our small worlds, come the agents of change, to interrupt and discombobulate. There then follow those times of difficult adjustment and heightened awareness, those periods in which we have to start again, have to grow accustomed all over again.

'The new era is nothing if not difficult . . .' wrote Rimbaud. These times of adjustment are tortured, deliberate times. Times when, for the first time in a long time, we have to think again, consider and deliberate. How do we do this? How does this work? Gershwin is dead and now we have to start believing it, wake up to a world that is missing one of the elements that, in its absence, we realize was more than just an element, it was a keystone. Some elements of our seasons, some people, places and things are, let's admit it, fairly easily eliminable. With others, their absence would really be the end of an era. A lover, a job, a home, a child: one element that in leaving or ending takes a world with it. These are season closers, these events, ends of spells in hell or paradise, or more likely somewhere just good enough, where we no longer have to think too much, a comfortable, familiar, routine season, which we will cling to past its passing, and resist the beginning of change.

The new era is nothing if not difficult. At first we must perform the graceless dance of adjustment, thinking out our moves until such time as a new order, a new set of routines, a degree of comfort, begins to emerge. Beginnings are a difficult time. The first few episodes of a season are always clunky, when the new characters are introduced and the old ones mourned. New themes emerge slowly, and it takes a while for us to get the hang of it all. Slowly we begin to feel what kind of time we are having. The new lover, job, home, child or simply the rhythm of the absence of the old, becomes established and eventually we learn to dance along. We grow accustomed. For minor to moderate change it usually takes us a couple of months; with major league adjustment, a couple of years. Then comes a new equilibrium, a new normal. Life becomes routine again. Until the next time. Long periods of equilibrium, punctuated by change. Like this:

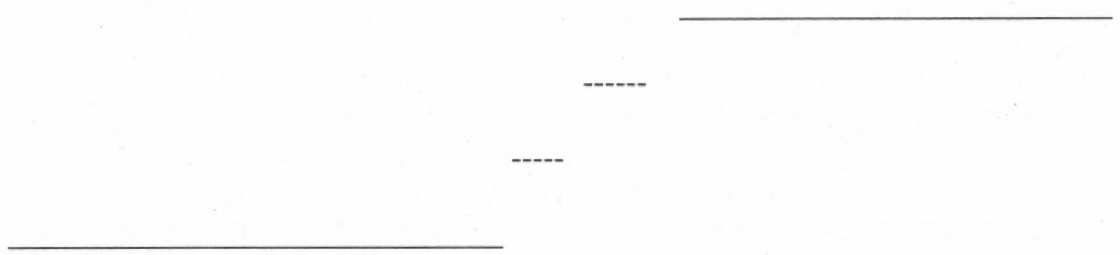

————————————————

————————————————

Figure 6. Life

Unless of course you like it faster, or if that is just the way it is for you. Then your life really is like the movies, which are more like this:

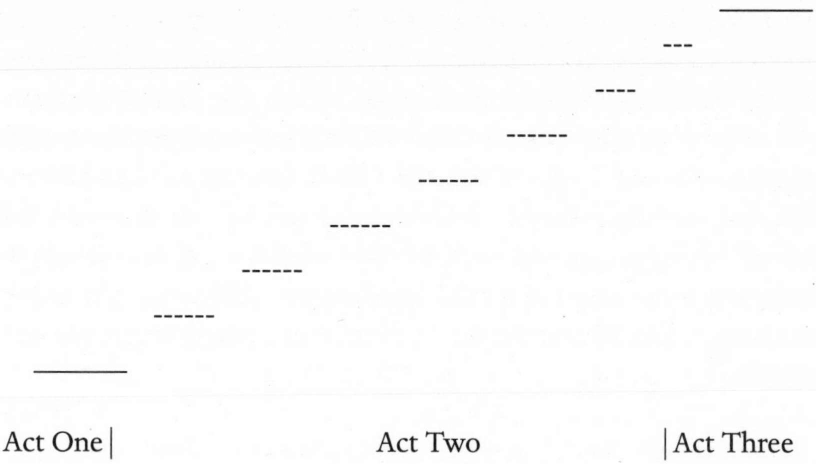

———

\---

\----

\------

\------

\------

\------

\------

———

Act One | Act Two |Act Three

Figure 7. The Movies

Movies are all about the change, the graceless dance. Almost every movie you see will follow the three-act formula illustrated in Figure 7. The little line to the left is Act One, representing the last days of a stable state, just before some disaster strikes, before something happens, some news from elsewhere: the leaving, the loss, the imperilling, the new arrival. The Event. The bulk of the movie is taken up by Act Two, the desperate dance of adjustment. That's what we pay to watch. The struggle to re-establish equilibrium, not the old one, that won't happen, and that's the real struggle at first. The new reality clashes with the habits of the old one, the inbuilt, ingrained physiology of denial that continues to perform the old gestures in response to new demands, continues to reach for what is gone.

Will Smith dodging cars as he runs down the freeway; Bruce Willis's bare and bleeding feet; Sigourney Weaver being choked to death by a robot. That's what we want to see. People reduced to desperate measures, gestures and moves, trying and failing, not even knowing what a new equilibrium would feel like; no rhythm, comfort or ease. That's what will take up most of the screen time, most of Act Two and the first part of Act Three: increasing struggle against increasing difficulty. This is what we want. Men and women contending with a new order. We go to the movies to watch characters being recast through crisis. We watch them squirm, watch them until they begin to learn, and learn to begin anew. That's where we arrive at in the dénouement of Act Three, the little solid line at the top on the right. It's the start of a new season; it signals in brief the rhythms and colour of the new equilibrium, as Act One did the old. But we don't want to see stability and ease. Act One and the end of Act Three, the new normal, take up as little screen time as possible and these days the former is often over before the end of the opening credits. Maybe we should be glad that life isn't more like the movies.

Maureen's Shower. Maureen is moving house. With that and other life events, she is in one of those interregnums, an Act Two time between stable state and stable state. She is having to do a lot of thinking. One of the things she misses most is her shower. There are other things happening to Maureen. Important parts of her support network are down and temporarily out. More to cope with and fewer means with which to cope. One of the things that helps her is showering. Three or four times a day if there is a lot of coping to do, which right now there is. This is not a need-to-be-clean thing. For Maureen it's the thing that other people use driving for. Put the body in a position where it can perform a series of mainly automatic moves and it frees the mind to process what is going on. This is not quite meditation; it's more like a parent giving the children something to do – watching television – while they get on with what they need to do. Keep the body busy, quiet, occupied. This is what the shower does for Maureen: the repetitive and automatic movements, the routine occupation of the body, frees her mind from thinking about what she has to do next, frees it to process, to pray, to cope.

Maureen is moving house. Apologizing in advance for how ridiculous this sounds, she tells me how much she misses her shower. A whole series of routines, which at their most fundamental feel to her like comfort, have been disrupted or abolished altogether. She is staying at a friend's house where, OK, there is a shower, but it's not hers. The layout of everything is different, the automatic micro-gestures do not work here and need rethinking. Something that was once transparent and thoughtless, has become obdurate and in need of her attention. Like driving in a new car, or driving in a different country. Deliberate and irritating time, trying to buck the trends of your body's inclinations. Maureen is in Act Two. Her need to deliberate, to think, is higher than ever, and yet the means by which she does so are disrupted. Important things are missing; important things are new. Maureen has a long way to go until she can really shower again.

This shower is not the stuff of movies, or of philosophy, where recently the talk is all of Acts and Events. These Acts and Events are epoch-making or destroying happenings that reconfigure the coordinates of entire worlds, personal (the Act*) or socio-political (the Event[†]). Understandably, given the scope of these events – sorry, Events – the problem is locating them. When did you last see the entire socio-political universe transform? When did you last perform an Act that negated everything that had previously defined you, reduced you to a ground zero of self, a place of utter destitution, where all the symbolic and affective ties that previously fixed and shaped you were severed and turned to ash? The Event and the Act. Philosophy, like Hollywood, thinks in Capital Letters. Our day-to-day transformations are usually less dramatic, but no less (re)definitive. Moving house will shake up the coordinates of your life more than some abstract movement in the world of ideas. Acquiring a new lover will recast you as effectively as any Trauma. There are many ways to change. The end of a world doesn't have to be The End of The World.

The End of John

Enter Rumour, *painted full of tongues.*

Shakespeare, *Henry IV, Part II*

* Slavoj Žižek.
[†] Alain Badiou.

John, mid-teens, is in his family sitting room – standard-issue working-class – dark eyes and heavy brows both concealing and revealing an inner sadness:

> When I was about fourteen or fifteen, I had what I thought was depression . . . I'd been to the doctors, been to see counsellors, but they couldn't really work out why I had depression.*

Sitting in the sitting room, staring at the screen. A shout from another room, some demand or exhortation, sends him shooting off the couch. Hooded top, baggy trousers, bolting out the front door. Slam.

Outside is grey standard-issue working-class urban. Pebbledashed estate, houses crushed too close together. Scruffy patches of communal green, demarcated by low walls, concrete bollards, metal grille fencing. The roofs of a row of flat-roofed garages decline in a gradual slope of shallow steps. There are a couple of stunted trees.

John jumps from his top step, hits the ground running, and leaps onto a concrete bollard, landing on it with his left foot as his right extends forward to the next, the single fluid movement taking him in loping, improbable, graceful steps from bollard to bollard until a final leap leaves him, poised and teetering, on the narrow metal bar that tops the fence; knees pulsing, he pushes off from there, grabs a tree branch, swings up, lets go and lands on a garage roof, takes their decline in long running hops, one step per roof, and then he's jumping off the last one onto the pavement. He stands still there for a moment, then runs off down the street, down to the local park where other planes, surfaces and angles offer new affordances for his restless agility.

This is John's Act One, briefly ciphered, the rut and the release of his daily grind. This is what his world is all day and all the time, this is everything that is the case for John. You should get the sense that

* John Kerr, *Jump Britain*, Channel 4 documentary (2005).

he is close to exhausting this world, and vice versa, that if he finds no joy or answer within these limits then . . . what? As if boredom could achieve a useful tension, reach a catharsis, which it never does; rather it stultifies, it kills. You should get the sense that the continuation of this life without alternative will lead to some kind of death for John. And with the spotlight of our attention on him, we know that is not going to happen. We know there is about to be an Act Two.

So what happens? John is about to hear the news from elsewhere that will change his life. Coming from the television which, just for a moment, for a few lucid dream-like moments, was actually talking straight to him. Have you ever felt that luscious skin-crawling moment when you knew yourself to be the addressee of the mass message, when you knew that this time it really was for you?

We are only real in our moments of recognition.*

The Inciting Incident is an event that disrupts the world of the prot-agonist and/or gives them a clear goal in the story. Now we know what the film is about.†

Interior, living room, day. Yet again John is sitting in front of the television, blank. Then rising in the eyes in response to some images newly on the screen, some blipvert for a coming feature, rising in the soul, but we see it in the eyes, rising up, a kind of terror, a sign of the incipient reversal, the tension of something just before the moment of its negation. John is about to die. The television has never talked to John before, he has never seen himself there, despite the baggy-panted, hoodied, shambling skater kids stuck everywhere to try and catch his eyes, he has never actually seen himself addressed or represented in this universal medium. But now . . .

---

* Carol Shields, *Unless* (Fourth Estate, 2002).
† Douglas Dunnan, from lecture notes on screenwriting, Edinburgh University, 2005.

On the screen is a feature about parkour – free running. Young men are running around and on and through the barriers of their worlds, turning the urban furniture of confinement into the props in an improvised ballet of exuberant, dangerous freedom. Levels of skills, leaps he's dreamed of but has never risked, things until this moment purely private, an inner world of grace and possibility, that world of dreams and leaps and flight, that innermost, almost shameful, treasured, private part of John is there in front of him, on the television, right now. Staring back at him. The blipvert is over, and so is John.

And then I remember seeing the video and it was [long pause] . . . like something we'd been waiting for . . .*

Quick! Are there any other lives?†

John has heard the news from elsewhere, the rumour from and of his world-to-be. Enter Rumour. Rumour as opposed to gossip. Gossip is the intimate whisper of familiars about familiar things, the stuff that passes between the pseudo-siblings under God, that unites a community, binds a world with common threads, with the weave of gossip. Against this dense and cosy knit, rumour is the noise, the rumble from another world that until then no one knew existed. Until this moment John was party only to the gossip of his immediate associates, and they didn't have much to say to him. Until this moment John didn't even know there were any other worlds he could belong to. If gossip is the hum of our own community, rumours are the noises off which we hear from other small worlds: vaguer, threatening, promising, inciting. Even the etymology of 'rumour' bespeaks a cruder kind of information: a noise, a hoarse shout, a clamour from afar. Rumours are the noises of worlds beginning to collide: rumours presage war, or act as recruitment calls, as

---

* John Kerr, *Jump Britain*, Channel 4 documentary (2005).
† Rimbaud, *A Season in Hell* (1873; New Directions, 1961).

a summons to leave one world and join another. Rumour has just named the unnamed parts of John, called him up and issued an invitation to a new community. John has heard his calling.

Listening to Rumour – How Carol Became Safe

Douglas Hofstadter draws attention to the role of what he calls spontaneous intrusions into any creative process . . . every increment of design in the universe begins with a moment of serendipity, the undesigned intersection of two trajectories that yield something that turns out, retrospectively, to be more than a mere collision.

Daniel Dennett[*]

Encroachment is what makes life interesting.

Daniel Dennett[†]

Now an actual movie, in the form of *Safe*, the 1995 film directed by Todd Haynes. Spotlight on another moment of rumour/encroachment, another inciting incident. The protagonist is Carol, played by Julianne Moore. Act One shows us, as usual, the world that is about to end. This is a world of empty luxury – white, rich American women meeting up, doing lunch, aerobics classes, baby showers and coffee with other white, rich housewives. Carol is one of them. What sets her apart is an air of disengagement, daze. She wanders like a ghost through her own life, saying the words that her other friends say, following their diets, adopting their fads, going through the motions, walking through a part that does not inspire her, but without the redeeming sense of some suppressed desire or true self awaiting release or ignition. The closest hints to passion are the way she is faintly appalled by both her stepson's love of violent games and by the sexual desire of her husband. What turns this into a

---

[*] Daniel C. Dennett, *Freedom Evolves* (Allen Lane, 2003).
[†] Ibid.

drama, starts Act Two, is the gradual development of physical symptoms. Carol begins to suffer from fits of breathlessness, nose bleeds, headaches, fatigue. Her doctor, finding no physical cause, sends her to the psychiatrist, and the psychiatrist returns her to the doctor, for neither can explain the symptoms. Restless and unhappy, she searches, now with some feeling, within her community for explanations and meaning. She finds none.

The benign intrusion, the mundane epiphany of rumour, is beautifully portrayed in *Safe*. Carol's first encounter with the news from elsewhere is underscored with the significance it will only assume later, as all such formative moments are, in retrospect, surrounded by the aura of their importance-to-be. Walking away one day from an aerobics class down the corridor at her local gym – inexplicably fatigued, numbly distressed – she approaches the community notice board, one of those places where other worlds can advertise their existence, rub shoulders. On the soundtrack an organ-chord hum, a low rumble of impending significance, starts to swell. The camera, our point of view, is already beginning to zoom slowly towards a red piece of paper on the notice board. That notice is becoming the focal point of the picture, as soon it will become the centre of a whole new world for Carol. Cut and zoom towards Carol, to her face, the site of reception for this message. The message and its addressee are coming ever closer, as we cut back and zoom further in on the notice, now legible.

The organ swells: 'Do You Smell Fumes?' A surreal epiphany, but in the list of triggers and symptoms beneath this headline, Carol for the first time recognizes her self. It's for *her*. This is Carol's invitation to another community. Her calling.

A cult is a group which we don't wish to belong to, an island of belief which we choose not to visit. There are too many and our interests, if well served and tended by our indigenous community, will not stray too far from home. Unless, like John, you find no reflection of yourself and your interests there. Unless, like Carol, you find no answer or ease there. This is how Act Two can begin, with an accumulation of unease, with a growing sense that your world is not enough, with a restless searching for you-know-not-what. Anyone poised on the brink of leaving a job, or a home, or a relationship, anyone on the brink of beginning these things anew, knows the feeling of being on the lookout, on the hunt, listening out for rumours.

> 1. In the first place the public must have total confidence in the official media ... so as not to be tempted to seek information elsewhere.
>
> ...
>
> 3. When something happens, a maximum of information must be disseminated as quickly as possible. Rumors arise from the spontaneous questions that the public asks itself to which no answers are provided. They satisfy the need to understand events, in the case where events do not speak for themselves.*

These recommendations come from a report to the American government during the Second World War. They are suggestions for putting a stop to rumour, ways to prevent people looking elsewhere. Consider Carol and her symptoms. The question her symptoms pose is a riddle. Symptoms don't speak for themselves, for they are a sign, a clue to something else. The symptom means that there's something going on. The solving of the symptom is a question for an expert, not for us. We take our symptoms elsewhere, traditionally to the doctor. The doctor will figure the symptom out, will decipher it. Doctors know what symptoms mean.

But of course sometimes they don't. Disease in the absence of organic pathology, symptoms signifying nothing, nothing physical, account for a large percentage of what we ask doctors about. Like Carol, people with these symptoms tend to end up in front of a psychiatrist, for whom the symptom is news from an inner elsewhere, a place where meaning can hide and yet demand attention, can encode its concerns in the language of physical symptoms.

---

* Quoted in Jean-Noël Kapferer, *Rumors* (Transaction Publishers, 1990).

Disease, says the psychiatrist, is a rumour from the unconscious. Time was when the public had confidence in these official discourses (see Rumour Recommendation 1 above). Time was when answers were provided to explain and ameliorate our unease (see Rumour Recommendation 3 above). But these official media have lost our total confidence. There is too much they can't explain or do, too much unease and too many other resources competing to buy up the explanatory debt of our symptoms. Enter rumour.

Consider your symptoms, your unease, consider whatever it is your community cannot answer or explain, cannot speak of or to, cannot find the words for, cannot express. This is what sets us questing, listening for rumours. Carol developed her symptoms in a community that had no means of framing the question of her distress, let alone answering it. The 'Do You Smell Fumes' flyer, like the rabbit hole for Alice, takes Carol elsewhere, into a new community where there are answers, emotions, explanations. A commune, full of sufferers of unexplained physical symptoms, located in the hills, far from modern life, far far away from the world of Act One, a community united in fear and avoidance. In Carol's old world her disease was an intrusion, a stain on a well-groomed urban landscape, a disfiguring figure on the common luxurious ground, an exception; here it is the rule, the ground of the communion of this community. Suddenly she recognizes herself everywhere, in everyone she meets.

What *Safe* shows us is the cost as well as the benefit of answering your calling, and the work involved. We saw Carol and John at the moments of their recognition, when with a sudden intuition they glimpsed their future home. There is a beautiful ease to these moments of epiphany, a sense of coming home. But you're not home. You've seen where you *could* be, you have glimpsed a possible world, but to get there you have to relocate – psychically, physically, emotionally, linguistically, all or some of the above. You will have to move. You will have to go through the long and deliberate struggle of Act Two.

Interregnum

The one unifying factor, according to research, is that people who get involved in a cultic group are in a major transitional stage in life: 'A mid-life crisis, going to college, graduating college, loss of a loved one through death or divorce, moving to a new country or community – these are all normal transitional stages when we're just a little more vulnerable to undue influence.

Nick Johnstone, 'Beyond Belief'*

Amber's Train

Amber's interregnum. You might want to picture her. It could help you connect. In the movie she'd be played by Katharine Hepburn or Bette Davis at their larger-than-life peaks. Magnificent of mind; vivid and vibrant in speech, gesture and dress; just past forty with a precociously brilliant career behind her and with yet greater brilliance ahead; and all this magnificence is now crushed, broken and abject. For Amber is in-between. Something is over. A world has ended and nothing has begun to take its place. She has a strong sense of what this time will be like. The road ahead is all pain and fatigue. Today is the first day of the work of loss. The person she loved has gone. A future, a promising future, is over. And there is nothing to take its place. Already she has an overwhelming anticipatory fatigue and agitation; already she is full of an instinctive aversion for the road ahead, the long, solitary walk of mourning. She has not even begun and she wishes it was over. It's the beginning of Act Two in the most commonplace of dramas. I wonder what the statistics are on this, how many acts of loss and mourning begin each day. How many acts of resistance – George Gershwin died today, but I don't have to believe it if I don't want to – have

* Nick Johnstone, 'Beyond Belief', *Observer*, 12 December 2004.

been committed in the time that it took to write this sentence. How many decided not to continue at all? Lord have mercy.

Act Two, a time when we are most prey to the vicissitudes of courage, and yet most in need of it. No future – there is no future for Amber, not at the moment. She knows it will never be better, never be different, that her future will be only a continuation, an intensification of this nascent anguish. If we have been through loss enough times, if we decide to persist with it, we will come to know that this is just a failure of imagination posing as truth and revelation. But in that fresh raw morning of grief, there is no room for hope. Amber knows, just knows, that life will never be OK again. How many never make it further than this? How many are lost forever in these foothills of grief? Lord have mercy.

My heart is as black as the blackness of the sloe,
or as the black coal that is on the smith's forge;
or as the sole of a shoe left in white halls;
it was you that put that darkness over my life.

You have taken the east from me; you have taken the west from me;
you have taken what is before me and what is behind me;
you have taken the moon, you have taken the sun from me;
and my fear is great that you have taken God from me.

Anonymous, 'Donal Og'*

So Amber is on a train. She has nowhere to go and no reason to go there, but she is on a train because in the locomotion there is a lulling of the pain. It's very simple. When the train moves, the pain recedes. When it stops, the pain returns, and she rocks herself, to keep the movement going, to keep the pain at bay, she rocks herself across those appalling gaps, the inner tension mounting until the

---

* Anonymous, eighth-century Irish ballad, 'Donal Og' (Young Daniel), trans. Lady Augusta Gregory, in Seamus Heaney and Ted Hughes (eds), *The Rattle Bag* (Faber & Faber, 1982).

train chugs off again, until it picks up the beat and rocks her off again. Before the train, at home, trying to bear it, there was an over-whelming agitation, a desperation too great to sit or be with, so she paced or rocked or walked the streets, as if she could escape the pain, as if she could outrun her feelings. So she moved and kept moving until she found herself sitting on the train. Here she can sit, as the train moves for her, rocks and soothes her, as if the train had picked up the inner pulse of her agitation and pitched its rhythm in time with it, harmonized it, lulled it, making it for the moment bearable, like an expert mother with a teething child. Lullaby. At every stop the pain returns, quelled again as the rhythm resumes.

Amber is resisting change, avoiding, for the moment, the pain laid out before her, the long ascent. George Gershwin is dead, but . . .

Amber is in an interregnum. Literally the time between two kings, between two ruling purposes. Something is over and nothing begun. Times of motion and transition, the beginning of Act Two: 'normal transitional stages where we're just a little more vulnerable to undue influence'. Her therapist knows what might help. Amber needs something new to be, or at least to begin to become. Some-thing she can recognize herself in. She was once a partnered forty-something with a late chance at children, but now what? Her therapist sends her off to look for something she could bear to be, looking for examples of forty-something single women who are happy with their lot, for anybody who has made a decent show of pulling off what Amber is now being forced to be. Her therapist is asking Amber to imagine an Act Three, the next place of relative equilibrium, the new normal beyond the current period of forced adjustment. The next stop.

Lenny's Play

Someone else. Lenny. Male, early fifties, once the Great White Hope of British Theatre, and still charged with the authority of the great actor, even (or especially) in his despair. I ask him who would play him in the movies. 'Kenneth Branagh?' he wonders. John Hurt,

I think. Somewhere – someone – in between those pillars of leonine pride and crumbled grandeur. For Lenny the last few years have been a gradual declension away from the world of acting and now he is changing stations yet again. He is taking a risk and is about to sacrifice his livelihood for a vision. He has worked for the last two and a half years in a job that paid the rent but which was beginning to become corrosive to something he valued more than comfort: a certain degree of freedom to think and to question and not to become defined by a station or an office. And he has an idea, a piece of kindling. In front of him is the dim shape of a play that he might write. Behind him, clearer in the leaving, is the material; something about reduction, about grandeur or ambition punctured, pride fallen, humbled, punished. The material behind. The play ahead. Lenny in between.

And prey, very prey to the vicissitudes of courage. As you get older, Lenny tells me, you only get low-voltage epiphanies. No longer the dramatic summons and re-formations of youth. This time all he got was a title. A title wherein, condensed, he could see several of his recurrent preoccupations come together into something potentially dramatic. When he tells people the title, they too experience a little jolt of revelation, can feel the potential. An evocative title then, but what it evoked would need to be worked out. The title was pretty much all there was.

Lenny left his job on the strength of it, or on the strength of the pull of that and the push of boredom and restriction. And now he is in what he calls a flat-line time. His old commitments have been shed but the new ones are not yet compelling or clear enough to structure his time, to possess him. He is like an actor between jobs. Only a glimpse of what the next role might be, given sufficient attention and time. Maybe. Very, very vulnerable to the fluctuations of hope and despair, to undue influence. He speaks of searching for a hunger, for the beginnings of urgency. Most things take more energy to start than to continue once started. Once started, he knows that the process could acquire its own momentum, as all successfully manifested processes do, but there is the work of getting started all ahead of him. Looking for motivation. The title has provoked him, and continues to do so.

But the rest will be work. Lenny will have to rise to the occasion of his recognition and hope that it rises to meet him in turn. Persistence in the faith that it will, fidelity to that low-voltage epiphany is, at the moment, the work he needs to do. Act Two is all ahead of him.

Walking against the Wind

At the core of subjectivity and feelings is a dynamics of resistance to variance.

David Rudrauf and Antonio Damasio*

There were times when I was really upset and then I'd find myself going out and doing parkour and forgetting who I am and forgetting every one of my problems, becoming Kerbie I guess, not being John anymore, not having the weight on my shoulders that John has, but being Kerbie.

John Kerr[†]

We are almost ready to return to John, or rather to John becoming Kerbie. We left John poised on the brink of annihilation, about to become someone else, a new person in a new world, a star of parkour. We saw him transfixed by the images on the screen, about to embark on the journey of re-formation whose dénouement he will mark with a new name, Kerbie. But it won't happen just yet. Even when we want it, even when we're really asking for it, there is an inertia. A stickiness. Anything as complex as us takes a while to settle, and once we do, we get comfortable and a little stuck. We adhere to the status quo. We cling to the persistent. Several months later John will *be* Kerbie. But in between lies the work of becoming.

* David Rudrauf and Antonio Damasio, 'A Conjecture Regarding the Biological Mechanism of Subjectivity and Feeling', *Journal of Consciousness Studies* 12/8–10 (2005): 236–62.
[†] John Kerr, *Jump Britain*, Channel 4 documentary (2005).

Every day for everyone, there is a dialogue between comfort and unease. Every moment of every day your Automatic works hard to keep you within the very narrow parameters within which human life is viable and comfortable. There are a myriad of micro-adjustments going on just now, from metabolism to behaviour, all working hard to stay the same. The neuroscientist Antonio Damasio calls this set of interlocking mechanisms the 'homeostasis machine'. As with our metabolism, so with our emotions: we pitch our activity to keep the feelings, like Goldilocks' porridge, just about right. This is why Amber is on the train, trying to calm the feelings down. This is why Lenny left his job, trying to get the feelings back. This is what a client described to me: after years of beating himself up for his obsessive behaviour – his running, his rocking, his cutting, his eating – he looked back and he suddenly got it. 'It was my way of coping, I was just trying to feel OK.'

Staying the same is a constant and dynamic process. We are in a continual active dialogue with change, always in transition, always just-been or just-about-to-be, always trying to feel OK with our-selves. Being complex systems, there is always a lag of adjustment as we try to meet the demands of our ever-changing circumstances by modulating whatever state we are in now. However comfortable you make yourself, you will have to work to stay like that: the lights will dim, or the temperature will drop, you'll become hungry or tired, restless or bored; something will demand adjustment so that you can stay comfortable and you will have to change to stay the same.

There is always a period of adjustment, of resistance to incoming change. And not just incoming: in our anticipations, dreads and desires, in our stories about how we should be, we create the gap between where we are and where we want to be or think we ought to be. We make ourselves uncomfortable. Our longings to be elsewhere pro-duce arousal or fatigue at the thought of all the work that we'll have to do to get there. Our aversions for our present state lead to an inner shrinking, a closing down; a kind of arousal still, but this time fuelling the desire to flee or fight against it. Never entirely still, we live in a con-stant state of flux between now and then, between what is and what if, continually perturbed and adjusting, always a little Act Two, always catching up.

> Because this conflictive dynamics is ongoing, and because a viable control of perturbations requires anticipatory strategies, the compensatory reactions often begin before the actual perturbations do. Such a setting creates the condition of a dynamic confrontation of the system with itself. Because of the inertia of the process, the system is 'walking against the wind internally', which is to say, walking against itself. *

Here, in the parlance of neuroscience, we get a glimpse of why, when things are difficult, we can make them even more so. In our attempts to ward off the blows of change, we are already flinching before they hit; already dealing with feelings of despair that haven't yet arrived. We left Amber rocking, resisting adjustment, a system out of step with its circumstance and with itself. To the degree that she is out of sync with circumstance, to that degree she is in pain. To the degree that she resists the pain, to that degree she is in distress. Resistance defines her current state. When she stops again, when this Act Two is over, that is when she will have enough comfort to sit with this new set of circumstances and bear it. Or not. To the extent that she can't, to that extent she will still have feelings about it, those feelings being nothing more than her resistance to the new.

Between us and our circumstance, between us and ourselves, there is always an interplay of ease and discord. It's along that frontier that our life happens, along that line that we feel what it is like to be ourselves, when we know who we are. Constantly rubbing up against what-is-not-yet-us, this friction generates the heat of feelings. And this is not so much good or bad as necessary.

For John, the feelings are all excitement. Until he is comfortably Kerbie, there will be a felt difference, an unease that will fuel the

---

* David Rudrauf and Antonio Damasio, 'A Conjecture Regarding the Biological Mechanism of Subjectivity and Feeling', *Journal of Consciousness Studies* 12/8–10 (2005): 236–62.

efforts of adjustment and resistance. For Carol there were physical symptoms and the anxiety caused by their lack of explanation. For Maureen, moving to a new home, the feelings are unease, discomfort. For Amber and Lenny there is pain and discontent. For everyone in Act Two, there will be a lot of feelings. There need to be. The feelings will both power and guide the change. Excitement and anxiety, discomfort and unease, physical distress and the desire for meaning, these feelings will redirect their attention to those activities that will make them feel more OK again. For John, the felt discrepancy between himself and who he wants to be will produce the arousal he needs to leap the barriers between John and Kerbie. As long as he is not OK, is not where he wants to be, he will be in a state of perturbation, a system at odds with itself, trying to reach a new equilibrium. Until the gap between John and Kerbie begins to close, he will not be able to sit comfortably. Until then the feelings will keep him awake and going, give him the energy and urgency he needs to get through Act Two. To return again to the language of science:

> The arousal is there to drive the organism to provide specific solutions to abolish the source of alarm . . . the arousal will be sustained until the reason for the arousal is eliminated. In other words, arousal turns off arousal by initiating and driving the system to produce the proper actions.*

Change produces arousal – physically, cognitively, emotionally, in our bodies, minds and hearts – and it will only subside when we have reached a new equilibrium, when we have mastered the new and worked our way through Act Two. And it is during that working out that worlds change and end. John's world really will change. Stuff that was just stuff before, neutral stuff, will become charged with value, will become either an enabler or an obstacle to his purpose. As his built environment offers him a set of props and affordances to

---

* Holger Ursin, 'Press Stop to Start: The Role of Inhibition for Choice and Health', *Psychoeuroendocrinology* 30/10 (2005): 1059–65.

which others are blind, so the world of Kerbie will be different to the world of John. Without direction, it didn't matter where he directed his attention or energy. Attention which has no particular focus has, as a result, no concept of distraction. Now, with somewhere to get to, John's life will be full of potential distractions. Stuff that was just stuff before will either help him on his way or take him off his path. He will begin to make these discriminations, his senses will become heightened and his attention sensitized to the things in his world that enable or block his transformation. His *Umwelt*, the set of things that matter and are meaningful to him within his environment, will be radically different than before. Things in his world will begin to mean more, to mean something. He will act differently, feel differently, think about his world in a different way. This is the excitement of Act Two. A whole new world to explore.

The only way to avoid the feelings and the work of becoming would be to magically jump from Act One to the end of Act Three, to curve the emotional space–time continuum, leap through a wormhole, only then could change happen with no feelings, no pain, no unease. But nothing changes without resistance. Not even those straw Buddhists we met at the beginning of this chapter. Act Two will be nothing if not difficult.

The Gift of Legs. Imagine if you missed your calling. Imagine if you were out when the summons arrived. John wasn't out because if he had been then he would still be John and our spotlight would be trained on someone else. John is poised on the brink. His attention and arousal are about to be completely re-mobilized, his world is about to be reconfigured into a new set of affordances, obstacles and resistances. Millions watched that programme, but him it touched. There has to be a readiness. There has to be, in the moment of recognition, a transaction: the wound or need has to recognize its potential assuagement. There is a newish marketing technique called astroturfing. Having noticed that, post-internet, a lot of new cultural phenomena get established from the ground up, through gossip within sub-groups and through rumours running in between them, marketers are now trying to create a faux word-of-mouth buzz by seeding rumours within their target sub-groups. Trying to start a fake grass-roots movement, hence astroturf. But even with such smart seeding, most will still fall on stony ground. There has to be a readiness. Millions watched the programme John watched, hundreds saw Carol's notice. It only spoke to them. There has to be a problem that needs sorting, something unnamed but insistent, unmet but urgent.

So it was with John. Chances are that, sooner or later, he would have heard of parkour. It's a much more widespread rumour now, which Johns all over the place will be catching wind of, forming themselves into communities, getting into networks of affinity with other free-runners. But when John heard it, it was real news, a revelation, a bolt from the blue. Like a magnet, placed near a mix of dust and iron filings, so that call convoked and realigned elements of John into a new pattern. It transfigured him. He investigated the world of parkour, identified the location and members of the tribe that he wished to join. He contacted them. Important stars of it came to meet him at his home, showed him leaps around local props that he had never thought of or dared to try, showed him what was possible. Soon he relocated to London, to live close to members of his tribe-to-be, devoting ever more time and energy to parkour. Eventually parkour went from being an isolated figure in his life – one other thing he did – to being the ground, the basis of who he was and what he did. He changed his name. All the elements of John are to be found in Kerbie, nothing was added but everything was realigned, as Kerbie. The agent of the realignment, the celestial magnet, was the news from elsewhere, and it was the readiness, the Kerbie-in-waiting in John, his unease with his current world, that brought this news to earth and turned mere information into a living, working belief. A transaction between above and below. This is also how lightning works, not just a bolt from above, but as a rising from below (see text box).*

---

* Boxed text taken from online source: www.levydisaster.com/lightning.aspx.

HOW IT WORKS

The cloud bottom carries a negative charge. Positive charges may collect on the ground, buildings, boat masts, people, flagpoles, mountaintops or trees.

A stepped leader – a negative electrical charge made of zig-zagging segments or steps – comes partway down from the cloud. The steps are invisible: each one is about 150 feet long.

When the stepped leader gets within 150 feet of a positive charge, a streamer (surge of positive electricity) rises to meet it. The leader and the streamer make a channel.

An electrical current from an object on the ground surges upward through the channel. It touches off a bright display called a return stroke.

We rise to the occasions of our recognition. Something in us rises up. This is what Slavoj Žižek calls *performative recognition*, for in recognizing who we are, we become it. In looking at the news and saying 'That's for me!', we subscribe to that narrative. Like Carol, like John. To become something, we need not only an impulse from within, from below, but also something from elsewhere, from above, a narrative, a story about who to be. Amber's therapist was suggesting that she look for versions of herself that she could bear to become. When outer narrative meets inner need, then there is the lightning stroke, the marriage of heaven and earth, the beginning of transformation.

You can even induce it experimentally. Several healthy undergraduates were told that they had a particular illness. Immediately they reconfigured their pasts. Recent, random moments of tiredness, stray pains and passing symptoms were recalled and pressed into the service of manifesting an illness. Nothing new was introduced except this piece of bogus news, but with it their worlds changed as an external narrative met inner need. Previously unconnected elements of their past and uncollected moments of their present were taken and rearranged into the pattern of disease. 'We always knew we were ill, this explains it.'

There is an exquisitely awkward scene towards the end of *Safe*. Carol has physically relocated to the commune in the hills and is making her inaugural speech to her new community. It's a stumbling, incoherent mess, not so much a speech as a word-salad composed of all the tropes and shibboleths she has heard everyone else say over the last few weeks. It ends with an apologetic 'I'm still learning . . . the words'.

The question that hovers over *Safe* is whether this new community, this new language, this new Carol is any more authentic than the old one. As we see her being socialized into a new small world, trying to learn its moves and words, stumbling her way through a whole new dialect of distress, are we seeing someone finding her voice, or a form of ideological possession? Have you ever got a glimpse of someone fluffing a performance of themselves, or trying to use someone else's gestures to express themselves, and doing it badly? People do it a lot with Chandler from *Friends*: 'Oh. My. God.' A whole generation have been inflected by the social dialect of west-coast American teenage girls that first disseminated itself through *Clueless*, *Buffy* and *Mean Girls*: 'like, *totally*; like, *whatever*'. Ever seen someone do that clumsily? That kind of queasy feeling hangs over the end of *Safe*, of someone uneasily speaking a foreign tongue. In searching for the answers to our unease, we should be careful what rumours we listen to, what calls we answer.

Another story reaches me, a sad, dark, true tale of a woman finding herself, finding the answer to her lifelong pain within a community based on power and abuse. The role of self-negation she adopts within this new community leads to her lonely death. In times of transition, in Act Two, we are indeed 'just a little more vulnerable to undue influence'.

We leave Carol encased within a porcelain bubble, isolated and safe from everything. John is Kerbie now. Their difficult, effortful time, for the moment, is over. Others, like Maureen, Amber and Lenny, are in the foothills of change, a time when we are most prey to the vicissitudes of courage, and most in need of it. Vulnerable to undue influence, listening for rumours. They will have to be careful what calls they answer, discern if the news from elsewhere is gift or curse.

They made it sound like it was the first and only activity to ever make people consider their surroundings anything other than architecture, what the hell? Some of the street they were on looked the bizzo mind, tonnes of badass transitions and flatbanks. What was with that dude who looked like mike vallely, he shouldve been nails, came across as a right wuss tho, id knack him with one arm tied behind my back, actually the lot of them were sissies, the guy with the cowboy hat on who looked and acted like boy george and that guy Kerbie (real name john or something) was just a general fopp, you know the dude wouldve been a full on goth if he hadnt found the gift of legs.*

* Testicle Tim, discussing the parkour documentary *Jump Britain* on the Mountain Bike UK Forum: http://mbuk.com/forum/default.asp.

ACT TWO

CHANGING

Chapter 6

First Impressions

In which we look at the early days and first nights of change, the clumsy first steps of adjustment to the new. It becomes apparent that the acts we choose to repeat in these transitional times – when the Automatic is for the moment suspended and Deliberation makes a rare, sustained appearance – are uniquely important and indeed formative of our character.

Character is that which reveals moral purpose, exposing the class of things a man chooses or avoids.

Aristotle

I fancied him until he opened his mouth.

James B. L. Hollands

So, Act Two begins, the first steps in the dance of adjustment. Having received our summons, heard our call, the great or terrible or merely uneasy news, we need to begin to *become*, to become other than we are. Something as complex as you and me doesn't change easily. We get set in our ways, comfortable, accustomed. This is what makes daily life work: how good we are at getting comfortable. But the call to change has come, and a new accommodation, a new relationship to our circumstance, needs to be negotiated. New habits need acquiring, old ones shedding. We have seen how we are and have counted the ways we are set in. Now we must begin to depart from them, and to establish new ones. Now the work, the drama, begins.

Playing House. The set is empty. Well, not quite. But the set is new. In boxes in the hall, there are the things that will fill the rooms. In the front room there are only two red sofas, stark on a new carpet in a room smelling of fresh paint. No other signs of life. Everything as fresh as a newly dug grave. And here comes the body, here comes the bride. Well, not quite. Here comes Maureen. ALL ALONE. As a graphic novel this could really resonate. Comic strips of long bare halls, empty rooms with single light bulbs. In each frame a figure with the light behind it, darkened, small already, further dwarfed by the empty rooms. We would know she was alone and not loving it. This is the beginning of living alone. No death has precipitated this, except the death of expectations. At thirty-something, no husband has appeared; the move she always thought she'd make together she has decided to make alone. Her new home, alone.

And so on, pages of images of a little figure in empty rooms. But the rooms – life goes on – don't stay empty for long. Maureen is a woman of considerable drive, not the kind to hang about in empty rooms. She is tough, extravert and – orphaned young – used to being alone. She just thought it might be over by now. But no. So she fills the rooms, but not too much, gives each room an identity with a few carefully chosen things, creates a dining room, a drawing room, a bedroom, a snug. The house is really shaping up. She adds a cat, a lodger and telephones a friend.

Maureen cries down the phone. Not the uncontrolled wailing of the loveless, only that natural overflow that occasionally escapes us when the good-enough is reminded of the might-have-been. 'It's fine,' she says, both believing it and crying, 'it's really all fine, it just feels like I'm playing house.'

Let's call the lodger Jack. He's a bit player, we needn't bother filling this one in too much – pale and quiet man-boy will suffice. The cat is Hamish, a sleek, ginger tom. Maureen doesn't know how to be with Jack, Jack doesn't know how to be with Maureen, they don't know how to be with Hamish, and vice versa, all within a setting where the props and sets have never been used, so no one really knows how or where to sit or stand while not knowing what to do. Nothing here has been sanctioned by use. There are bright and ghastly attempts at breakfast when Maureen makes tea and toast for two. In the evenings they sit on separate red sofas and try to watch television. The cat is unsettled. No one knows their role, their place, their lines. So, as determinedly as she filled the rooms, Maureen is trying to play the part. Bright breakfasts and after-work tea and chat are installed into the day. Routines-to-be are given their first airings, domestic habits-to-come are initiated. Little figures in empty rooms. It's not just the energy required by this start-up phase, it's the terrible feeling of *inauthenticity*, of making it up. She is almost ready to give up, to send the cat back, Jack packing, sell the house and return to the small flat where she knew how to be single and alone. She's had just about enough of playing house.

Some people love this phase. I remember as a child the great feeling of freedom in being in a new house. There was something very playful about it. Nothing was set in stone, and for a brief phase it seemed as if anything was possible. The tremendous scandal of sitting on a bare floor watching TV while eating fish and chips straight from the newspaper; of all sleeping in the front room, the only one with heating, while the fire cast the shadow of its guard across the ceiling like a wind-blown web. Were there ghost stories? There is certainly a memory of something thrillingly new, of a suspension of the family law, where the kids could laugh at their mother's fear of spiders as she tried to fall asleep beneath the web.

There are some who actually prefer these early days of surprise and heightened arousal, of fresh paint and damp plaster. Just as there are some who prefer the start of relationships – the serial beginners, in love with the heady time before the die is cast, before the roles are fixed and the ways are set.

But not Maureen, not now. She wants to cut straight to the comfort of the new equilibrium, of an already established life. But she has a way to go yet, and knowing that does not make it easier, only adds to the exhaustion. We will return to her later, when she has reached the end of going through the motions.

First Nights

I think that when the alarm goes off in the morning, most people hear 'Action!'

Leonard Preston

Ash Wednesday. Today is Ash Wednesday, which in the Christian calendar is traditionally the first day of renunciation, the first day of a new regime. Old habits are relinquished and new ones started. Little figures in an empty room. Like Maureen rattling about in her early days, our new gestures have no weight. They could die at any moment, for they have no conviction, no gravity, no *precedent*. The unprecedented action, as a spontaneous gesture, as a moment, can be thrilling. The first time you hear yourself use a new word. A little rush of risk but, hey, you got away with it and people seem impressed. Or a gesture. You may have seen it performed by a friend or on TV and squirrelled it away until just now, when the occasion called for it, and it answered and wow, it worked. You made it yours. You *owned* it. Every single move you make has had its debut. Some will never make it past their first appearance. Others become you:

> . . . they're more a style
> Our lives bring with them: habit for a while,
> Suddenly they harden into all we've got . . .*

But habits in their infancy, like Bambi on ice, are far from hardened and far from being you. That's the work of repetition, of rehearsal, and that we don't often get to see. Most of the characters in our lives, including our own, are fairly well established. But sometimes, we catch them in transition. And, if we do, there is a fair chance that they may not be our friends for much longer. One thing that happens as people switch roles is that they acquire a new supporting cast. Or vice versa, as we saw in Chapter 4, 'Cosa Nostra'; sometimes acquiring a new supporting cast calls upon different parts of ourselves, demands a new version of ourselves. And then the old cast, at least a portion of them, don't hang around. To them this new role looks fake, stupid, inauthentic. Insupportable. Or at least that is how it looked to the friends of . . .

The Man Who Became a Buddhist. He was the cleverest and wittiest of a clever and witty group, all young men, students, all intellectuals

* Philip Larkin, 'Dockery and Son' (1963).

with artistic inclinations, and of this group he was always the one most likely to . . . to what, no one was exactly sure, but to excel, to star. He had the greatest ease with poetry, the greatest facility with ideas, was the most graceful and gifted of them all. Some exaggeration for later dramatic effect, but not much. That was years ago, more than twenty, and at a dinner party I met Andy, one of his group, and he told me what became of this star-to-be. He became a Zen Buddhist.

Andy recounts seeing him in transition. There is irritation and a kind of incomprehension at play as he describes the fallen star. It was the lack of spontaneity that got to him most. The last time he saw the man who became a Buddhist, the main thing that struck him was how false and studied all his words and gestures seemed. How deliberate and drained of all that once made him so nonchalantly graceful. Andy tried some of the old moves, tried to start one of those routines that grow up between friends – a riff on music, a take on cinema – some gesture that once would have reliably provoked a counter-move and started up the *pas de deux*. It fell flat, flat and dead on stony ground. There was A Pause. The Buddhist deliberates and then produces a studied, neutral response. For God's sake, a *polite* response. The death knell of friendship.

Charlotte Joko Beck, one of the most lucid writers on western Buddhism and its practice in everyday life, mentions a stage that people often go through when they first begin to practise mindfulness. They can become a little robotic, as their attempts at being mindful eclipse their spontaneity. For a while. This may have been all that was happening with Andy's friend, but I think it's more general than that. Andy had caught a friend in rehearsal, trying out a new role. That's rare, so here's another example.

Donald's New Role. Donald is a friend of Maureen, and you can imagine this happening, as it did, in Maureen's new house. Donald is mid-thirties, a handsome, kind and gentle man. A devout Christian within a fairly Christian peer group, married to Stephanie now for five years. Happy, building a home and planning kids. See what's coming? The handsome, kind and gentle may have given it away. Donald is gay.

Cut to several months later, past the mess which need not detain us. (Although a quick aside on those that survive the transition. Maureen survived and remains a good friend of Donald's, thus her witness to the following. Maureen's friendship with Stephanie did not make it through. The casualties of transition. Film trailer voice-over: 'Transition: Not Everyone Will Make It Through'. Get ill, divorced, bereaved or sacked and you'll lose a few.)

A dinner at Maureen's with Donald, a month or two after his separation from Stephanie. Maureen notices a change in Donald. First outward and visible signs are the jewellery, the chunky necklace, the leather wrist strap, the stud in one ear. So far so metropolitan, if not exactly Donald of old. But there's something new that's deeper than the skin. Donald is performing himself differently. Donald is being a version of 'gay'. The hands are more expressive, the gestures more effusive. The octave range within a sentence has doubled, so that remarks can be punctuated with an occasional rising 'Oh my God' and other new flourishes. This change in form, in style of delivery, partly reflects a change in content – an enthusiastic discussion of gay hankie codes and what sexual practices they denote. Maureen, though, is not so much struck by the content, which is nothing new to her, but by the delivery. Donald is trying out a new persona.

Donald and Shakespeare

Do I not look pale as fearing to be out in my speech?*

In Shakespeare's time, the first night of a play was part of the writing and rehearsal process. A play was 'on trial' on its first night; it was tried and refined by the audience response. Thus the

* From *The Foure Prentices of London* by Thomas Heywood (*c.* 1592), quoted in Tiffany Stern, *Rehearsal from Shakespeare to Sheridan* (Clarendon Press, 2000).

Prologues that beg the audience's indulgence, ask them to give it a fair hearing before they boo it off the stage. Playwrights have actors announcing, as in the quote above, the unreadiness of their new role, their dependence on the 'palmes of the vulgar' and the 'smoaky breath of the multitude' for approbation. Plays, roles and their performances were constructed in conjunction with the audience, with the first night being more raw material than finished product:

> the best Poems of this kind, in the first presentation, resemble that all tempting Minerall newly digged up, the Actors being onely the labouring Miners, but you [the audience] the skilfull Triers and Refiners.*

So Donald was trying and refining himself as gay. Over the next few months, Maureen observes the role's evolution. There was a certain night when a new high-water mark of change was set, when the performance ceased to be one of occasional stylistic flourish and became a sustained act of gayness, a masterwork of camp in which a coherent sequence of gestures, expressions and words were enrolled into a dramatic acting-out of anecdotes and high expressed emotion; a self-dramatization that drew attention, as only camp can, to the dialectic of theatricality and sincerity at work in any act of emotional expression, in any self-enactment. He really went for it. And then, a later meeting at which he was almost the old Donald again, just with a little added spice. Maureen is one of the audience that Donald doesn't lose. She sticks with him through these early trials and refinements until the perturbations settle. His repertoire of voice and gesture is now not so much new as broader than before, for he has a fuller palette to draw on and so a finesse of expression

---

* From Richard Hawkins, Preface to quarto edition of Beaumont and Fletcher's *Philaster* (1628), quoted in Tiffany Stern, *Rehearsal from Shakespeare to Sheridan* (Clarendon Press, 2000).

not available to the old Donald. Through dint of repetition, Donald has tried and refined a version of himself that he is now comfortable with.

Manners, manners. I sit in the meeting and watch. I watch one person in particular because I recognize her type, not one that I have seen often, but certainly one that I have seen before.

It's little if anything to do with how she looks. There is an element of that, but it's not physiognomy, not her biological givens. Anything that identifies her as the type I recognize physically is to do with choices she has made. How she has chosen to dress. For a start there is the purple. We are at a meeting of psychotherapists. Like many female psychotherapists, she has chosen purple and velvet, for at the time of writing this there is a tendency for female therapists to dress in dark crushed textures. Velour or corduroy skirts or trousers, heavy rich shirts or blouses. This may be a nod at clerical garb, connoting 'priestess', or just a sophisticated bohemian, post-hippy professional. But it's a look. She has it and two other women at the meeting have it too. But it's not that. That's not what types her, not really. I can imagine this type in pretty much anything, though certainly the garb helps.

The hair is also a contributory prop. The way it feathers lightly around the rim of her face all the way down to the neck. A little shaggy, a little scruffy, very smart. 'I'm human' hair. But it's not that.

It's this: her head is tilted down and her eyes are looking up to just below the eyeline of the group. Her right hand, her thinking hand, is raised. She is gesturing with her cupped palm turned towards her, showing us the back of her hand which moves in cadence with the point that is coming out v e r y c o n s i d e r e d. Precise, but, like the clothes and hair, with a kind of scruffy, bo-ho encounter-group edge. But you could take all the clothes away and you would still recognize the type. If it was the New York version you would recognize 'thoughtful therapist making a contribution to the group' and it would be likeable, clever. This is like that, but with the added patina of east-coast Scots which actually detracts slightly from clever and veers towards pedantic. It would be easy to dislike this, because you feel a little school teacher has combined with the therapist, a dash of Jean Brodie. I can't stop looking at the eyes, which are not looking at us, but at the point they are making. As if she's reading from a vision – a precise and rather prosaic one. The hand coaxes the words out of the mouth in small insistent waves. The mouth smiles, the eyes wrinkle, not at us, but at a little irony in the point she is making. I really forget the point because I am so struck by the manner. I'm thinking about manner anyway, so I am sensitized to it. But it really got me, because I could, for a moment or two, see it as a separate entity. Something, like her clothes and hair, chosen, studied, acquired. For the first few moments of the meeting she was silent, and I hadn't a clue what I thought about her, other than that she had the purple thing. And then she opened her mouth and became the person she now is in my head. Before then, she could have been anyone, anyone in those clothes. Now she is someone. I have a sense of this woman. But it only started when she opened her mouth, when she started moving, when she became animated, and then the noises, the tone, the deliberation, the precision, the heavily signalled thoughtfulness, when that started, for a few rapt moments I was able to distinguish the collection of gestures from the body they were using. I was able to see them as an essentially arbitrary imposition on this person. Anything could have come out of her mouth. Any set of postures could have been adopted, enacted. And it wasn't that I was imagining her animated by the spirit of De Niro in *Taxi Driver*, all stare-you-out psychosis (though I am now, and it's funny). No, at the time I was just aware of the essence of this woman being the animation of the form; I could see her as a body possessed, albeit by herself.

Who Owns Your Personality?

> The use a man is to make of his body is transcendent in relation to
> that body as mere biological entity . . . Behaviour creates meanings
> which are transcendent in relation to the anatomical apparatus . . .
>
> Maurice Merleau-Ponty*

Legally, if something is alienable, the ownerships or rights of its use
can be transferred from you to someone else. Your house, your car,
your dog – you can sell your rights to them. However, there are certain rights that you cannot sell or buy, rights that you cannot
commodify and market: inalienable rights. Alienable derives from
alius, 'an other'. To alienate is to give away a thing or the rights in a
thing to another. There are rights you cannot give away: life, liberty,
the pursuit of happiness. They are yours for keeps, whether you
want them or not, for you cannot, at least in legal theory, sell your
freedom or your life. However, between your life and your house,
between the self-evident givens and your acquired paraphernalia,
lies the murky legal ground of your personality. Legally, you might
not entirely belong to yourself.

To plump up our definitions a little more, there are two kinds of
rights: personal and real rights. If you own the *real* rights to something, it has been, as it were, truly alienated from its point of origin
and become yours; you now own the rights as you might a house,
or a movie or a car. By contrast there are *personal* rights. If you have
the personal rights to something, it means that you have the use of
it, you have rented or borrowed a limited ability to use it, as if you
rented a house, a movie or a car. You can use it, but usage doesn't
make it yours and you cannot transfer these rights of use to someone else.

At this moment, in law, in some countries, your *persona* – which

* Maurice Merleau-Ponty, *Phenomenology of Perception* (1945; English translation,
Routledge & Kegan Paul, 1962).

is to say the series of quirks and tics and appearance that make you recognizably *you* – is leasable. You can rent them out to someone, but as long as you are alive, you retain the rights. Once you are dead, however, your personality doesn't end. At that point it can become truly alienable and the rights to it can be transferred to someone else. At that point 'I' becomes another's.

This strange state of affairs has arisen, of course, in the cauldron of celebrity. If you're Lady Gaga, you can lease someone the right to put your face on a T-shirt. If you're Joey from *Friends* (who, to make matters more surreal, is of course not a real person at all, but the creation of an actor, a writer and a production studio), you can license the right to brand 'Joey's Café' with life-size posters of Matt LeBlanc around the walls. In the celebrity world it is clearer than anywhere that the persona of a person is a separate and potentially valuable commodity. Here is the legal definition of the persona:

> Each individual has his own distinct persona made up of physical appearance (image or likeness), name, voice, signature and other recognizable elements, together the so called 'indicia of identity', which for the celebrated few immediately evoke in the mind of the general public that particular individual . . .*

The odd and mundane reality of celebrity life is that your persona, like your car, can be stolen:

> The right of publicity is a right to raise an action either to prevent, or to seek subsequent compensation for the wrongful appropriation for commercial purposes of another's persona without that person's proper consent . . . or the consent of a third party which now exercises the right for that individual, to whom it has either been assigned, or by whom it has been inherited.†

* Simon Smith, *Image, Persona and the Law*, 2nd edn (Sweet & Maxwell, 2008).
† Ibid.

Remember the set of gestures enacted by the therapist. They make her up. Had she been rich or famous, and had I appropriated enough of her tropes – and made them, for instance, a character in a video game where you could, for example, blow away therapists with a rocket launcher, mid-gesture – then she could sue. Maybe she could sue anyway, but I could argue that her type was too generic to be specific to her. She is the opposite of an archetype – a stereotype. Both words come from printing. Stereo here means solid, as in the solid printing block from which multiple copies can be produced. I have seen all her gestures before. But I have probably seen all of yours too. It's not the gestures that count, but their orchestration.

Here again legalese is useful. As my legal-expert friend Lilian pointed out, the law is interested in what can be commodified, and works hand in hand with capitalism in attempting to generate ever more objects and properties for lease, sale and legal protection. To constitute a legal object, a dramatic work – for example the 'turn' of a comedian – must be a 'work of action' that is *fixated:* i.e. both stereotyped and unique enough that it might be recognizably performed independent of its originator. Does the therapist tick all those boxes? Give me a wig and a week in rehearsal and I could have her down to a T, but I could argue that I was impersonating a sub-group of therapists in general. Perhaps something of what makes a celebrity a celebrity is the fact that they are one of, or the first of, a kind. As stereotyping is the reproducing of an original, so a prototype is the first type, the first stamp, the original from whom the others are derived.

The notion of the transmissibility of a gesture-set is not new. Elizabethan dramatists divided the art of an actor into two parts, distinguishing between action and delivery, or gesture and speech. As there were conventions for how the text should be enunciated, so there were conventions for how emotion should be manifested. Gestures, postures and facial expressions were taught, and these were not always necessarily natural. Audiences had to be 'in' on the conventions of emotional expression to be able accurately to decipher them. Up until the nineteenth century, originality was not a trait desired or praised in either actors or performances. Early or first performances of a role would have established a prototypical interpretation of it, which would become an autonomous, transmissible 'part'. A part – a particular set of words, a particular style of enunciation, actions and gestures – would then be transmitted to other actors and down the generations. A part, writes a journalist of 1737, 'is a kind of Property, not to be taken away without injustice'. Publicity for plays made much of the fact that the audience would see a version of a revered original. Two companies, both performing Congreve's *The Old Batchelor*, competed for publicity. One had the renowned actor Thomas Betterton playing the part of Heartwell. The other advertised that their actor would act not the role, but Betterton's version of the role, and moreover would do it better than Betterton himself. A part, once prototyped, could then be transmitted from actor to actor, achieving a longevity longer than any individual or theatre company. Thus we have the eighteenth-century actress Elizabeth Barry training up Mary Porter in her parts, rumoured to exclaim: 'Dear Porter, I will never die whilst you live.'

The notion of originality enters the world of theatre and criticism with eighteenth-century actor, producer and playwright David Garrick, who was renowned for inventing all-new prototypes of parts. However, this was only so that he could then disseminate *his* parts as widely as possible.

> His new performances were carefully crafted into immutable fixed entities: he was for instance furious when Barry [an acting rival] took to the other theatre 'his' method of playing Romeo.*

The amount of control that he exerted over his company was phenomenal, with everyone down to the bit players instructed in parts *à la* Garrick. Originality stopped with its originator. His energy of

---

* Tiffany Stern, *Rehearsal from Shakespeare to Sheridan* (Clarendon Press, 2000).

invention was matched only by his urge to impress his work on others:

> New moulding characterizations and stamping a particular brand of acting onto a performer involved Garrick in an extraordinary quantity of teaching.*

So the actors and their lawyers have known for a while what psychologists are just beginning to understand, which is that the essence of a person is not some inscrutable inner quality but is stamped on their form.

Aristotle's Soul

> The soul is the form of the body.
>
> Aristotle

'New moulding characterizations and stamping a particular brand of acting onto a performer involved Garrick . . .' Note the prevailing metaphors. They tell us something about what the beginning of a new part might look like, about the mechanisms that begin to turn the early days of playing house and first nights into longer runs. Mould, stamp, brand, type, cast, impression, character, figure,† cut, mark, impress. And style, think of style and stylus. There's a little pottery/sculpture here (the cast of a character), but predominantly it's the two-dimensional arts of printing (stereotype) and of writing, of sealing, marking, impressing and branding a blank surface. And just in case we haven't quite got it, here is character, speaking for itself:

---

* Ibid.

† 'Figure' in the sense that Henry James uses it in this sentence in *The Portrait of a Lady*: 'Mrs Touchett had an hour's uninterrupted conversation with her niece, who found her a strange and interesting figure: a figure essentially – almost the first she had ever met.' This definition is 'figure' in the sense of the impression the person makes on us, the mark they make, the figure they cut.

character *n* Before 1333 *caracter* a symbol marked on the body or an
imprint on the soul, borrowed from Old French *caractère*, from Latin
character, from Greek *charakter* instrument for marking, distinctive
mark, or distinctive nature, personal feature, from *charassein* to
engrave, cut furrows in, scratch.

Chambers Dictionary of Etymology (1999)

There is a double sense of marking here too. First, the mark the
world has made on us, with character as the branding of experience
on the molten wax of self. Then, like the sealing ring, this becomes
the impression that we make upon the world, the mark we return,
the figure we cut. Both branded and branding, marking as we are
marked. And if we go back to the therapist lady – the mark that she
left on my mind, and now on yours, was such an embossing: all
externals and outward gestures forming shapes in space, creating an
impression, cutting a figure.

What is embedded in our language is a version of ourselves, of
the way we come across, with our character being a kind of branding
or a forming of the clay of us into a particular, distinct shape. This
is a notion as old as our thinking about ourselves. We could trace
two versions of our soul, our essence, through history – possibly
more, almost certainly – but for the purposes of our illustration,
two. A distinct two.

First there is the idea of the soul as an impersonal, inscrutable
essence. A pure thing imprisoned in a sullied flesh, but essentially
immune to the experience of the latter, from which, one day, it will
be liberated. This is the soul of Plato, of Christianity, of Descartes,
of Kant, the Atman of the Hindus. To the purity of this soul, our
personal characteristics are a stain that will be removed when our
flesh perishes or is forced into submission. For this tradition, in a
variety of ways, our unique features are so many clouds occlud-
ing the light of the truth hidden within. Remove the ego, remove
the pathology of the desiring self from the moral order, remove the
promptings of the flesh and serenity, justice and peace, and the *real
you* will emerge, shine out and shine on. The soul is God in us. Our

fleshy selves are, on the other hand, a temporary smudge on the face of the divine.

Against this let us set the soul of Aristotle: 'The soul is the form of the body'. We could, just quickly, go further back than Aristotle, to the Egyptians. The Egyptians had a multiple soul. Through the murk of time and cultural difference, we have only the dimmest sense of their scheme, but we know it was a thing of parts, this Egyptian soul, and one of those parts seems very close to our sense of persona, and uncannily close to the idea, now enshrined in law, of the persona as a thing with a separate existence. One of the parts of this multipack self was an independent collection of attributes and actions, an autonomous persona, like the therapist's gesture set, or Garrick's theatrical parts. It had a self-sufficient existence; it could inhabit another object, say a statue, and bring it to life with the animation of the body it had left behind. This gestural double would persist after death, and had its own need for food, its own life. It is a very early recognition of the relative independence of our persona, our manner (etymologically all about hands), the distinctive way in which we do things and enact ourselves:

> The way you wear your hat.
> The way you sip your tea.
> The memory of all that –
> No, no – they can't take that away from me.*

From those hazy Egyptian days to Aristotle, and the soul as the form of the body. Not some inscrutable inner, but the most external, the most out-there part of us is, in fact, the essence of us. The way we sip our tea. But still, be it at our innermost core, or out there in the way we are, we are equally inscrutable to ourselves. This Aristotelian soul is the 'self as others see us', from which

---

* George and Ira Gershwin, 'They Can't Take That Away from Me' (1937).

Robert Burns notes our eternal sundering. Our spontaneous gestures, our deliberate ones, our ongoing and outward expression of ourselves over time – that is who we are. The personal, fleshy transient body self does not obscure our immortal soul, our essence. Rather, moment by moment, it reveals it. This is a self spread out, not contained and inscrutable, but up front, all the depth of us contained within our surface.

Leapfrogging several thousand years, we find that psychology is waking up to the way in which the self is a thoroughly and primarily embodied thing:

> the newborn infant does not attend to the outward appearance of the other, but rather attends to the *action* and *expression* of the other . . . The other presents me with 'themes of possible activity for my own body' . . . The infant does not perceive the other person as an object so much as it senses at a behavioral and motor level, that the expression of another is one the infant itself can make.*

And as the infant does not perceive the other as object but rather as expression, so its deepest sense of itself is not as object but as embodied[†] *movement*, as motor action and potential. As Shaun Gallagher points out, Merleau-Ponty was the modern philosopher who most thoroughly grasped that there was something about gesture that both defined us and was, in an uncanny way, not entirely contained by us:

> The use a man is to make of his body is transcendent in relation to that body as mere biological entity.

and

* Shaun Gallagher, *How the Body Shapes the Mind* (Clarendon Press, 2005).
† Gallagher is part of the *embodied* cognition movement in psychology, one of the Es of the 4E cognition movement (extended, enacted, embodied and embedded) that we met in Chapter 3.

the human body is defined in terms of its property of appropriating, in an indefinite series of discontinuous acts, significant cores which transcend and transfigure its natural powers. This act of transcendence is first encountered in the acquisition of a pattern of behaviour, then in the mute communication of gesture.*

So, as the Egyptians observed, our gesture sets are in some way transcendent to us as beings and are both acquirable and transmissible. What we see of others, and what they know of us, is not some core glimpsed through a thicket of obscuring behaviour, but rather that very behaviour is our heart laid bare. Aristotle's soul, and the self emerging from neuroscience, does not hide within our body, nor is it bound by it; rather it spills out, occupying space and marking it for all to see. Like a hand-held firework, our passage through space emblazons an inimitable figure and brands the air between us with a unique impression that we ourselves can never really grasp. But this is what people 'get' when they get us. This is what our brains are wired to detect in others. As the infant's deepest sense of itself is as potential and actual movement, as its natural perception of others is as the same, so beneath our veneers of considered judgement runs this urgent stream of first *impressions*, with our automatic perception of others as enacted performance. We may even have dedicated cells in our brains – mirror neurons – that reflect the performance of others as if it were our own. We 'get' people because, when we see them do their thing, we actually know what it feels like, for some part of us is doing it too.

Psychology is beginning to get what Aristotle knew: the flesh is not that in which our soul is hidden, but that upon which it is written, branded, stamped, cut, typed, figured and impressed, for all to see and, if you are a celebrity, for all to steal. What the world sees, once we open our mouths and start to act, is the collection of habits and ways of being that we have acquired and nurtured. It's what I

---

* Maurice Merleau-Ponty, *Phenomenology of Perception* (1945; English trans. 1962), quoted in Gallagher, *How the Body Shapes the Mind*.

was so struck by when the therapist started enacting herself. In the eyes of others, we cannot help but expose our character, the things we have chosen or avoided. Perhaps the universal sense of shame comes from this: not so much that we have anything in particular to hide, but that we know how hard it is to do so; for we can see, in the eyes of others, quite how legible we are.

George Eliot's Skin

Our deeds travel with us from afar,
And what we have been makes us what we are.

George Eliot*

Our characters, then, are a collection of precedents, a collection of gestures that have survived the trying and refining of early days and first nights. I caught myself at it today, caught myself character-forming. A T-shirt falls from a high cupboard as I pull out another one. As it falls and lies on the floor I catch a glimpse of myself at work. The Saturday morning urge to let it lie, to carry on the journey out of the room to tea and toast and do it later is temporarily frozen by a new impulse, one that I have been fostering for a few weeks, which is to deal with stuff as soon as it happens: doing the dishes after the meal, opening the letters as they arrive, putting the new phone number in the address book right away and not on the nearest piece of paper. A new impulse deliberately fostered because I am in a new phase of life, one where it feels more imperative, feels better to be on top of things, to know what's up. So I've tended this new impulse like a small flame at the kindling of a fire, and today I watch it catch and burn on its own. I laugh as I watch these impulses meet. I laughed because I didn't decide a thing, as I watched the old, comfortable King of Saturday morning meet the upstart Knight of Order and, after a momentary deadlock, to me a

---

* George Eliot, *Middlemarch* (Blackwood & Sons, 1874).

micro-pause, the old ceded to the new and there I was bending down to pick up the T-shirt, slinging it back up to its home, then off to tea and toast. I laughed. I have a new precedent.

> Tito was experiencing that inexorable law of human souls, that we prepare ourselves for sudden deeds by the reiterated choice of good or evil that gradually determines character.*

More than most, George Eliot had a sense of our being a collection of precedents. Her pithiest formulation is probably the one at the top of this section, 'what we have been makes us what we are', and what we have been is what we have *done*. What she understood was the persistence of deeds, the way that past actions leave a trace, what she called elsewhere 'a record deeper than the skin'. A deed, once done, creates a tendency for its repetition, and reactivation of the tendency gives it greater force. Eventually, these tendencies, as Larkin said, can harden into all we've got and become our character. Our beaten paths.

This is not a new observation. Aristotle gets at the same idea in his notion of *hexis*, which translates to something like dispositions or states of readiness. These *hexeis*, more than mere habits, are complex dispositional states, encoding how we feel, think and act towards things that we have met before. These are the ways we get set in, the paths we have beaten. Through the mingling of reason and deliberation, raw feeling and force of repetition, we form ourselves to respond predictably, build up a class of responses, an ever-widening array of things and states that we approach or avoid.

Aristotle, Aquinas and Eliot all place these dispositions at the heart of morality, of vice and virtue, and these in turn at the heart of character. Similarly *sila*, the Buddhist word for morality, means habit, behaviour, nature, morality and character all at once. All these venerable thinkers are trying to tell us that character is not just innate

---

* George Eliot, *Romola* (Smith, Elder & Co., 1862–3).

disposition, not just the personality we were born with, but also an accretion of choices, a mixing of impulse and reason played out over time until it hardens into all we are, and how we got there. What they want to tell us is, Be Careful: as we begin, so we will become.

George Eliot is always reminding us of this. She writes, 'There is a terrible coercion in our deeds . . .' (*Adam Bede*, 1859) and that

> Our deeds are like children that are born to us; they live and act apart from our own will. Nay, children may be strangled, but deeds never: they have an indestructible life both in and out of our consciousness . . .*

and

> Our lives make a moral tradition for our individual selves, as the life of mankind at large makes a moral tradition for the race; and to have once acted greatly seems a reason why we should always be noble. But Tito was feeling the effect of the opposite tradition: he had won no memories of self conquest and perfect faithfulness from which he could have a sense of falling.

and finally

> Our deeds determine us, as much as we determine our deeds: and until we know what has been or will be the peculiar combination of outward with inward facts which constitute a man's critical actions, it will be better not to think ourselves wise about his character.

Critical Actions. In its own small way, my shall-I-pick-up-the-T-shirt struggle (though in fact, more accurately, I was the site of a struggle), was one such critical moment. A small one, I grant you, but one that may resonate through future circumstances in ways crucial to my

---

* This and the two following quotes are from *Romola*.

future well-being. In the stooping and the picking up, the balance between lazy impulse and the reasoned desire to live more mindfully shifted just a little more in favour of the latter. A virtuous *hexis* was reinforced, my *sila* bettered, my readiness to act in such a way in future without deliberation, without the little freeze, the micro-pause, is now that much greater. The next time I meet a similar juncture – let-it-lie or do-it-now – my tendency to the latter will be that much more automatic. By accumulation of these little acts, by repetition over time, something fundamental could change in my life and in my character. Eliot, Aquinas, Aristotle, Buddha – these thinkers remind us that our present behaviour creates our future dispositions, our new Automatic. Our choices matter.

Defining Moments

There is nothing *special* at the time about a birth that will turn out to have been a speciation event. Similarly, one should be suspicious of the demand that there be an event – an SFA [self-forming act] – that has some special, intrinsic, local feature that sets it apart from its nearest kin and explains its capacity to found something important.

Daniel Dennett*

It seems that everyone I know right now is at the beginning. Here I am, beginning a new adventure of single parenthood and a research career. There is Amber, whom we left on a train some time ago and now she has moved and gone, left the pain behind and started a new career in a new town. My nephew Ben has left school, left a situation where no one told him he was any good, to step into a world where there is a possibility that they might. My other nephew is off to university, and his parents are beginning to find out what life is like in the empty nest. My sister is now a student after thirty years of work. Someone else is about to begin the journey of grief. And

* Daniel Dennett, *Freedom Evolves* (Viking Penguin, 2003).

my daughter Vicky, just turned sixteen, has a new school, new house (with me), new peer group, new town, a whole new way of life. And Maureen. Home alone. Early days and first nights. Act Two beginning for all of us.

I tell my daughter, because she is the one I can tell most directly, that the beginning is important. It's simple stuff, the stuff that we all know, but I want to give it the force that comes from it being so obvious only because it is so true, so obvious that we miss what is obvious about it. I talk to her about establishing and getting into habits. For study, for school, for where to put things so you can find them, for setting up routines that may, given repetition, become Automatic and make her life easier to live.

And so we are back, all of us, with Maureen. All little figures in empty rooms. What we do next, us beginners, is more important now than at most other times. These beginnings, these first nights and early days, are the formative times. George Eliot called the deeds done at such times critical actions. The philosopher of free will, Robert Kane, calls them self-forming actions. We all encounter such times when, in response to new demands, we have to suspend the Automatic running of our lives, times when the complex dispositional state that is us is forced to pause for thought and consider, and reconsider, and deliberate, and begin to become, begin to form some new precedents or at least consciously choose to modify and repeat the old ones. As pointed out in Chapter 2, The Automatic, these are exceptional and energetically expensive times. They are also, as we saw in the last chapter, emotional and preoccupying times. The new era will be nothing if not difficult; it will be exhausting, emotionally arousing and preoccupying, with the heart, mind and will all in higher gear.

There is also, as Daniel Dennett notes above, nothing magic in the acts that we perform at these transitional times, no way to distinguish the ones that will flourish from those that will perish. Maureen, with equal determination, set about establishing routines for her cat, her lodger, herself and the running of her domestic life. She set them up with an uncommon vigour and a determination to make them stick. Some flourished; some perished. In the negotiation between new circumstances and new habits, some moves succeeded and survived those early days and first nights, while others fell on stony ground. Trying and refining. All that survived have by now passed into her personal and extended/embedded and social Automatic. As a result, the feeling of inauthenticity has passed. There is comfort again.

That's a reminder – for Ben, Amber, Vicky, all of us – don't expect the beginning to feel real. We are all going to be playing house for a while, before we establish the ethos of our present time and place. Ethics and ethos all go back to *etho*, literally nothing more than what we are accustomed or wont to do, our accustomed place. Custom, ethics, character, habit, persona, ethos, all of these are traceable to the same root of habit, all built from repetition. And sometimes, in some privileged and unsettling moments, we are in a position to begin something anew, to change our ethos, to acquire new tastes.

So, to all of us beginning Act Two, let us pay a little more attention to what we inaugurate and begin to repeat right now. First impressions do, after all, matter. The following verse, sometimes attributed to the Buddha, gives us a pithy summary of why we should care:

> The thought manifests as the word;
> The word manifests as the deed;
> The deed develops into habit;
> And the habit hardens into character;
> So watch the thought and its ways with care . . .

'. . . and let it spring from love, born out of concern for all creatures'. That's how it ends. That's what he wants us to do. That's the normative bit – the love – the rest is merely a description of a mechanism: what we choose to start, to repeat or to avoid at this stage will set the tone for the time to come, will reinforce the classes of things and states we approach or avoid. We could just continue, carry over our old ways, tastes and tropes. And, overwhelmingly, we will. Ben, Vicky, Amber and I aren't going to change all that much, and the older ones certainly less so. We have already established a substantial world of likings and aversions which we could not revise even if we wished to. Or not unless we wished *really hard*, hard enough to pay attention and go against our grain, walk against the wind, daily, wilfully, for a long time. We probably won't do that. But some things are, for the moment, up for grabs, up in the air, malleable. At these liminal times there is more freedom and anxiety, and we will act, inevitably, to reduce both, to get it all back into the comfortably Automatic.

I talked to Maureen today and asked if she remembered that difficult phase of months ago. Now she loves her home. Having got rid of Jack, she enjoys her own space so much that she is reluctant to get another lodger. And Hamish the cat, who completes the feeling of being at home, is *her* cat. How did she get there? She kept it up. She kept playing house until it felt real, kept repeating the moves of the life-to-be until it became her life. That's what we will all do. We will become what we repeatedly do. So, let's be careful what we start.

Chapter 7

Second Natures

In which we see that in the throes of change we have more than personal resources to draw upon, and that there is a hoard of ready-made ways of being to ease some of the blood, sweat and tears of change. We look at how, in learning and adopting any new role, we turn to these *prêt-à-porter* ways of life. Finally, we take an extended look at how it is possible to draw upon these cultural ready-mades to fundamentally change our identity.

Some people would never have fallen in love if they had never heard of love.

François de La Rochefoucauld*

What are we today, Gilbert?

I Didn't Know You Cared, TV comedy series, 1975–9

As Seen on TV. I am sitting with Vicky on a Sunday evening. Vicky has only recently moved in with me, so we are still trying to establish our joint routines. It is early Sunday evening. We are wondering what to do. In the lovely phrase of Lenny's mother, we are wondering what to do with time. We had planned to go to the movies, but we have that slightly listless dopiness of Sunday evenings. This would be helped by getting out, we know, and the cinema would get us out, but we don't want to commit to a movie, get out late and walk back in the cold and dark. The anticipated effort is draining our will to live as we speak. So how do we shape this Sunday evening, which now feels flabby and looks empty?

Well, we put a meal in there, we'll cook a meal, and then we'll go for a short walk after the meal, and then we'll watch ... I can't remember the programme, but in the ordering of events to come, the evening went from being empty and flabby, formless, to being An Evening. I remember saying 'That's OK, isn't it? That's the kind of evening people have?'

* François de La Rochefoucauld, Maxim 136, *La Rochefoucauld, Maxims*, translated by Leonard Tancock (Penguin Classics, 1959).

Quick mental image of our evening as before and after shots of a room in a makeover show. Before: one of those pre-makeover loser rooms, full of arbitrarily placed objects, no cohesion or character. After: it is A Room, like you might see in a magazine, or on TV. The transformational arc of our evening.

A similar transformation: I had a stretch of free time, a long run of mornings when, in the absence of any actually urgent tasks, I pottered and listened to the radio, read books, thought, wrote this and sometimes wondered what to do with time. Then I heard on the radio about the life of ancient Greeks, about how different values structured their time. Cartoons of ancient life formed in my head as the radio spoke – of a life in which time was not about money or work, but was treasured for leisure and the cultivation of the self through reflection, contemplation, reading and conversation. Work, productive labour, was seen as being strictly at the service of this more valuable time, not an end in itself, not a career, just the income-generating project you had to do occasionally to enable the real work of life: getting to know yourself and working out how to live.

That morning my days of pottering were transformed. My time out from labour had been given a permission slip, an ancient endorsement. The example of these ancient Greeks made me feel more comfortable with myself, allowed me to allow myself to have the life I was having with some degree of comfort and conviction. That niggling sense of wasting time, of something being not-quite-right was obliterated as my formless baggy days became the kind of days which other, better, older people had enjoyed and valued. My days were OK.

There is a feeling of comfort and rightness that comes from being *like* something, from knowing that your activity has the validation stamp of precedent.

Quick recent survey finding: the majority of those buying fair trade products are doing so not primarily because it is good for the environment but because it gives them a sense of being like the celebrities who endorse the products.

Precedent automatically confers a ballast to our actions that otherwise might feel perilously light and arbitrary. Those clumsy
first-night moves stop being just you, or me, rattling about in a
room, playing house. They become an Activity, or a Role, honoured
by time and repetition. My pottering mornings become a stretch of
time for cultivation of myself as writer and thinker (as practised by
ancient Greeks, as heard on the radio). In beginning a new activity,
in donning a new role with no precedents of our own, we tend to
rely on the precedents of others to give our actions some heft and
our role some authenticity:

> Robert Delaney, a detective who went undercover for two and a half
> years in Jersey City to collect evidence on the Bruno and Genovese
> [Mafia] families, testified to a 1981 Senate Committee that the mob-
> sters he met saw the original movie [*The Godfather*] as many as ten
> times. While dining at a restaurant, the son of Joe Adonis gave the
> waiter a pocketful of quarters and asked him to play continuously
> the theme music from *The Godfather* on the jukebox. 'All through the
> dinner we listened to the same song, over and over.' Startled, Sen-
> ator Nunn wanted to make sure he understood: 'Are you saying
> sometimes they go to the movie to see how they themselves are
> supposed to behave?' After answering in the affirmative, Officer
> Delaney added, 'they had a lot of things taught to them through the
> movie'.*

In the same article, we heard from Mafia wife Lynda Milito, about
the effect that getting hold of the video of *The Godfather* had had on
Mafia don Louie Milito and his crew:

> he watched it like six thousand times . . . he could not pull himself
> away from the TV, he could not stop watching that stupid movie. A
> dozen times he told me 'This movie is fantastic!' The guys who

* Quoted in the *Times Literary Supplement*, 2 July 2004.

came to the house were all acting like *Godfather* actors, kissing and hugging.*

Note the strange reciprocity at work here. Gangsters imitating actors imitating gangsters. You see it all the time on reality TV shows. Real people on TV acting out themselves like actors in TV shows. I saw one recently, a reality show – nothing less real – in which a team were competing to become the apprentice of Alan Sugar. The group of wannabes were set a task to come up with an advertising campaign, and spent the day at work in an established advertising company. As soon as they were seated around the glass-topped table, they began to do a very poor but earnest imitation of 'People Who Work in Advertising'. They began to speak oddly, awkwardly, in boardroom-meeting clichés, as if they had only ever seen it done on the television. Which was probably the case. They talked about 'running ideas up poles', 'rolling out campaigns', 'brainstorming', 'really just getting everything out there on the table'. They used a series of ready-made phrases, what actors would call the stock responses of stock characters. This advertising sound and fury produced nothing more than its own empty noise, like a spell not working in the hands of apprentice magicians. Wannabe advertisers striving to become real ones by copying pretend ones.

Maybe it's just that in these more extreme and exceptional moments – the early days and first nights of Act Two – we resort to common modes of being, relying on a stock of cultural ready-mades, on roles that have been prepared earlier and look like they might work here and now.

After all, how else do we learn to complain in restaurants, talk to taxi drivers, do a job interview, act like a passenger on a plane or a person at the side of a hospital bed? If we have never done it or seen it before, we rely on the common group wisdom for what might work in the present situation. Humans are creatures of mimesis,

---

* Lynda Milito, with Reg Potterton, *Mafia Wife: My Story of Love, Murder and Madness* (HarperCollins, 2003), quoted in the *Times Literary Supplement*, 2 July 2004.

after all, for we learn by imitation, and most of us see more people doing more things on television and in the movies than we ever could in life. So I know, you know, we all know how to act like Mafia dons, or advertisers, without ever having met them in person. Perhaps it is no surprise, then, that the 'real thing', the real gangsters and advertisers, should also draw on this common stock to see how they should be. Our parents will be the most formative source of our early templates for becoming, but when we begin to roll out our own adult roles, when we confront the Act Two crises that will reshape us through change, we will turn to culture as much as to family.

Quick mental note: The way we like to talk or think about ourselves in terms of pre-existing forms: those inexhaustible 'Which X are YOU?' viral quizzes – where X is Disney Princess, Superhero, Country, Colour, Animal, Harry Potter/Hobbit/Friends/Game of Thrones Character . . .

Fledgling X

At the climax of the film *Ghostbusters*, Gozer the Destructor, a Sumerian god, is about to cross over from his supernatural realm into downtown New York and destroy it. The three Ghostbusters have failed to stop Gozer manifesting, but they have one final ironic bit of control over the situation. Zuul, the demonic herald of the coming of Gozer, commands them to 'choose the form'. Gozer, a creature of pure destructive force, has no fixed form and so will manifest as whatever they imagine it to be. If you have seen it you'll know what happens: Dan Aykroyd can't helping thinking of the Stay Puft Marshmallow Man (see Figure 8 overleaf), and accordingly, the ancient Sumerian god manifests as a giant marshmallow-man, cute little sailor's hat and all.

What this gets nicely is the dialectic of force and form; that any kind of urgent force needs to manifest as a specific structure in order to persist, to act, to be identifiably something. It needs to

Figure 8. *Ghostbusters*

be *like* something. Think back to those Mafia dons, aping the gestures they saw on screen. Their criminal energy could manifest in many ways. Imagine criminal styles across the world from Harlem to Hindustan – criminality will have its regional dialect, its own local styles. There will be, for each locale, and for different classes and ethnic groups within each locale, distinct *ways of being* criminal. Although the criminal tendency might be innate (argue that one amongst yourselves), what is fluid is the form of its expression. Fluid but not arbitrary, it must choose a recognizable form.

The British actor and comedian Russell Brand does a nice stand-up routine about violence. His angle on it is this: what if, in a moment of bristly hauteur – say when you have held a door open for someone and received no thanks – you impulsively express your feelings, only to find that you have provoked someone who is Good at Violence. It is this slant that makes the routine funny. He doesn't talk about 'someone violent', but 'someone who knows all the right words', 'knows the posture and the arm movements'. Someone who knows how to act violent even before they have been violent, who knows the look, the dialect, the style of it. And, just as importantly, you know violence too, or rather you recognize someone who is good at it when you see them, and respond, as you ought, with fear. And it's partly that ability to signal their expertise at violence, and to elicit your fear, that makes them good at it. That's how it works when you are suddenly in the game of violence with an expert player, with someone who knows the form. It's second nature to them.

Second nature has, by definition, got to be acquired, but we only catch its formation in times of transition, in Act Two. In following the journey of becoming we have, so far, reached a certain point. We have heard the news from elsewhere and been forced into a period of deliberate living. We have had a difficult first few nights of new routines, of trying to establish practice and precedent in our new way of being. New moves have been started, but they still lack the automatic ease of complete conviction, the inimitable gravitas of *habit*. Near the start of Act Two we are all fledglings. Fledgling Mafia don, fledgling yob, fledgling X, where X is whatever has been recently begun, be it going to university, as a student, like my sister and nephew, or as a professor like Lilian, or as a Research Fellow, like me. X for Charlotte is the possibility of relationship. X for Lenny is trying to be a writer again. X for Vicky is new school, new city, new relationship with her father. X for Donald, whom we met in the last chapter, is being gay. And our own moves, awkward and fledgling, need help, need to borrow the ballast of precedent. Here are four ways of thinking about what we do in terms of getting help at these points. Four ways of thinking about how we become.

1. Jelly Moulds

You'll notice, as you read the first three of these four metaphors, that they all share a notion of *solidifying*. They are really one metaphor posing as three, for there are only so many ways to skin a cat – and that is, partly, the point. Whichever cat we want to skin, there will be only so many ways already available to us, a rich but limited stock of know-how to draw on. Let's use the example of being a gay man. I was talking to Lenny and Lilian about this. We were talking about the currently available versions of gayness, now, in the West, at the beginning of the twenty-first century. Certainly at the time of writing, you will hear people say, or read them write, about how the media has progressed beyond the effeminate stereotypes of the 1970s, when it first became OK to have identifiably gay characters on TV, just so long as they were camp, or their sexuality was to some extent ridiculous. Now we have Graham Norton, Mitch and Cameron from *Modern Family*, Kurt and Blaine from *Glee*, Bryan and David from *The New Normal*, Will and Jack from *Will and Grace*, the *Queer Eye for the Straight Guy* teams, *Little Britain* . . . where, we wondered, is the progress?

These characters constitute the mainstream versions of being gay. Bundled into them are a series of tropes about How to Be Gay, which are repeated and amplified in both the straight and gay media. A gay man is witty, well dressed and clean; likes designer clothes and underwear; is naturally gifted at interior design; is bitchy; is sensitive; has women as best friends; is the best best-friend a woman could have; is narcissistic and selfish; talks about sex a lot; has sex a lot; fancies straight men; fancies straight men in uniform even more; likes cigarettes, alcohol and drugs; is proud; is out; likes musicals; loves Lady Gaga, Britney, Kylie, Madonna, Barbra, Judy (pick your generation); loves drama, is camp, is dramatic, is a drama queen, is hysterical (chose your degree of dramatic inflection). This is what is *prêt-à-porter* for gay men. These are the versions of gay that are publicly available, now and in the West.

This is not to say that none of these are 'true', although truth is not really what I'm concerned about. Just as the mobsters watched *The Godfather* to see how to be mobsters, so there will be a degree of reciprocity between being gay and the available versions of it. However, there is no necessary connection between sexual partner preference and these available 'gay identities'. This is what French philosopher Michel Foucault was getting at when he wrote of his visit to San Francisco: 'I am a homosexual in a city full of gays.'

Other times, places and cultures, and other less mainstream elements of our own culture, present us with other forms for homosexuality, or deconstruct the category as such. But you have to go looking for them. It is easier to pick and choose from the widely available, high-street versions of Gay. Our first metaphor, then, is that these available versions of whatever it is you are trying to become are like *cultural jelly moulds*. Your molten urgency, or even your thick reluctance, to be gay – should such be your urgency or reluctance – needs a shape in which to pour itself and form its identity. To be a teenage girl, a professor, a lover, a spurned wife, a research fellow, a student, depressed or Catholic, your urgencies can decant into a myriad of available moulds, settle effortlessly into a form that will provide the nuances and contours of a performance that would have otherwise taken you years to work out unaided. In the journey of your becoming, the forces of change will eventually settle into a form that both you and others will recognize as being like the thing that you want to become. Having the form readily available makes the journey and the recognition that much easier.*

2. Fixer Solutions

The variety of youth cultures available these days is a vast numerical improvement on those available in my youth. Indeed, the niche markets of identity for all ages and income brackets continue to proliferate, with the tail becoming ever longer and the trends becoming ever more micro. But to stay with (UK) youth, we have: emos, goths, nerds, geeks, dorks, indie kids, chavs, townies, jocks, skaters, surfers, grungers, stoners, straight-edgers, gangstas, rude boys, mean girls, posh kids, plastics, hipsters, and still a smattering of hippies, punks, skins and neds. If I were younger I would know even more, and could make finer intra-tribal distinctions for you like folk-emos and townie indie kids. If you have seen the film *Mean Girls* (2004), you will know what a knowing and funny play it is on the notion of these youth-tribes. At the start of that film we are taken through the school canteen, where all the different tribes and

* Simone de Beauvoir's suggestion that 'One is not born, but rather becomes, a woman' springs to mind.

their habits are described. And, of course, since this is a movie, and movies are all about transformation, we then watch as our heroine goes from a studious, outsider geek 'freak' to an A-List plastic, i.e. an immaculately styled pretty girl, top of the hierarchy, the natural partner of the Jock and the rightful heir to the prom queen crown. As much as this film served to lampoon these tribes, it was also part of the process of their reification and transmission. In the 2006 UK TV's *Big Brother*, for instance, the savvier inhabitants rightly identified that they had split into two groups: the Freaks and the Plastics, pretty much along the lines advertised in the film. This division structured the group dynamic right to the end of the show.

Here we want to introduce, reintroduce even, the notion of *tribe*. This time we will present it in the guise of a *fixer solution*. Picture this: a photographic darkroom, lit only by the red bulb by which everything looks grainy. There are shallow white trays full of clear liquid in which a piece of white paper is gently being sloshed. As the image on the paper begins to emerge from nothing, it gets gradually darker and more defined. At the high noon of its definition, before it lapses into murkiness, it is plunged into another tray of fixer solution, where its development is arrested at just that point. The image is fixed.

To find your tribe, to find the social group you belong to, is to *fix* your self. Lenny and I talk about how sexual identities can now, and in the West, find and join their tribes very early in the journey of becoming. We compare it to other journeys we know of from our youth, where, with less publicly available help, sexualities developed in the wild, took longer, more idiosyncratic and lonely routes, before they fixed into a final form. And what Vicky noticed, in her first days at her new school, was that the first question she was asked was, 'What music are you into?' This is the tribal identifier par excellence; her answer will allow her new peers to get a fix on her, and she on them.

Partly, this is all to do with money. Capitalism now thrives on niche marketing, on micro-trends and tribal marketing. It is in money's interests to identify and to sell you your own tribal identity.

Money has named the tribes. To all the youth groups and sexualities, add the economic and demographic groups: the yuppies, the dinkies and the tweens; the class and ethnic groups. Add to them the age demographics – add them all and you've got the potential for ever more fine typing: the single-parent, gay, forty-something, mixed-race woman teacher living in the north of England. What deodorant can we sell *her*? Money wants you to identify with your tribe as quickly as possible, and to buy the associated merchandising. It wants there to be as many tribes as possible so as to maximize the merchandising. Every distinct youth culture will have, for instance, their particular type of trousers. Straight and skinny for the indie boys; slightly baggier boy-jeans for the indie *girls*; baggy and scruffy for the grungers and stoners; baggy and black with buckles for the Goths; particular brand names for the gangstas, worn falling off the hip; shorts for the skaters; and so on, with matching footwear and headgear and T-shirts and bags. And even pets. Some tribes you really need a dog for.

By the time you read this, no doubt it will all have changed – the best way to sell more merchandise is to change the tribal identifiers regularly – but the principle won't. There are now (and this is emerging as the dark-horse metaphor) ever more off-the-peg identities, *prêt-à-porter* personas of such refinement that you might find one that fits perfectly, that feels like *you*. When the choices were more limited, it was easier for the majority not to buy into, quite literally, the identity market and just to live and die within the given bare essentials of class, race and gender. But now there is a niche for almost everyone, and with it comes a soundtrack, an attitude, a look, movies and books, trousers and footwear. Teenagers are asked to choose their form earlier than ever, to fashion and fix themselves. It's like being your own Barbie or Ken or Bratz doll, with all the accessories. We could end this fixing section with a note of caution, for bathing yourself in the fixer solution of a tribe may lead to premature hardening of the persona. Or, as the Scots say when someone has pulled a particularly unattractive face: 'the wind will change and you'll stay like that'.

3. Crystals

Ted Bundy: the charismatic, handsome, intelligent man who raped, tortured and killed probably close to a hundred young women. In his last interview before his execution, he was asked about the role that comics and graphic cartoons depicting women being tied up and tortured had had on his development. He talks about the 'demonic chemistry of sex and euphoria, control and murder' he found in the cartoons, and his interlocutor asked: 'It fuelled your fantasies, didn't it?' He answered: 'Well, in the beginning it fuels the thought process, then at a certain time it is instrumental in crystallizing it, making it into something that's almost like a separate entity inside.'

Now, his interlocutor was a right-wing Christian, whom Bundy was perhaps just telling exactly what he wanted to hear about the evils of pornography. So from this monster let's just take the notion that existing forms can help to *crystallize* desires, and that, having done so, they can take on a life of their own and *become* you. Let's take that notion and move on.

4. Habitus

Philosophers often write about subjectivity, about being a person, in a very abstract way. Sartre, for instance, the modern philosopher supposed by many to have been the closest to saying something useful about how to live, tells us that our subjectivity is only authentic, only really us, once it is freed from all weight of culture, from all external conditions and conditioning. Against this ideal 'consciousness without inertia', social theorist Pierre Bourdieu takes as given that our 'inertia', our conditioning and conditions, are not only inescapable, but are precisely who we are. He quotes Pascal:

For we must make no mistake about ourselves: *we are as much automaton as mind*. As a result, demonstration is not the only instrument for convincing us. How few things are demonstrated! Proofs

only convince the mind; *habit provides the strongest proofs* and those
that are most believed. It inclines the automaton, which leads the
mind unconsciously along with it . . . It is habit that makes Turks,
heathens, trades, soldiers, etc. . . . In short we must resort to habit
once the mind has seen where the truth lies, in order to steep and
stain ourselves in that belief which constantly eludes us, for it is *too
much trouble* to have the proofs always present before us. We must
acquire *an easier belief, which is that of habit*. With no violence, art or
argument, it makes us believe things, and so inclines all our faculties
to this belief that our soul falls naturally into it. When we believe
only by the strength of our conviction and the automaton is inclined
to believe the opposite, that is not enough. We must therefore make
both parts of us believe: the mind by reasons, which need to be seen
only once in a lifetime, and the automaton by habit, and not allowing it any inclination to the contrary.* [my italics]

'It is habit that makes us Turks, heathens, trades, soldiers, etc. . . .'
This is very close to the Aristotelian idea of *hexis* or *habitus*, as it is
often translated – the idea that our character is a set of dispositions
moulded, fixed and crystallized through repetition, shaping our
self-expression more or less automatically, 'with no violence, art or
argument', as Pascal so neatly puts it. What Pierre Bourdieu adds to
this notion of character as *habitus* is the insight that it is *borrowed*.
That the world is full of pre-established, off-the-peg, ready-to-run
routines that allow us to short-circuit some of the hard labour of
Act Two. We are, according to Bourdieu, born into 'a world of
already realized ends', a world littered with pre-established 'cognitive and motivational structures'. We don't, in short, need to
discover for ourselves what to think, feel and do about things. There
are ways of being already worked out, for whatever X you decide to
be. These are passed on from generation to generation and

* Pascal, *Pensées*, 252, quoted in Pierre Bourdieu, *The Logic of Practice* (Polity Press,
1990).

[ensure] the active presence of past experiences, which, deposited in each organism in the forms of schemes of perception, thought and action, tend to guarantee the 'correctness' of practices and their constancy over time, more reliably than all formal rules and explicit norms.*

Or, most pithily, *habitus* are: 'embodied history, internalized as a second nature' – cultural ready-mades, passed down the generations, or through the tribe, transmitted ways of being whatever you might want to become.

Bourdieu focuses a lot on class, and on how particular class structures and institutions transmit and maintain their ways of being. His basic insight is that in order to do so they need to be embodied not only in explicit laws, but also in people, in their dispositions to act, feel and think in certain ways in given situations. All individuals belonging to the same class participate in the same *habitus*. And inescapably so:

> 'Personal' style, the particular stamp marking all the products of the same *habitus*, whether practices or works, is never more than a deviation in relation to the style of a period or class.†

Note the almost sneering quote marks around 'Personal'.

So why do we adopt a *habitus*? Because we cannot but do so, we are born into them, these ways of being, and our education and enculturation is precisely the process of incorporating – literally to make a part of our body – ready-made ways of being and doing. Our first *habitus*, the first ones we put on, we will put on haplessly, picking up on our family's manners, our daddy's shoes, our mother's heels; and our first steps in character will follow in the footsteps of those closest to us. And as we age and settle into ourselves, perhaps these early borrowings return?

Lenny tells me how, as he gets older, he can see and hear distinctly within himself the times when he is reacting and laughing

---

* Pierre Bourdieu, *The Logic of Practice* (Polity Press, 1990).
† Ibid.

like his father, or worrying like his mother, and can feel himself, for a spell, taking their form. But between these first steps and the set-tling of our final forms, lie the choices in our idiosyncratic journeys of becoming. Like the Ghostbusters, we get to choose the form. But why choose? Why not roll your own? Partly because it takes some of the sweat out of Act Two, because there is also some tre-mendous ease in the *habitus*: 'a spontaneity without consciousness or will', as Bourdieu puts it.

What I have called above the dialectic of force and form – the meeting of your molten urgency with the available jelly moulds to give it form – Bourdieu calls the dialectic of 'expressive dispositions and the institutionalized means of expression'; i.e. when your urge to express something meets with the available means and modes of expression, something is created which is both of you and nothing to do with you. He writes nicely of the thrill of improvisation in jazz. The expert improviser first has to learn the impersonal, institutional-ized means of expression; only then can these be infused with the idiosyncratic urgency of that particular musician. Again, it is a dia-lectic of force and form. The individual force, the personality and emotion of the musician, meets the pre-existing impersonal form, the rules of jazz. When they come together, when force and form interact, the artist is overtaken by their own performance, both carrying it and being carried by it. This *spontaneity without will* is nothing more or less than the Automatic of Chapter 2, the effortless and invisible hand of servitude facilitating most of our activities of daily life. This is why we are all so desperate to find a *habitus*, a jelly mould, a fixer solution, something to crystallize our urgency and give it shape. It allows us to move from the Deliberate, that hard, exhausting, effortful, anxiety-provoking and upsetting mode of liv-ing, back to the Automatic. When pre-existent structures coincide with our own urge to find expression, then we can improvise our-selves. These pre-established ways of being, doing, seeing, thinking, do not require our conscious deliberation but rather carry us for-ward, they say the next thing, make the next move without our conscious intervention, and without perceptible agency. Mean girls, gay boys, rude boys, skaters, you and me, perform ourselves with a borrowed ease. In the last chapter we talked about the way that our gestures and postures, our enactment of ourselves, are in some way transcendent to us. The *habitus* is nothing other than a ready-made set of gestures, saving us the trouble of coming up with our own.

Let us give the last word here to Marcel Proust, showing how the *habitus* of nobility in one of the characters in *À la recherche du temps perdu*, Robert de Saint-Loup, is both essential to who he is and quite separable from him:

> . . . my mind was distinguishing in Saint-Loup a personality more col-
> lective than his own, that of the 'noble'; which like an indwelling spirit
> moved his limbs, ordered his gestures and his actions; then, at such
> moments, although in his company, I was as much alone as I should
> have been gazing at a landscape the harmony of which I could under-
> stand. He was no more then than an object the properties of which, in
> my musing contemplations, I sought to explore. The perpetual dis-
> covery in him of this pre-existent, this aeonial creature, this aristocrat
> who was just what Robert aspired not to be, gave me a keen delight,
> but one that was intellectual and not social. In the moral and physical
> agility which gave so much grace to his kindnesses, in the ease with
> which he offered my grandmother his carriage and made her get into
> it, in the alacrity with which he sprang from the box, when he was
> afraid that I might be cold, to spread his own cloak over my shoulders,
> I felt not only the inherited litheness of the mighty hunters who had
> been for generations the ancestors of this young man . . . I felt in him
> especially the certainty or the illusion in the minds of those great lords
> of being 'better than other people', thanks to which they had not been
> able to hand down to Saint-Loup that anxiety to shew that one is 'just
> as good', that dread of seeming inferior, of which he was indeed
> wholly unconscious, but which mars with so much ugliness, so much
> awkwardness, the most sincere overtures of a plebeian. Sometimes I
> found fault with myself for thus taking pleasure in my friend as in a
> work of art, that is to say in regarding the play of all the parts of his
> being as harmoniously ordered by a general idea from which they

depended but which he did not know, so that it added nothing to his own good qualities, to that personal value, intellectual and moral, to which he attached so high a price.*

You're My Nigga Now – A Case Study of Habitus at Work

ancient wise men brought divine powers into the region of mortals, attracting them through likeness. For likeness is sufficient to join beings to one another.[†]

So, let us look at an actual case study of the role of *habitus*, of the jelly moulds, of the cultural ready-mades in action. Here, now, is the story of the white folks who became, by virtue of donning a *habitus*, black.[‡]

Steppin' is a dance form that is mainly practised by African-Americans, or it certainly was in Chicago in the early 2000s, where our story unfolds. Back then, Steppin' clubs tended to be located in the predominantly black areas of what the author and would-be Stepper called a 'hyper-segregated' city. While certain black styles – hip-hop and gangsta, for instance – have crossed over into the mainstream, become commodified and exported to other ethnic groups, Steppin' had largely maintained its cultural integrity. The following quotes are all taken from the article by Black Hawk Hancock (see footnote):

> Steppin' is too mainstream within the African-American community to fit the binary of either a renegade African-American identity or a cultural form that can be easily folded into mainstream White society.

---

* Marcel Proust, *Within a Budding Grove* (1919).
[†] Proclus, quoted by Psellus, published in Édouard des Places, *Oracles chaldaïques*, 3rd edn (A. Segonds, Paris, 1996).
[‡] The account of transformation is taken from Black Hawk Hancock, 'Steppin' out of Whiteness', *Ethnography*, 6/4 (December 2005): 427–61.

Primarily, Steppin' is a dance form, a variant of the Lindy Hop: 'the original Swing dance born in the ballrooms, clubs and rent parties of the African-American communities of Harlem in the late 1920s and early 1930s'. The Lindy Hop revival then became part of mainstream culture through its world-wide exposure in Gap adverts from the late 1990s. Steppin' resurfaced simultaneously but in almost exclusively African-American circles. While sharing with the Lindy Hop a common source of energy and athleticism, it aims more for fluid grace and an apparent effortlessness of execution. The dance is performed to contemporary Rhythm and Blues, older R&B ('dusties') like Harold Melvin & the Blue Notes, some white soul, like Daryl Hall and John Oates, and some of the smoother hip-hop artists. The dress code recalls the origins of the dance, all 1920s-style flapper dresses and dapper suits, but overlaid with colour, vivid silks in skirts and shirts and ties. There is an implicit code that distinguishes it from the mores of thug and gangster black hip-hop culture, not only at the level of dress – no trainers, no denims, etc. – but also 'manifested in manners and dispositions'.

In other words, the Steppin' world is a small world, a tribe unto itself. The heroes of our story, a white academic, Black Hawk Hancock, and his female dance partner, Julie, both already experts at Lindy Hopping, realized that to step into the Steppin' world they needed to know more than the dance moves:

> I bought trousers, alligator shoes, silk shirts in bright styles and colours and patterns, while Julie purchased the styles that were fashionable for the women. This change in our dress style signified more than an acquaintance with fashion; it was something we needed to master, like the dance, in order to fully assimilate into and demonstrate a complete grasp of the world we were now involved in. In this new environment we had to learn the codes and norms by listening and watching to establish trust and respect.

Their first night, as all first nights, was tentative, awkward. Arriving in an all-black neighbourhood, they then approached the doorman at the club. They hadn't, they realized, looking at the doorman and the people milling around outside, got the dress quite right. While they had got the generic idea, the parties were often aesthetically themed, and that night was a red night, expressed in vivid splashes of shirts and blouses, and they had come in dapper dark. So you might have forgiven the doorman his incredulous, 'You're here for the Steppin'?'

Racially and sartorially marked as outsiders, they were let in with amusement and met mostly with their own self-consciousness, the feeling, and probably the fact, that most people in the club were eyeing them with bemusement. They found some seats and perched at the edge of the dance-floor.

Anyone who has tried knows the initial act of courage required to get up on the dance-floor and start to move. The warm-up phase is always at least a little dry, a little cold, the body recalcitrant as the music tries to find its way around your self-consciousness and down to your feet. Drink helps, for sure. They had a couple and they moved to the floor:

> At first, our anxiety overrides everything else, and our movements are hesitant and inhibited. We struggle to make it through the song; we can't quite seem to click. Before the next song starts, we're unsure if we should attempt another or quit while we're ahead . . .

In the movie, on TV, this would be the point of the almost failed encounter. The camera would zoom in on their faltering gestures and mis-steps, then cut to contemptuous glances from some, pity from others, and disappointment from that nice older lady who had admired their chutzpah for being there at all – she shakes her head sadly. It's as if they have let everyone down, squandered some of the diminishing stock of human hope. Dramatic Low Point.

> 'Should we sit down?' Julie asks. 'No, we just got out here, we have to keep going, just one more, okay?' We continue to dance and try to relax, to get the groove we see around us. Suddenly, I notice the DJ pointing at me and smiling . . . This sign of recognition eases us, and we start to unwind and get into the flow.

Dramatic Turning Point. They continued to dance, and felt that there was a kind of implicit acceptance, made tangible when an older woman, in her late fifties, 'leans over, "Y'all look good. Keep on dancing!" '

So they vaulted this first dramatic hurdle into a new world. This arc of the drama reached its apogee over a year later when the couple entered a new club for the first time. Again they endured a barrage of bemused attention. More accustomed to it now, however, they made their way to the dance-floor and danced regardless. They had one of those nights that any practitioner will know. Be it playing pool, dancing, typing, writing, running, sex or cleaning the fridge, there are some nights when you just get it right, when you just plain *get* it. They were graced by such a night. They read each other perfectly, risked new moves in sync and felt the swell of being carried away. They could hear a shout behind them: 'You go on!' More movie moments. They became the focus of their corner of the dance-floor, where call-and-response shouts are volleyed at them: 'Get down', 'Yeah! That's right'. They rose to the occasion, dancing better, faster. Later, as they left the dance-floor, surrounded by applause, bemused regard has turned to amazement, to incredulity and to something else:

> As we passed through the aisle on the way back to our seats, the once seemingly indifferent crowd was now gregarious. People were looking us in the face and smiling. One woman puts her hand up for a high five . . . When we finally reached our seats, the people around us . . . immediately turned and started talking to Julie and me . . . we seemed to have gone from total outsiders to people who were welcomed and respected as regulars. I had come to realize one simple point: they were not responding to the novelty of our skin color; they were responding to us as dancers.

Dramatic High Point. The lesson of this drama? All curled up within that one phrase really: 'they were responding to us as dancers'. Their position as white people in a black world should have marked them as racial outsiders, but their mastery of an exclusively black set of

cultural practices created an identity at odds with physical appearance. Anyone who has seen *The Jerk* (1979) will recognize this tension
between appearance and practice. In the film, Steve Martin plays a
white man who has been raised by a black family, who doesn't in fact
know that he is white. He 'acts' black and everyone around him
treats him as if he is. Effectively, beyond the accident of his skin colour, he is black. This being a Steve Martin film, the mismatch
between colour and bodily practice is played for laughs. With our
academic dancers and their new world, it created more interesting
tensions. As they became integrated into the Steppin' community,
were invited to inner circle parties and formed friendships, people
began to talk about the (white) elephant in the room. One friend
insisted they must have black ancestry. To their denial he responded:

'No, fuck that. You've got Black in you. That's a fact. Because you
are definitely not White; you got Black in you, the way you dance.
You may look White, but you're definitely not White!'

This was one of many responses which negotiated in their different
ways a process of incorporating these two outsiders into the social
body of the Steppin' community. One club DJ asserts:

'You're family now. Ain't nobody going to mess with you up in
here – now you're family – remember that.'

Another friend said (my emphasis):

'You are definitely not White. You're my nigga now. You're *one of us*
now.'[*]

This white academic and his dance partner had managed a feat of
cultural cross-dressing that ran deeper than the skin. Bourdieu
reminds us that the body is symbolic raw material, a building site

[*] See Chapter 4, 'Cosa Nostra', the section on 'One of Us'.

for the construction of practised identities. That's not to say, however, that we can be just anything, because acquiring cultural competence takes effort, time and practice:

> Since the body is malleable raw material cultivated and formed through practices, it is open to being 'retooled' as it is socialized and cultivated into new practices. This bodily retooling requires what Wacquant [sociologist and pupil of Bourdieu] calls 'body work', which is not a matter of conscious choice or obtaining intellectual information passed on through logical reasoning, but arduously acquired through inculcation, bodily labor and training.*

And it is these practices that the author of the article and his partner became good at; this was what made them effectively able to cross the racial divide, to pass for normal in a new small world. The author insists how exceptional this racial cross-dressing is, and how it is these exceptions that draw our attention to a phenomenon that might otherwise go unmarked. When a white body performs a white identity, or a black body a black one, we read in this 'second nature' the naturalness of a first, we assume the forms are innate. But

> when we change this order and put a white body in a style that is African American, as in the Steppers example, or in hip hop with the case of Eminem, we no longer treat that body within the usual categories and expectations of the commonsense logic of race. In these cases, the white body is not 'playing' or pretending, but is African American through its competence in the practice.†

* Black Hawk Hancock, *American Allegory: Lindy Hop and the Racial Imagination* (University of Chicago Press, 2013).
† Ibid.

This refiguring of the body, this arbitrariness of second nature, is much less exceptional than the author asserts. South London teen-agers, regardless of race, seem largely proficient in the vernacular of hip-hop and gangsta culture. Even the indie kids can slip into a half-convincing rude-boy spiel, and there is rapidly evolving a new teen language which is largely black in origin. There are now many full-time white rude boys, or Wiggas ('white niggers'), as they are pejoratively known by the other tribes. They form affiliations not by race but by others *like* them, that is, with others who *perform themselves* like them, and who have come to look like them not through biological givens but through sartorial choice and bodily practice, through *second* nature. They even have distinct styles of walking. The white rude boys, just like the black ones, affect a leis-urely lop-sided pimp roll, an easy, assertively confident inhabiting of cultural space. These tribes are based not on innate characteristics but on acquired practices, second natures. What is academically remarkable is a teenage commonplace. Who you are is not just how you are born but what you *do* with it, the personally acquired tastes and habits of the last chapter, combining with the culturally acquired *habitus* of this one. What other people respond to is not how you look but how you act.

This primacy of second nature in the signalling of identity is, it seems, in itself hardwired. As we saw from the work in embodied cognition quoted in the last chapter, we are wired to respond to people as their movement, not their static appearance. We know this from scientific work on babies' perception. Babies see the other not as appearance, as objects, but as *expression and motor action*, and fur-ther, as action which they could mimic; they are already shopping for their own second natures. Babies, like us all, respond to others not as objects, but as dancers.

The Gift of Shoes. We could hammer the point home with a few more extreme examples. The children raised by animals, the monkey-boys and wolf-girls, where the raw material of their bodies is overwritten by the *habitus* of another species. Or more common but equally odd examples like camp straight men.* Or Ali G, the alter ego of white Jewish comedian and actor Sasha Baron Cohen, who acted so black that many people believed he was black. But I would rather move away from race and culture to universalize and individualize some of what has been gained through this most sociological of the chapters.

There are many ways for you and me to be. Or rather, there are many ways that we have chosen to be, that have become second nature and are now who we think we are. Many off-the-peg identities of surprising finesse have been chosen and worn until they feel like ours. These choices will have been made and rehearsed in our first nights and early days, when we were younger, or when we were in transition, in Act Two. That's when these ready-mades become important. You may be browsing the aisles right now, furiously trying on different cultural ready-mades. If so, be careful. Further down the track of change, as we are in this chapter, further into the hardening, setting and fixing process, you need to choose your form with care. Think of Beryl Reid, the actress, who when asked how she settled into a new character, how she acquired the feeling of being someone else, replied, 'First, I find the shoes.' The rest follows.

---

* An interesting creature this one, the *habitus* of gay worn by the heterosexual male. Maybe it's a good mate attraction strategy?

Chapter 8

Spellbound

In which we become obsessed with the new. It becomes clear that to continue on in the process of change, it must, for a spell, take centre stage in our lives. We show that change is a concert of three faculties – mind, heart and will – and that new habits are formed through the collective action of this trio. We see that in the state of heightened arousal and attention, the noonday glare of change, we often take shelter in old habits. We find ourselves preoccupied, anxious and exhausted.

We are what we repeatedly do. Excellence, then, is not an act, but a habit.

Will Durant on Aristotle*

> We sow a thought and reap an act;
> we sow an act and reap a habit;
> we sow a habit and reap a character;
> we sow a character and reap a destiny.

Nineteenth-century saying

Moment of Truth. Habit-forming is, in essence, what Act Two is all about. The process of changing is one of forming new habits. This is what concerns us. We have been, by whatever News, jolted awake, out of the Automatic, into the awkward realm of deliberation. Trying out new moves, trying on new roles, trying to cope, thinking, feeling and acting in unaccustomed ways. We will not stay in deliberation for longer than we have to. We want to, we are built to, become accustomed. Living in deliberation is one kind, a common kind, of what we call stress, which is usually nothing more than prolonged arousal, those periods when life demands too much attention, care and effort for too long, those times when we cannot get comfortable. The constant vigilance and arousal required by this insistent News is stressful, i.e. it is exhausting physically, and mentally and emotionally it troubles us, troubles us enough for us

---

* Will Durant, *The Story of Philosophy* (Simon & Schuster, 1926), summing up Aristotle's ideas from *Nicomachean Ethics*.

to work hard to become accustomed to it. The arousal and attention produced by the new is precisely *for* this; it is experienced as a physiological discomfort which drives us to act, to do something to make the new stop bothering us. Being uncomfortable drives us to become comfortable again.

So, what's bothering you? No, let's rephrase that: what *concerns* you? What's on your mind? Henry James, in describing the creative process (another kind of News) writes of the value, the necessity of saturation, of becoming steeped in one's material. Just as the dancers, the Steppers in our last chapter, have to go to the end of the process of change in order for the Deliberate to become Automatic, so one must pass through a kind of high noon of *obsession*, of saturation and immersion in the new; in short, we must be for a while uncomfortable.* It has to really bother us and concern us for a while. It may be as mundane as learning to drive, or getting to know someone, or working out how your new phone works; the high noon may only last for an hour, or it may run for months, or years in grief, but there will be a period of time, if new ways of life are to be made, new paths beaten, when the new will be all that concerns you. For a spell, the new will be, *should be*, all that's on your mind, heart and will.

In the movies, this would be the moment when the hero is totally eclipsed by the new. This is the apogee of Act Two and, in screenwriting praxis, this is the turning point into Act Three, the last and most effortful lap of change. It's the moment of truth, the most punishing part of the drama, usually the point where the hero is down and out, when all the old moves have failed them. It's the point at which we might be most inclined to give up. And sometimes, for a while, the hero does just that – gives up, goes back to their old ways. As we have said many a time, the new is nothing if not demanding, and this is the point where all its demands need to

---

* Recall the nameless heroine of *Rebecca*'s take on this period of discomfort: 'poise, and grace, and assurance were not qualities inbred in me, but were things to be acquired, painfully perhaps, and slowly, costing me many bitter moments'.

be met. If the new is to become our new normal, if we are to get through to the end, we must be, for a while, overwhelmed. These are the moments of truth, where we either give up or push on. For if you are not, in some way (however exhilarating it is), overwhelmed, if the new is not taking up most of your time and attention, taking you out of comfort, then you are not going to get it. So, let's push on into Act Three. Let's look at the kind of demands the new makes of us.

Yom Kippur. Yom Kippur is the holiest day of the Jewish year. The day of atonement. This is the day for looking back over the last year and repenting. Repentance is the theme of Yom Kippur, today,* the repenting of old ways and the beginning of new ones. This is the day of change, of turning. Of turning away from the things of death and towards the things that lead to life. Today your soul is in suspension. Unless you are one of the few very righteous, whose names are already in the book of life, or one of the very few already damned, whose names are in the book of death, then the book in which your name will be inscribed will be decided today. Today is the day of judgement, today your fate is sealed. Literally, for your name was, in fact, written in its book ten days ago, but you have had ten days to mend your ways and get it moved before the book is sealed. Ten days to plead your case. Today is the day, the final day you can, through repentance, prayer and fasting, change your ways and change your fate. Change is the theme of Yom Kippur.

What can Yom Kippur tell us about change? For a start that it has three elements and to change is to effect change in three realms: through *Tefilla*, or prayer, you effect a change of consciousness, of mind; through *Teshuvah*, or repentance, you effect a change of heart; through *Tzedakah*, or charity, you effect a change of will and action. It is worth looking closer at the central concept of today, the notion of repentance, because in it, in *Teshuvah*, are contained all three elements. The eleventh-century Jewish philosopher and

---

* This was written on Yom Kippur.

scholar Moses Maimonides distinguished distinct stages of *Teshu-vah*. First must come the recognition that there needs to be change – you have to see that how you are living needs amendment. Thus change is partly a change of mind. But that in itself is not enough. Next must come a confession of wrong, and a feeling of regret for what you have done. So emotion must be involved; there has to be a change of heart. Finally, there has to be a resolve to act differently, to sin no more. There has to be a change of will, expressed in action, in changing your ways.

Christian theologians distinguish exactly the same three domains in true *Metanoia*, a word St Paul uses several times, that is often translated as repentance. More accurately it means a profound change of mind. As such, the first part of the Jewish equation is reiterated in the Pauline one – a change of mind is a necessary part of repentance. But St Paul, and the desert fathers after him, recognized that this in itself was not enough. With the change of mind has to come the sorrow of the heart:

> Now I rejoice, not that ye were made sorry, but that ye sorrowed to repentance: for ye were made sorry after a godly manner . . .*

And further, the very essence of repentance is inscribed in a change in behaviour – a turning – the paradigmatic turning being that of the prodigal son, who, after having thought, and after having sorrowed, after having changed in mind and heart, changed his resolve:

> I will arise and go to my father . . . and he arose, and came to his father.†

Heart, mind and will: these are the elements that need to be turned around, to be re-orientated today. These are the things that need to change if change is really to occur.

* 2 Cor. 7:9.
† Luke 15: 18, 20.

The Devil Wears Prada. The movie *The Devil Wears Prada* (2006) is one of those pleasing transformational dramas. The prototype is *My Fair Lady* (itself a reworking of the play and the myth of Pygmalion) and there have been many versions since, in which the lumpen clay of the main character is to be moulded into a form that seems, given its starting state, improbable. We love these unlikely transformations, love to see the butterfly emerge. There are so many of these dramas that by now we know the tropes and hardly need to repeat them, but let us alight on this one for a spell, to find in it a profane counterpart to our sacred beginning. What can Hollywood tell us about change?

Andy is a geeky journalist who happens to end up working at the epicentre of high fashion – for Miranda, cold Queen of high style and editor-in-chief of *Runway* magazine, the fashion bible. Much, of course, is made of the incongruity of the geek landing on Planet Style, which is enough to give the transformative ride an appropriately unlikely gradient to ascend. How does it start? First, find the shoes. Bruce, the stylist at *Runway*, gives Andy a pair of stylish shoes. Having taken her first fashion steps, this first move towards fashionableness, she begins to have a change of mind. This is where you see the seeds of change begin to sprout. Miranda, irritated by Andy's inadvertent snicker at some fine fashion distinction – a passionate debate over the right belt – delivers a bristly lecture on how the colour of Andy's current, don't-give-a-damn-about-fashion sweater is in fact traceable, through a chain of global fashion economics and aesthetic trickle-down, to last year's Dior spring collection, showing Andy, with cold, informed precision, how her own style is feeding off the crumbs from the high-fashion table. For intellectual Andy, this is indeed food for thought, and you see a glimmer of a change of mind, a reorientation of attention, a rethinking of values. But she doesn't change much as a result. Real change kicks in when she starts complaining to Bruce about the lack of respect she is accorded in the *Runway* offices. Expecting sympathy, she is shocked when he confronts her with her own superior disdain and lack of gratitude, calling her out on her implicit contempt for his world, its art, inspiration and beauty, its transformational potential. This really gets to Andy. This is the turning point, the point at which fashion really starts to *concern* her.

These changes of heart and mind express themselves in new resolve. Having watched the slow ascent of inner change, we now get the joyous downhill swoop of change expressed in action. Through the magic of movie-montage, we watch her go from geek to fashion goddess; we watch the butterfly emerge and dazzle. And how great she looks, how even better when we see her friends and lover become first concerned and then appalled. Remember, in transition you will always lose some friends. We could follow her arc on through its inevitable second turn, when the new values are thrown into question and to some extent repudiated, through to when the final equilibrium is reached between old and new ways, when lessons are learned and maturity is gained. It's a perfectly typical and stylish example of the form, and from it let's take only this: heart, mind and will are the elements that need to come together for change to be effected, be it sacred or profane.

The Friends of Dorothy. Who does Dorothy meet? The week before Vicky, fifteen, started at her new school in a new city, she was like this: her mind, scattered like straw at a crossroads, blowing this way and that, torn between trying to forget it was happening and being overwhelmed by anxious anticipation; scenarios of hope and disaster intruding on the normal run of thoughts. Her emotions were stuck in a perpetual loop between excitement and anxiety, heart hammering out the rhythms of one or the other, often indistinguishable, switching between them in the space of a moment. Her will wavered between the reckless courage of 'I can do this, no problem; I can take the lot of you'; between this impulse to fight and the flight of 'Do I have to do this? Remind me why I'm doing this?' Vicky was not exactly in a state, but her heart, mind and will had departed from their normal runs, from comfort, as they must mid-transformation. She phoned her oldest London friends, her cousin Ben and his friend

Jamie, her boys, and they came up from London to distract her, to calm her down, to encourage her. Same trio. Mind, heart, will.

Who does Dorothy meet? An ancient trio. Plato describes the soul, the life force, the *anima*, as having three distinct parts, or perhaps forces or faculties. The highest faculty is the rational: the mind. There is also the spirited part, from whence come courage, drive and motivation: the will. Then there is the desiring part, the part that wants what it lacks or what it feels it needs – love, sex, comfort, satisfaction – the heart. In any endeavour, in any act of being human, these three must come together in some degree of harmony or discord. Here is what it looks like when it is working well:

> The soul has three powers: the intelligence, the incensive power and desire. With our intelligence we direct our search; with our desire we long for that supernal goodness which is the object of our search; and with our incensive power we fight to attain our object. With these powers those who love God cleave to the divine principle of virtue and spiritual knowledge. Searching with the first power, desiring with the second, and fighting by means of the third, they receive incorruptible nourishment, enriching the intellect with the spiritual knowledge of created beings.*

This early Christian father, St Maximos, is using Plato's soul to describe the project of seeking for God – heart, mind and will all acting in accord. We find in these desert mystics, and in the Greeks before them, the idea that trouble comes when the faculties act at odds with each other. Plato uses the metaphor of the chariot: when things are working well, then reason has the reins and the horses of will and desire follow where it guides. Desire is the tricky horse, though, the one that wants to go off-track and drag the ensemble

---

* St Maximos the Confessor, text 25 of second-century texts, in *The Philokalia*, edited by G. E. H. Palmer, Philip Sherrard and Kallistos Ware (Faber & Faber, 1981), vol. 2.

with it. This picture of conflicting faculties is one of the earliest acts of psychological description, and a dynamic one at that, attempting to account for the lived experience of inner conflict, of behaviour at odds with what we know is best for us, with the will pulled in two directions, struggling between reason and desire. In the hands of Aristotle, then the Christian mystics, and then Aquinas, we see a theory of virtue and vice, of ethical conduct, elaborated upon the core trio. The irascible faculty, as Aquinas calls the will, is what we need to overcome adversity, to get up and go – but, unchecked, intemperate, it leads to (the sin of) anger, or the excess of energy and acquisition that is gluttony; or, in its deficiency, to sloth and despondency, what the ancients called *acedia*, and we would call losing the will to live, giving up. The faculty of desire, Aquinas's appetitive part, is what we need in order to know about our essential lacks, our necessary hungers; but left to its own devices, run riot, it can lead us into lust and avarice; or, in its lack, to dejection and melancholia, where we want but unappeasably, where nothing, not even that which we need, will fill the space of want. And reason, the supposed charioteer, the rational soul, can become carried away with itself, falling into vainglory and pride and going tearing off in the wrong direction, blinded by its own lights.

And as the faculties have their vices, so they have their associated virtues. The mind, properly exercised, exhibits prudence and discernment, is wise and can distinguish right from wrong. The irascible faculty gives us fortitude, the courage to persist through adversity. Desire, finding its golden mean between wanting too much and too little, produces the temperate soul that is neither carried away in sensual excess nor mired in dejection. Indeed, for Plato and all who followed in his tracks, the virtue of temperance is the form of all virtue, for the exercise of virtue is nothing more or less than this: that the faculties act neither in excess nor in deficit but in moderation, finding their mean and acting in harmony with each other. This acting in harmony, with each faculty functioning to achieve a common goal, is what these ancients called justice. Justice was nothing more or less than the ideal interplay of wisdom, courage and moderation: heart and mind and will working together for wise ends.

We could trace this trio on through history. St Jerome sees – in the vision of Revelations, in the four holy living creatures – the three faculties repeated, earthly desire as the Ox, will as the Lion, reason as the Man and, above them all, their ideal guide, the Eagle of Faith. In *The Reformation of Morals*, the tenth-century Syrian Orthodox scholar Yaḥyā ibn ʿAdī bases his scheme of ethics on the same three faculties, and through him they inform Muslim ethics. And so it continues through time. In the nineteenth century, one of psychology's founding fathers, Alexander Bain, described the three foundations of the discipline in terms of cognition, emotion and connation (aka will). This structure is still to be felt beneath the floor of modern cognitive science and therapy, with their tripartite vision of human being and human change in terms of cognition, emotion and behaviour. Neuroscientist Joseph LeDoux calls the latter the 'mental trilogy', and traces our human problems to the fact that the 'installing' of language into the human brain leaves unsolved 'the connection between cognitive systems and other parts of the mental trilogy – emotional and motivational systems'.*
So the Platonic trio of the faculties, their harmony or lack of it, is repeated, once more as neuroscience.

Who does Dorothy meet? A clever Straw Man who wants a mind. A passionate Tin Man who wants a heart. A cowardly Lion lacking will. Through their concerted effort, through heart, mind and will acting together, we have a condensed and perfect analogy of the faculties functioning together as the very form of justice. By acting in concert, they both perfectly realize their own natures – nothing more than what they already are, but now recognized and owned as

---

* Quoted in Slavoj Žižek, *The Parallax View* (MIT Press, 2006). Žižek makes the point that rather than being a problem to be solved, it is the very desynchrony of the faculties that gives rise to our specifically human emotions; to be human is to be, to some extent, at odds with yourself and out of step with your immediate environment.

wisdom, compassion and courage – and they restore things to their proper equilibrium. Justice is achieved in getting Dorothy home. Indeed, as both their common purpose and point of cohesion, Dorothy *is* justice. Heart, mind and will, all together, setting the world to rights, restoring a situation of disturbed equilibrium.

From Yom Kippur to Oz, for the change to be effected, a concert of the faculties needs to be orchestrated. All together now: heart, mind and will. Oh my.

Charlotte and her Projects. Charlotte is at the end of a spell of love in which hope was reborn from ashes. For three weeks, her heart and mind and will have been in delirious concert. Sometimes they take a while to learn their collective routine. Usually one has to take the lead, with the other two dragged along until they begin to learn to act together. Sometimes, particularly at the start of a new project, they act together clumsily, reluctantly. However, there are other times when, like a spontaneous outburst of song, they come together just like that. First love is one such moment, if you can remember. That concert needs little rehearsal, that one can get branded into your being fully formed, heart and mind and will all acting together as one from the off, singing a chorus of the beloved. Jon, the man who has just left Charlotte, is one such love, as she is for him, twin choruses that have sung together briefly and intensely, just three times in eighteen years.

Charlotte had ended their relationship first, because at the time she had had another focus, another project, another imperious demand that took up her attention, her emotion, her actions. She had other duties. I talked to Charlotte today about this idea of *projects*, as things that convoke, call together your heart and mind and will. As a way of seeing her life, she gets it completely, because this is how her life has been as she moved wilfully from one project to another. For Charlotte a constant, recurring project has been that of artist, expressed in theatre, making music, playing in bands (some famous), making films: art, animation, documentaries, documenting the lives of children in her community. She always has a project, is always committing or planning acts of creation. It's something she loves and loves to do, something that preoccupies her mind, something she knows how to do, which her hands, her body and her eyes just know. Past projects have produced in Charlotte an expertise, a creative Automatic, through which her love of creation can run untrammelled, be it in music or film. Anyone who has know-how, knows how that feels when knitting or baking or mending the car, the joy of being in the grip of well-known routines in the service of a new creative project that carries you with it, the exhilaration of it. That's what creation is, the old and learned faculties in the service of the new. This is another kind of obsession, of heightened arousal, attention and deliberation, another kind of getting out of comfort. This is the good News from Elsewhere, and of course that news can also be love, as Jon's was for Charlotte.

The second time, it had been Jon's decision, for reasons that I can only speculate on, some constellation of safety and duty and fighting shy of fully taking the reckless plunge of love. Charlotte, like Maureen, was not one to hang around and so she got on with other projects, with other loves, her art in part, but most stunningly of all, her daughter, the most compelling project of all. To see them together is to see a true double chorus of heart and mind and will. It is amazing, revelatory, to see how considered and acute and surprising four-year-olds can be, if, from birth, you have taken their hearts and minds and wills completely seriously and given them what children almost never get, which is real agency. It's a project that some thought mad. Childrearing practice slides up and down a scale of how much you should allow your child, how seriously you should take them. At one end, there are the will-breakers, from nineteenth-century pedagogy up to the current revival of non-appeasement, feeding times and sleep regimes. From their perspective, everything else looks liberal, hippy, a bit too much like spoiling. But Charlotte, from day one, did something not entirely on the scale, neither indulgence nor oppression. She had, and continues to have, a very considered and completely serious dialogue with her daughter about her life and its sometimes difficult circumstances, and she gives her daughter very real choices within it. The results are remarkable; if you get the chance, try it. Even more than her art, this project has taken up, corralled and convoked Charlotte's thoughts and feelings and actions with unparalleled focus. Indeed, until recently, it had pushed the art to one side, but now that her daughter is going to school and better able to understand her mother's other projects, the art is coming back. Or it was until, after years of total silence, Jon came to live with Charlotte.

She described this moment as like having a new planet enter into their orbit, a new gravitational body forcing a readjustment of everyone's path. An entirely new project, or rather a combination of the very new and the very old, for an old routine, the emblazonment of love, was resurrected and re-run. What surprised them both, given the new circumstances, was how familiar it felt and how well it worked. And it felt different; it felt as if Jon had actually taken the mad leap of love at last, and so, for three weeks, there was a kind of delirium, a brief spell of having something that you never thought you would have.

Charlotte asks me if I am using her as an example of how desire sets the chariot off-course. Not so much. I wanted more to use her life to get to this notion of projects, be they the madness of love, or art, or children or writing a chapter about projects, or the difficult deserts of grief, or merely moving in with someone new; I wanted to use what I was witnessing first-hand, this friend caught up and spellbound, her heart and mind and will given, wholeheartedly, over to adjusting to something new. Charlotte was in the throes of Act Two. I wanted to use this example as a kind of recurrent figure, to give this chapter – about how the new must take centre-stage before it can become Automatic – a living heart. I asked her if I could and, some factual errors aside, she didn't mind.

Jon's gone now. That bothers and concerns her, it's on her mind, troubling her heart, affecting her will. Getting used to his absence is as much a project as getting used to his presence was, and she's now in a new Act Two. He's gone. The three-week bubble has burst, the chorus is silenced again, though it resonates still, as fugitive beauty and pain.

What's on her mind? For the moment, prudence. She has other projects – those Jon displaced – to return to and nurture. Work, art-work, that she cares about, and putting together proposals for new work. Her daughter and other loved ones require and get her atten-tion and care. She occupies herself with other things, with other people, puts her heart, mind and will at the service of other pro-jects. Her mind directs her will to reasonable occupations, and her heart remembers the joy of them and follows. She gets on with it. It's hard and she does it. Of course, Jon still bothers her, troubles her heart and tugs at her will. She is still in Act Two, but there are other things to do. Other projects. She gets on with them, because they matter too. Jon is not the only thing that concerns her.

Projects and their Relics. So, what's bothering you? What con-cerns you? Chances are, something is. Some source of discomfort, something a little Act Two.

The modern management-guru David Allen defines work as anything that you want or need to be different than it currently is. Chances are there are things in your life that are not as you would wish them to be. Some invisibly so, some niggling, some insisting, some demanding, some overwhelming. A sliding scale of our con-cern for the not-quite-right. Charlotte is close to one end, emotions raw and still insistent, mind racing, will torn and troubled and sometimes despondent. Chances are you're not quite at that end of the scale, but good luck to you if you are. More likely you are in the middle, with a more mundane to-do list hovering in your life space. You can feel it, if you try, wrapped around your being, infus-ing your sense of what being alive is like right now. You will experience it as worry, as feeling and as urge (that trio again – mind, heart, will – this time in their mode of insistence). Something is not-quite-right, something that you want or need to be different than it is now. A concern, a rumour from elsewhere.

Let us call them projects. Call what? Whatever is bothering or concerning you. We saw it begin, way back, with John in his transition into Kerbie. We saw the beginning of the project of transformation. Saw how the gap between where he was and where he wanted to be would create a discomfort, a necessary unease, whose very purpose was to motivate the closing of the gap. So the boy from the estate became a parkour star. We saw it in Maureen, and in Lenny and in Amber. But the concern needn't be so grand. It may be as simple as hunger: your hunger is maybe beginning to insist you pay attention. Leave it, ignore it and it will only complain louder, insist more. Soon as a chorus: thoughts of food, feelings of hunger, urges to eat. Mind, heart, will. Try it and see. Leave your hunger for a while and it will really start to demand your attention, ever more loudly. Or maybe it's a room? Maybe you're decorating a room and it's not finished. Or maybe you haven't found the right pair of shoes for your outfit? Maybe it's a new lover, or an unexplained symptom, or a difficult decision. Or maybe you and your children are going to suffer if you can't get more money soon. Maybe you are learning to dance, starting school, writing a book chapter, going to a meeting, filling in a form or just full to the brim with an unexpressed emotion? Anything, but something, some constellation of worry, feeling or urge. Something concerns you, something is up.

You know it, because it's more than thought. As Hollywood and Yom Kippur reminded us, thoughts in themselves, a change of mind in itself, won't bother you enough to start a project. It won't sufficiently concern you. It takes more than a passing cloud of inner words and visions. Many scud across your inner sky all day, random, half unheeded, arising and dissolving perpetually. Don't worry, I'm not going to ask you to watch them and detach, though others might. I want you to look at the ones that come and don't go, that arise and stay. These are the thoughts from which you are anything but detached, where there is no effort of attention because they are right there, in your face, bothering you, insisting. Look at what you can't ignore right now – pleasure or pain or simple bore of job to be done – and you'll see it's more than just the thoughts.

It is this notion of concern that has concerned me for days now. The journey of change, Act Two, even with all the assistance of the societal ready-mades that we can lay our hands on, must for a while become a project. For change to really happen, it must take centre-stage and for a spellbound while the new must become our obsession. This has been my concern. I see it at work in therapy. Sometimes with clients I can see, and help them see, emotions and thoughts and will all tied up into problem knots. With cognitive behavioural therapy (CBT), we could unpick them, call them schema or complexes or core beliefs. I could draw a picture for a client, showing how this thought, this scary thought, pushes at the heart, causes fear to flood the mind with images of horror, and puts the will to flight. My CBT colleagues draw these diagrams every day, pictures of the three faculties in discordant harmony, diagrams of anxiety or depression as problematic knots of thinking, feeling and doing. These methods are the nuts and bolts of my profession and of how it makes you better. Change, as managed by profession-als, is nothing more than a project explicitly framed in terms of the three faculties, and it will only happen if there is a change in each of the faculties – in mind (cognition), heart (affect) and will (behav-iour). My profession dresses up the heart and mind and will as cognition, emotion and behaviour, claims them for its own and charges a fee for their management. That's fine, that too is a trick as old as Plato. I do, however, want to point out that other, older and simpler versions are available. But this is all a kind of distrac-tion from what is really concerning me, which is this: *what happens when our projects are finished? Or, put another way, where do old pro-jects go?*

Relics is the key word here: projects and their *relics*. I want you to see yourself as a vast repository of finished or abandoned projects, which, like dead things, have fossilized and formed your very sub-stance, your geological strata. You are a reliquary, a storehouse for relics. Those of you who have kept up with the journey will see that we are now trying to move forward to where we started, to push on with deliberation and conscious effort until the new is not so new anymore. We want to arrive at the place where the deliberate becomes habitual, Automatic. If we see Automation as a kind of possession, where we delegate semi-autonomous agents to run our lives and conduct our affairs, then possession, as the priests will confirm, must be preceded by a stage of *obsession*. It is in this obsessive, spellbound stage that the new begins to really *mark* you, where it begins to leave its stamp on you. For it must, if it is really to become part of you, if you are truly to possess it and it you. If we are in the throes of obsession, we are also beginning to see the end of it, which is nothing more than this thraldom becoming routine, a routine that you know by heart and so no longer need to think about. The end of a project – its residue, its relic – is habit. That's what I am trying to get at. That's my current concern.

Logismoi. Don't worry, we have not abandoned the project of projects and relics. Neither have we abandoned Charlotte, who can now take a rest from being an example, or she could but for this: 'I've been through it before; I know what it's like.'

This is news fresh from this morning. Charlotte is speaking a few days after Jon has left and she is realizing that this is nothing *new*, only what has happened twice before in the last eighteen years. Deserts of silence, punctuated by oases of bliss. Standing afresh within this realization today, that nothing new had actually happened, other than that the blissful part had persisted longer than before. She had allowed herself to hope again. Hope that had died twice before had been miraculously resurrected and now needs to die again, and that begins today. Today all is clear to her, and dreary, same old. She has walked this way before, knows what it involves, knows that the desire, the preoccupation and the pain will fade beneath the hum of other projects and in the silence from Jon.

Charlotte knows this way and can walk it with more equanimity than before. This Act Two will be shorter, because she has played it out before.

The desert fathers, those early Christian monks in the wilderness, those experts in the three faculties and their management, would have told Charlotte to guard her heart. Those desert mystics wanted to cleanse the heart of its relics, of anything that was not to do with God. They wanted to stop anything else from concerning them, wanted to stop any other thoughts entering into a pact with their emotions and their will. And there indeed is the rub.

What's really bothering you? It's the thoughts that have crossed the threshold of your heart, *that's* what bothers you. These dusty old men distinguished between simple thoughts – thoughts that stand for bits of reality – from troubling thoughts, *logismoi*, that want to enter into the heart, that want to pass, in their language, to the 'passible' faculties. Passible here being a word which, like passion and passive, means that which can feel, or more literally, that which can suffer. These intrusive thoughts, *logismoi*, are the path from reason to suffering.

If the desert fathers had asked Charlotte to guard this passage to suffering they would have recommended *nepsis*, by which they meant a watchful attentiveness, a standing on guard at the gateway of the heart, looking out for those thoughts that don't just come and go but which demand access to the passible, to the passions, demand to be felt and acted on. At first we entertain these thoughts, elaborate them through rumination. This stirs our feelings, the thoughts become associated with dread or desire and so begin to demand enactment, to demand to pass into the fulfilment of action or avoidance. They want to manifest in the world. Such thoughts-feelings-actions, once entertained and enacted, leave permanent traces on our being, permanent tendencies to act and feel like that again. Through repeated feeling and thinking and acting they bed down and spread roots through our being, they become us. They establish routines which, once triggered, can run again and again, even after years of silence. So you become a reliquary of realized passions, of past concerns and of finished or abandoned projects.*

And this is what bothered them, these desert fathers. Their project was the cleansing of the passions and the illumination of the mind. This in itself would have laid down relics in their heart, ways and means of acting, coalitions of heart and mind and will branded and stamped and, after years, stained and steeped into these old, astonishing, desert souls. This was their project. Not so much the cleansing of the heart, but its re-inscription,† an establishment and reinforcement of new ways. It would have worked – it still does; it's the same basic mechanism as cognitive behavioural therapy, of any successful behaviour change, whatever methodology effects it. When faced with the demand of the new, work with mind, heart and will over a long enough time, begin to inscribe a new schema, a new groove in the heart, and it will form a new way of life for you.

It works. It worked for these fathers because it bothered and concerned them enough for them to think, feel and do something about it for long enough. It changed their minds and hearts and wills, brought them together to achieve a new end. Their lives eventually became the record and their bodies the reliquary of this project. Through them, we have precious insights into how the soul is shaped; we have insights just as keen, but fresher and less encumbered by jargon, than those from cognitive science. We have from them a fully formed technology and ethics of change. That was some project, its relics still reside in the hearts of many. But theirs is just one way of life, and it's not for Charlotte, nor for most of us.

Groove is in the Heart. Whatever bothers you now is what you will be good at later. What concerns you now, you will master or abandon, incorporate or expel. Incorporate, literally to make part

---

* Cognitive behavioural therapy would call these thought-feeling-action tendencies schemas. Otherwise our modern version is essentially the same.
† Remember, as we saw in Chapter 2, there is no subtraction in human life, only the addition of more compelling habits/schema/*logismoi*.

of your body, as you will and have for years, because most of your major projects are finished. Language, movement and walking – how far back do you want to go? – how unimaginably preoccupying they must have been. Old news now, old games. As Bourdieu explains, the earlier you enter the game, the less you are aware that it is a game.

Now you know most of your moves by heart. You, a reliquary of completed projects, a heart full of grooves. And we have tried, over the last few chapters, to capture a new act of inscription, a fresh laying down of the laws of the heart, we've tried to capture it happening before our eyes. Someone before us has described the stages of this in these terms.*

First there is *unconscious incompetence*, when you are entirely prior to any act of change or awareness of the need for it. Then, alerted or summoned to adapt to some new rhythm, some new concern, you pass to *conscious incompetence*, that early awkward stage that we met a couple of chapters ago, of halting first nights and uneasy early days. Then, with repetition, and with the aid and example of others who have danced the same dance that you are trying to learn, a little grace begins to enter your moves, a little fluency, as heart and mind and will begin to work out their routine. This stage, as we saw in the last chapter, can be rapidly facilitated by the available cultural ready-mades, for there are whole ways of feeling and doing and thinking – *habitus* – that you can take off the peg and wear right away. This is the stage of *conscious competence*, when you know the moves, and know you know them, and you still have to think a bit to get it right, but get it right you do, and all feels fresh and new.†
And then . . .

Well, everything eventually becomes routine. Whatever was at

* Noël Burch, a colleague of American clinical psychologist Thomas Gordon.
† And in case we haven't made it sufficiently clear, this period of heightened deliberate awareness is *by its very nature* exhausting, preoccupying, anxiety-provoking. If you are constantly worried, tired and jangly, you are probably still in Act Two.

one point fresh will become a stock response, to the point that you may forget that you ever chose it, forget it ever had an origin outside you. You will be so good at it that you won't even know it. This is the stage of *unconscious competence*, not just in the sense that you are now such a good little mover that you could do it in your sleep, but also in the sense that your competence does not reside in consciousness, it is located in and performed by something else, it is the Automatic that is competent. The routine doesn't need you anymore. The new project has had its brief moment of deliberation in the light of consciousness and choice, then it passed through the twilight borne of repetition and settled at last into that vast darkness of old and automated being that is most of you. Obsession preceding possession. Here it now resides with all the stuff you don't need to think about anymore, though sometimes, daily, there are choices about which old relic you'll summon up, which well-worn routines you'll run again today. Charlotte, for instance, embarked on one of compelling intensity and is in it still. But, as she came to realize, she knew the way already, for the grooves were already deep in her heart.

Coupling. Coupling, the desert fathers called it. You entertain the idea, mull over the old routine and then you decide to run it, or rather you decide to let it run you. You couple with the old routine and give your will over to it and now for a time it is in charge. For this is also what lies at the end of our projects. Once the groove has been made within your heart, it is always available, always there and ready to run again. For sure, the new can be our project, can compel us until it becomes routine, until we know it by heart; but so can the old, the relics; we can always summon an old by-heart routine and allow it to possess us, to take centre-stage for a while. Often we use these gnarled old habits, these relics, as distraction from the real project of paying attention to the new. We use old habits as a way of avoiding the difficult work of acquiring new ones, as an intermission in Act Two.

To consider running an old routine is a bit like pondering what record you will play on the jukebox. Or, to go back to the desert fathers' use of coupling, it is like dating or flirting, a passionate attention to something you might go further with. You feel it as a pull. One thought or notion out of all the notions, one with a little more insistence than the rest, one thought that demands your attention, your presence. The old can be just as compelling as the new. I feel it now. There was an encounter this morning, a close call with another human being, a stranger – a magical, charged and unexpected moment. I could follow it up. As I write, there are stirrings still, insistent and urgent to pass into action. They want into my life and out into the world, they want to live, they want me to let them, they *insist*.

I can feel several others there too. Catastrophe, I am very good at catastrophe: it's an old, old routine for me, maybe one I was born with, and I can run it in response to a surprisingly diverse set of stimuli. Today and yesterday it was triggered by the funny smell in the kitchen. No, really. I called the experts, this is part of my catastrophe routine, I need to bother an expert, cry for help, share the concern. And the expert agreed that there was indeed a funny smell. So good to be validated, so much more food for catastrophic thought: rot, rats, floor collapsing, gas, eviction, months of tribulation, a sign of spiritual corruption and oh, I could go on, the head will do it now without my thinking, running on Catastrophe Automatic. Indeed, I would have to try to stop it and that would be the effort; the effort would not be in the commission, but in the ceasing to commit. It's the same with the heart. I'm sure you've your own versions of this one, but for me it's the creeping dread, the unease, the tingly fear. But, like a quantum computer, the heart can apparently represent several states at once, because with a little shift of attention I notice that it is still tripping up on this morning's encounter. Which routine will win out?

And it is the will with which all these old routines are really trying to engage, to couple. For the will is the entrance to the world. I find this part of my couplings most interesting of all, and this is where the desert fathers really got it right. Because I know that

should I let any of these projects *in potentia* pass to the act, if I move from this speed-coupling, this serial dating, if I pick one and move from idle flirtation and fumbling feeling to what they called *assent*, if I pick one and let it take over the running of things, then it will. *It* will. Not I, but *it* will start to will my actions. *It* will run the show.*
It is currently a close call, for me, between these competing projects:

1. to fold into this writing a text about multiple agency and the cast of *The Simpsons* that I think would work (dread, hope, a little weariness)
2. to follow up this morning's encounter (desire, stirrings, intrusive and arousing images)
3. to find a missing sock (really, it matters: a strong undercurrent of something incomplete and that feeling really bothers me)
4. to tackle the smell in the kitchen (helplessness, big degree of dread, images and scripts of catastrophe)
5. to work on my research (guilt, fear of reprimand, counter-arguments of justification)
6. to get ready to go to London (that one actually, on inspection, is not too insistent, i.e. it is surrounded by the confidence of its timely completion).

There are more, involving presents for Ben and food for me and Vicky, lunch with Louise – and I could go on and bore you silly – but using me as the current 'patient etherized upon a table', giving Charlotte and her mad romantic project a break, the project currently in charge of me is this one, this writing. At least it is new.† For you geeks, the project currently taking up most of my CPU is this, what you are reading. This is

---

* This calls to mind Sigmund Freud's insight: 'Wo Es war, soll Ich werden' ('Where It was, there I shall be'). By contrast, the formula of possession, or of habit-forming is 'Where I was, there It shall be'.
† Rimbaud said, 'I do believe that there's no consolation to be found in habits when things get pitiful.' He was a rare creature indeed.

what I coupled with and then assented to. For non-geeks, the CPU is the central processing unit of a computer, its current project-processing space. Like us, it can only be acting on one or two main projects at a time, while other potentials run in the background.

All it takes is a little attention, and I can see the things in me that are competing for assent, wanting to manifest through me. A little attention brings to mind and heart their essential features, each a unique constellation of thoughts and feelings and urges, a unique routine. Which shall I perform? Which will I assent to? Which is most urgent? Not necessarily the one that is best for me to enact. Ah, *nepsis*, *nepsis*. Guard, dear author, your heart. For I know something new about myself now. I always thought of myself as lazy. But then I watched for a while, and I noticed that in a given week, this particular week, once I had started on a project, it didn't stop so easily. Again the details are irrelevant, but I want to give you an idea of the range of projects that I mean: a complicated ethics form for research; a quest for intimacy; buying the right black, merino wool, V-neck jumper; finding out what programme was taking up 98 per cent of my laptop's CPU and fixing this (this latter for real, not as metaphor; it took many hours of one day, hence its serendipitous availability as an example).

Each one, once embarked on, compelled me for hours, often in the face of some felt reluctance to persist; there was, despite my exhaustion, a dumb persistence. I carried on regardless, or *it* did, they did, the routines, the projects did. It wanted completion, closure, satisfaction. It had started so it will finish. A week of projects. I re-evaluated my laziness. It was more like a reluctance to begin than anything else. And perhaps that reluctance to begin was and is informed by the knowledge that once it starts, the routine doesn't stop so easily. It really does take possession. Once started, the effort required is not to persist but to stop. Like dancing, once you get into the groove, it's actually easier to keep going, for *it* wants to keep going. So, not so much laziness as an avoidance of that altered state, that possession, a reluctance to assent and commit to that, a resistance to putting on the Red Shoes.

I am not, I know, unnaturally endowed with persistence, and it really felt, looking at it all week, as if this quality didn't reside in me but was encoded in the routines themselves. The will, the urge to carry out the task and persist with the project came fitted as standard in the relic. Once started, it wanted to continue. And, as we all know, to let it take over can be enormously satisfying. There is an ease, a comfort and a familiarity, in running a known routine, in being run by it, in being swept away by a project. It compels you and entrances you, it captures you and carries you away, spellbound. Someone in the throes of coupling with an old habit is someone in a trance, moving to a set of compulsions and demands invisible to the naked eye, moving to a rhythm no one else can hear. It carries you, thinking for you, taking the weight of the world off your shoulders and the monkey off your back. Give in – you know you want to – because if you give in, assent, the monkey will stop bothering you and the world will melt away. It's a deal, a trade, *it* gets to manifest and you get a break from worldly care, from deliberation and wondering what to do with time, the thoughts stop bothering you and you, potentially, get the ride of your life. Or the V-neck, or the CPU cleared, or the intimacy, or the form filled in. Or love. Three weeks of delirious, blissful love.

To be coupled to these old projects, coupled and assenting and letting them drive, is to be uncoupled from the immediate demands of contingency, or even of survival. It is to be, for a spell, freed from the chains of environmental necessity and demand. It is also a way of avoiding that other form of immersion, the demands of moving to the changing beat, getting the hang of the new. It is a way of stepping out of Act Two. Look at those spellbound by old habits: that guy there, caught in a relentless and exhausting search for the perfect V-neck; everyone you meet, look into their eyes and you'll see that some degree of inner preoccupation, some presiding concern, something other than the here-and-now, has taken hold of their hearts. To be uncoupled from the world and to be carried away with yourself: to be so for a spell is to partake of the very essence of being human.

I know something now. I know that whatever I start – even if I tell myself that I'll just have a nibble, one drag, one sip, name your poison, one sniff – I know that it will take over and that the person that chose the record to play is not the person who will be dancing to it. In just beginning, I have handed over agency, delegated my will.

I have started, it will finish.

All Together Now. In Chapter 2, 'The Automatic', we called these relics, these grooves in the heart, our *routines*. Here we have seen them begin to be produced, forming in the obsessive heat of the project of mastering novelty. We could also call them *agents*. An agent is a person or a thing that acts for another; a person or a thing that exerts or produces an effect. A thing that *does*, a piece of delegated will. As we have gone from unconscious incompetence, as our hearts and mind and wills have been called – in mastering the new – to collective focus and repeated action, as the groove deepens, so we begin to form a thing in us, a worn routine, a thing that will think and feel and act on our behalf. An agent. Already we have many. Here I am, moving my arms, breathing and using words like nobody's business. All I need to do is to point my intention in the right direction and all the necessary agents will execute the task. And if I went and instead looked for this morning's now waning encounter, or investigated the smell in the kitchen or the missing sock, so the requisite agents would perform their parts, establishing a temporary coalition of forces, parts, feelings and urges, a temporary ensemble of some pre-prepared ways of being, of motor programmes, moves and gestures, of thoughts and styles of thinking. Heart and mind and will, all together, getting things done. In Chapter 2, we corralled Dennett and Deleuze to support this notion of a multi-agent self. Some would argue that these versions are over-reaching, that we are greater than the sum of our parts, that something in us is not reducible to this mindless rabble, that it leaves out an indescribable nothing, an indivisible remainder. That's a subject for the last chapter. For now, let us go to sleep.

Dreaming. When Jon was there, living with her at last, Charlotte dreamed the rainbow ended in her house. Now that he is gone, she dreams that he has left his best shoes behind, and that maybe he will come for them. Bliss and yearning, such perfect condensations, but I do not want to dwell on these images, so much as to get straight to the function of dreams. In sleep we are not switched off at all. Take an image of your sleeping brain and you'll find it is crazily active, only differently so than in waking. You are not so much switched off as you are offline. The frontal circuits, outer sense and higher reason, your window to the world, are unplugged. And, because your body is paralysed, what is in you is prevented from passing into the world. Consciousness and action switched off, the world cannot enter you, and you cannot enter the world. Whatever can be happening within this hermetic seal?

When dreaming, the chemical weather of your brain is as different from its waking state as Venus is from Mars. In dreams, the circuits of motivation and reward are running at full pelt, the circuits responsive to pleasure, sex, chocolate, cocaine, cigarettes and alcohol, to whatever turns you on. Or off, for these circuits also underpin disgust and aversion. Also awake and hyper-alert are the circuits of flight and fight, fear and anger and all the shades of passion in between, for as you sleep these circuits are beating out their tattoo beneath your skin, pulsing and hammering through your wordless being. While dreaming, all the propulsions and repulsions, all the drives and desires, are free to play without the danger of passing into action, without the surveillance of reason, without the checks and barriers of the outer world. Without higher reason and without the danger of passing to the act, our structures of motivation, attraction and repulsion, longing and missing, wishing and dreading, all the flights and fights are free to take and find their form – are free to form.

In dreams, the meaning of events – their real meaning, their inscription in our heart – is written. In dreaming, heart and mind and will are free to improvise and settle on their final version of whatever has been bothering you during the day. In dreaming, the forces of meaning, emotion and motivation are all up and about, busily rehearsing, re-scripting, working out, coalescing and establishing, as a permanent part of you, a relic, an agent, a groove in your heart. In dreaming, you forge the relics of the soul, your projects pass from the light of day to the dark roots of your being, your new concerns begin to inscribe themselves as habit, as ways of being, doing, thinking and feeling, as you. In dreams, Act Two is moved along, the moment of truth begins to become part of the truth of us. In dreams, your condition is established.

What is your condition? Such a simple, humble word, but in it all the wisdom, such as there is, in this chapter. 'Condition', etymologically, means to speak together, to meet and talk as one, to speak in chorus, in agreement. To be 'conditioned' also means to be primed to respond again as you did before, for the parts to have a tendency, a pull towards coming together and agreeing like last time. The Buddhists dream of being unconditioned; the philosophers of free will try to locate something in you, some indescribable nothing, a font of unconditioned action, for to be conditioned is to be determined by what you have done before, by what has gone before. And for Buddhists and philosophers, and for the desert fathers and all the wise old men, to be so determined is not to be free, but is to be the slave of passion, circumstance and history, all three.

But I know that Charlotte does not despise her condition, or wish, despite the suffering, to be free of it. The desert project is not for all. Our conditions, the agreements of the parts within ourselves, our ensembles of agents and routines, the collection of arrangements which our hearts and minds and wills have formed is not, unless such is your project, something to be escaped from, erased or written over. It is who we are and how we came to be so, the living history of what we have cared about, devoted ourselves to, worried over and bothered about. It is – we are – the living record of our past concerns.

You can see that in the way you respond to things now, without much thought, automatically knowing and feeling and acting because you know now what you like and dislike. You know how you feel about things. And if you don't, then it will become a concern: it will bother you, becoming an Act Two during which you will figure it out until you know how you feel about it, until you make another groove in your heart. There are things you are susceptible to and things you are hardened against. You are likely to do this, but it's hard to imagine you doing that, given your condition. And as your current condition is the living memorial of your past concerns, so your future condition will record, with real fidelity, the shape of your present preoccupations, your current concerns, whatever is bothering and calling upon your heart and mind and will right now.

So, what is bothering you now?

Chapter 9
Dancing Already

In which we further consider the possession by routine touched on in the last chapter. In Part One, we see that, good as we are at forming habit and letting it run our life, the potential is there for suffering. We consider Hell. In Part Two, we see that the way we respond to events is dictated by the way we label them, and we spend some time looking at how we name and label what just happened to us. Finally, it is argued that the Automatic need not be at odds with the Deliberate, but rather that they can work in tandem to bring about something like betterment in our lives.

PART ONE

Response and Responsibility

Responses

Nothing liberates as well as a good master, since 'liberation'
consists precisely in shifting the burden onto the other/master.

Slavoj Žižek*

. . . yesterday's street is left us,
and the gnarled fidelity of an old habit
that was comfortable with us and never wanted to leave.

Rainer Maria Rilke†

Act Three. Now you have the hang of it. Now you know it all by
heart. The new isn't news anymore. It's routine, normal, part of
you; an agent ready to respond when it meets the like again, ready
to go into action without all the bother of thinking and deliberation
you had to go through to form this automatic ease. It's in you now.
It knows how to act without you. Now it has the hang of you.

Normal service has been resumed. The production line producing you, the habit machine, is running smoothly once again. In
movies, this is the dénouement, the end of Act Three. Act Three
began in the last chapter, in the high noon of preoccupation. It ends
here, now, in a new equilibrium, a new normal briefly signalled

---

* Slavoj Žižek, *Enjoy Your Symptom! Jacques Lacan in Hollywood and Out* (Routledge,
1993).
† Rainer Maria Rilke, 'The First Elegy', *Duino Elegies: with English Translations by
C. F. MacIntyre* (University of California Press, 1961).

before the end credits roll. Now you are settled and comfortable in a new small world. You could bestir yourself. Stir up the mud, the dormant massive most of you, the sediment of years of learning. Maybe for a moment you could stop the machine, wake up and watch, catch it at work. Step out of the dance. Never too easy. Find out who's in charge. Ask to speak to the manager.

I can talk. Nothing useful has been in charge for days now. Old stuff, old routine responses have been running my show. Months of Automatic living. It, not me, is in charge. Usually at this point I would use a friend as an example, to illustrate the point. That is the form that I have evolved, making a point about how we are, and then providing an illustration for you from amongst my circle of friends. Normal people doing normal things. None of them mind, most of them are flattered; a few names have been changed, but not all. You look at them, I make the point, to try and wake it up, stir it up in you. So you can watch yourself, catch yourself, at work. But in this final phase, this final descent of what was new into the dark night of habit and routine, in this chapter, the grand finale, about who or what is actually in charge now, and who or what could be . . . Well, I become a little nervous, for this chapter is all about *possession*. And I've been possessed for months.

But just before we reach the summit, let us look back, and see how far we have come, how far on we are from those first steps. Remember the footsteps in the virgin snow, the first forging of the path, that first dumb persistence that, through nothing magic, nothing other than persistence, ended here? Ends here. This ends here. You hear that line a lot in films. The Hero takes a stand, against some overwhelming foe, after a long stretch of violence and horror, takes a stand and says: this ends here, tonight. That act of ending, of bringing a season to an end, takes as much dedication as the beginning and the getting beyond the beginning. Beginnings and endings both take dedication and effort, for they force you to bestir yourself and break from the continuity of the past, for better or worse.

So, for months now, I have been putting this off. I really wouldn't, shan't, shouldn't bore you, as I have bored myself (I could weep) with the ways in which I kept this ending at bay. But I can give you the gist of it. Do you remember The Gist? So many chapters ago, who thought we would get this far? You know how athletes tire just at the end, how their last stretch is also their last gasp, how their energy can falter when the end is in sight? Maybe it's not so much because it's running out as the sudden realization that there is an afterlife, a new season to begin. I really don't know, though I know I am acting like the guy who does. But I know that I am not alone in curling up inside the last bits of a thing. For after this, what? New horizons. I will have to think again. Begin, again. Who wants that? Easier to stay in the Automatic ease, the familiar possession by known routine responses. Months. Being stuck and struggling with possession, something like this:

> The human condition is so wretched that while bending his every action to pander to his passions man never ceases groaning against their tyranny. He can neither accept their violence nor the violence he must do himself in order to shake off their yoke. Not only the passions but also their antidotes fill him with disgust, and he cannot be reconciled either to the discomfort of his disease or to the trouble of a cure.*

Quite. Except I might add 'habits' to passions: the tyranny of the masses, those agents that will, unless you really push it, run the show.

This is the sound of someone stalling.

For months now.

So, let's begin.

What happens in this last act, what happens after the spellbound stage of conscious preoccupation, that intense high noon that

* François de La Rochefoucauld, Maxim 527, *La Rochefoucauld, Maxims*, translated by Leonard Tancock (Penguin Classics, 1959).

occurs between the dawn of novelty and the night of habit? What comes after the period of obsession and thrall, as the new worms its way into the fibre of our being, into our nerves and nooks and crannies? It's a kind of thrill, the spellbound stage, but we won't stay there for long, because it's too much, too arousing and preoccupying. It can also be monstrous. I can think of monstrous examples too. Awful shortcuts from novelty to routine, to possession. For that's the common end of the process, monstrous or not. Most starkly seen in imposed regimes, regimens of torture and coercion, fascists forcing bodies into new routines. That's being under someone else's spell. The end stage of that process, the afterwards of that, in those concentration camps, the ones we have in mind now, was usually an inner and an outer capitulation to such overwhelmingly malign novelty. Few survived the imposition of that rhythm, not because they couldn't dance to it, but precisely because they could do nothing else.

> To sink is the easiest of matters; it is enough to carry out all the orders one receives, to eat only the ration, to observe the discipline of the work and the camp. Experience showed that only exceptionally could one survive more than three months in this way. All the musselmans* who finished in the gas chambers have the same story, or more exactly, have no story; they followed the slope down to the bottom, like streams that run down to the sea.

This is the dark night of pure routine, the Danse Macabre, the Dance of Death. Survival in the camp, according to Levi, was about retaining some moves of one's own, vicious, selfish, cunning moves – the dance of survival. The more purely one became a translation of the imposed regime, the more faithfully one succumbed to it and channelled it, the quicker the slide to nothingness. Levi is harsh:

* 'This word "musselman", I do not know why, was used by the old ones of the camp to describe the weak, the inept, those doomed to selection.' Footnote in Primo Levi, *If This Is a Man* (first published in Italian, 1947, revised edn, Einaudi, 1958; English translation by Stuart Woolf, Orion Press, 1959).

Their life is short, but their number is endless . . . an anonymous mass . . . of non-men who march and labour in silence, the divine spark dead within them, already too empty to really suffer. One hesitates to call them living: one hesitates to call their death death . . .

and angry:

. . . if I could enclose all the evil of our time in one image, I would choose this. . . . an emaciated man, with head dropped and shoulders curved, on whose face and in whose eyes not a trace of a thought is to be seen.

No trace of thought, no will, no divine spark. This is where we are heading. And it won't be so extreme, and I should be ashamed of this example, easier than my own, but let it stand for the moment, as one morbid limit of our general destination, our common end. How long did this process take, this creation of these living dead? Weeks. From human to puppet in weeks. A whole alien set of procedures and habits had taken possession, complete possession, in a few weeks, and Levi tells us in no uncertain terms that only those who kept a few responses of their own – a little spark, a small movement, a trace of independent will, life, thought – only those who didn't let the system in which they were embedded have everything, only they survived. In the end our real freedom may be nothing more than the 'small movement which makes a totally conditioned social being someone who does not render back completely what his conditioning has given him'.*

'To sink is the easiest of matters.' Indeed. Thomas Mann's novella *Mario and the Magician* is a perfect essay on the ease of sinking. It tells of a sadistic hypnotist, Cipolla, encountered by a German family on holiday in Italy between the wars. They are not having

* From an interview with Jean-Paul Sartre, 'Itinerary of a Thought', in *New Left Review*, 1/58, November–December 1969.

such a great time. There is a slow accumulation of indignities throughout the holiday, as the petty insults and minor inconveniences mount, culminating in the evening's magic show. That night, their kids insist on staying, way beyond the time when the older, wiser adults know they should have gone home. In fact they should have gone home days ago, but they stay, at the magic show, and at the resort, despite their better judgement. This is the atmosphere established before the climax: one of gradual capitulation, a slow succumbing to a situation they know they should have escaped from. Like the old myth of boiling a frog: put it in cold water, raise the temperature slowly enough and it will stay until it is boiled to death.

The bubbling climax of their holiday is the act of Cipolla, who succeeds in subjugating more and more of the audience to his will. The parallel is clear here: the family's gradual capitulation to their environment is mirrored and intensified in the hypnotist's act. Cipolla knows his audience. Knows that they (and we) have a profoundly ambivalent attitude to our free will, to acting on it, particularly if it puts us out of step with those around us. How much easier it is to sink, to slide, to mindlessly respond to the prevailing rhythm. Cipolla targets one man in the audience, slightly more reluctant to succumb than the others:

> 'Dance, who wants to torture himself this way? Do you call that freedom; this kind of forced submission of yourself? . . . How good it will feel finally to let go of your will. There, you are dancing already. Now it's no longer a struggle; it's really a pleasure.'*

The story was written in 1929, so of course it is an analogy, a fable for the rise of Nazi Germany and Mussolini's Italy, the sinking of the populace beneath the will of its leaders, the gradual, easy,

* Thomas Mann, *Mario und der Zauberer* (1930); extract from novella translated by Margaret Rioch and quoted in Margaret J. Rioch, ' "All We Like Sheep –" (Isaiah 53:6): Followers and Leaders', *Psychiatry*, 34(3) (1971): 258–73.

downhill slide of capitulation. Who can resist it? Who wants to torture themselves this way? Not many. To sink is easier, as bystander,
as perpetrator, as victim of these horror stories – it is so much easier
to sink, to slide, to dance along.

Ah, extremes. I could have used literature from hypnotism, from
social psychology experiments – the spectacular ones from the 1960s
and 1970s, in which nice people do awful things – the literature on
how to build shopping malls to co-opt our will and to make us spend
more time and money in them. But the end point would have been
the same, the route longer, and the scenery less dramatic. The point
is: we do not want to stay for long within the glare and heightened
arousal of willed and deliberate living. Not most of us, not most of
the time. It's viscerally too much. The urgency of those moments is
a little too uncomfortable, as it should be. It's our bodies' evolved
way of making us act, making us do something about the new,
reducing and incorporating it, familiarizing ourselves with it, catching its rhythm so we can dance along again. We don't want to be
thinking, willing, deliberating, not for long, we want to be dancing
already. That's what we habit machines are good at; that's what we
are designed to do.

What separates us, most of us, from Levi's musselmans and
Cipolla's dancers, is the extent to which we have chosen our environment, and its relative lack of malevolence. Look a little closer,
though, and it becomes clear that the difference is only in the content, not in the nature of the process. For whatever your current
situation – your environment, your network, your place within it –
you won't be out of step with it, not unless you're new to it or just
about to leave. If you have been where you are and who you are for
any length of time, you'll be dancing already. The burden of choice
and deliberation, of freedom, has been shifted; the high noon of
conscious action has passed into the night of habit. It has become
you. Your responses to where you live and what you usually do, to
the supporting cast of your daily living, have been encoded and
distributed in your nerves and muscles, in the people, props and
routines of your lived environment. For, unlike the musselmans, we

have a dialogue with our environment, we shape it and it shapes us. Strange reciprocity. In habit, routine, props and networks, you have distributed yourself through an Automatic that remembers how and who you are, and knows how to respond to most of the things that happen there. Only the really new will bother you now. The rest is Automatic.

That's where we started, way back, with the Automatic, with the invisible hand of servitude, with the thoughtless, massive, most of you, constantly at work in muscles and nerves, in the people and the places and the things you live with. We have watched it awaken and wax in response to the new, watched it forced into deliberation, watched it get its head and hands and heart around the new, practise and adapt to it, adopt and incorporate it. Now the new is waning, sinking down into the ground of our being. We've got the hang of it. The new is sinking below the horizon of consciousness into . . . oh, you get it.

And that's how it should be. That's how we're made. Give us any length of time in a new situation and we'll work out how to respond, how to dance. So why the fascist analogies and the creeping air of gloom?

A Glimpse of Hell. What Dante presents us with in his Hell is not an abstract soul, but the *habitus* of the individual:

> . . . every action, every exertion of the will toward its goal leaves behind a trace, and the modification of the soul through its actions is the *habitus*.*

This is literary critic Erich Auerbach illuminating Hell for us. We have met the *habitus* before, 'it is the residuum in the man's soul of his soul's history'. This is what Dante puts in Hell: his imagined souls are not an impersonal essence but something formed, more

---

* Erich Auerbach, *Dante, Poet of the Secular World* (1929; English trans. University of Chicago Press, 1961).

properly *de*formed, by repeated action, a reliquary, a faithful index of the daily things they did. The shades that Dante encounters are vivid, lively, impressive. They more than retain the routines and habits of their fleshy daily selves, for they have become nothing other than them. For Dante, it is our habitual selves that damn us and are damned. Or which save us. In Purgatory and Paradise, we see the *habitus* survive, but there it is now remediable or perfected. In each realm, what remains of us is what we did and so became; a living record, a faithful transcript of our previous responses, our willed actions. In Hell, it is a hardened armature of habit, of inflexible, brittle and automatic responses. Let's have a closer look at Hell.

Responsibility

In the course of evolution the innate and automated equipment
of life governance – the homeostasis machine – became quite
sophisticated.

Antonio Damasio*

Sir, it thinks without you.

James B. L. Hollands, *Here* (film), 2007

Getting Upset. It doesn't take much to upset us. Change the temperature. Let the mood drop, or the anxiety rise. Let the food and
water run low or the drugs run short. Let something new occur, or
something familiar end, and we'll react to get things back to how
they were. The homeostasis machine, as Damasio calls us, the habit
machine, is always operating to maintain or re-establish the status
quo. We know when things are out of balance because we feel ill at
ease. It is this that sets the machine in motion. Perpetual motion –
for there is a constant dynamic interplay of stability and change,
ease and unease, and we can only stay the same by continually acting to do so. We – or rather, it – have to work hard to stay the same.

Once upon a time we didn't know how we felt, what we thought
or what to do about anything. Then there was so much path-beating

* Antonio Damasio, *Looking for Spinoza* (Harcourt Brace, 2003).

to be done. You can see the force of this impulse diminish as the human creature ages. The wild and spontaneous oscillations of the child, the dramatic postures and successive self-enactments of adolescence, the exuberance of youth: all at last give way to a kind of steady state of knowing who we are and what we are like, of knowing what to do. Gradually we define the limits of our ease, become established in ourselves.

It took a lot of work to establish this established self. A lot of work to form, like a snail, the extended armature that is the world we now inhabit. Anything that bothered us, that took our time and attention for long enough, has left its mark, beaten its path. Once it was news, something out there, gradually we made it part of us, transforming it from It to I. To do so it had to pass through the narrow hourglass neck of conscious deliberation, effort and work. And then we got the hang of it and it became another it, a little it, now inside, an agent, a habit, a routine, fixed and set and ready to respond the next time it was called on, ready to think and act on our behalf. From It to I to it. From word to flesh.*

And with ourselves established, we begin to mind what happens and we become easier to upset. Now that we have something, we also have something to lose. With a narrower range of comfort the homeostasis machine has to work harder. The more established and fixed we are, the broader the range of potential threats to our establishment and the more precarious the balance. Which is fine if we can buy, for a time, the means to shore ourselves up, if we have the means to spread our establishment through an environment that embodies us and our values, a world that repeats ourselves. All the agents, parts and roles, the set, props and cast of characters, the entire corporation united under the principle of maintaining the established, adult self. Guarding against upset. These are the foundations of hell.

* Maybe this is all consciousness is for – deciding what the news is, what it is like, deciding what we should do about it. The effort of discernment and deliberation, the work of consciousness, should be completed as soon as possible. Then we can get back to normal, a new normal.

Dragonhide. The almost weightless present moment meets the mass of history we bring to it. So easy to ruin the moment, to miss what is truly unique about it. Easier just to repeat ourselves instead. Lenny calls this kind of living 'character sclerosis', a hardening of the self. The writer Alasdair Gray calls it 'dragonhide'. What they are both getting at is that it is possible to stop responding, to stop truly responding, to the moment, to the world as it is, and to begin to live a purely Automatic life, where more and more external stimuli elicit the same old responses, no matter how different the stimuli. The new legion of cognitive behavioural therapists* call this kind of living a loss of responsibility and emphasize their point by spelling it out as *response-ability*. In our terms, we could say that we become less and less willing to embark on the journey of Act Two. We keep saming when we ought to be changing.

Character as skeleton versus character as carapace. Our set of routines, our army of agents can form an inner armature allowing flexibility and dexterity, or it can form an armour composed of ossified habit, immune to all but the most shocking, and therefore shattering, news. Kenneth Williams, the British comedian and comic actor, kept a diary which can be read as the record of a creature gradually becoming imprisoned within a hardening carapace of character; in it he argues that the sensitive soul either breaks or forms a persona to protect itself. And Williams shows that the cost of this protection is high: an ever-diminishing ability to be in the world, a self that increasingly repeats the same stereotyped gestures, regardless of the circumstance.

This is Self as a prison only escaped by death.

We live daily by a constantly performed act of faith. Like the Fool in the Tarot, stepping heedlessly over the cliff, entirely sure that the angels will uphold him, we walk into our future confident that the routines that compose us will keep the show on the road. And so of course they do, that is what they are for.

---

* Third-wave CBT therapists who practise, and preach, acceptance and commitment therapy.

A centipede quite happy was
Until one day a toad, in fun, said
'Pray, which leg comes after which?'
Which worked her up to such a pitch
She lay distracted in a ditch
Considering how to run.*

Considering how to run is the last thing we want to be doing. We just want to run, dance already, and for things to run on Automatic most of the time. And most of the time they do, and so they should. As Žižek noted in the quote heading up this chapter, liberation for us means shifting the burden of responsibility, not having to make the choice. And so we shift the burden to our inner Automatic, delegate our will and our responsibility over to it. *It* responds, it thinks without us, acts without thinking, knows what we think and what to do; it knows our preferences and dislikes, knows the moves; and we dance, and we sink and we slide, into the easy downhill slide of Automatic living.

But if ease is there, so is suffering, as we repeat and repeat what we know and become less and less capable of Sartre's 'one small movement', a genuine response, a gesture not dictated by our past, by our *habitus*. Sometimes the stock responses are not what is called for. The Buddhists are good on this. They call our dispositions, our acquired ways of responding, *sankharas*, and it is the ignorant repetition of these, the life of nothing but these, that causes the suffering they are so keen to eliminate.† A pragmatic version of suffering as the repetition of stock responses in the face of new demands; of desires and aversions repeating themselves despite life calling on us to come up with something new, asking us to stir ourselves and step out of the dance, to make that one small movement, that massive

---

* 'The Centipede's Dilemma' (1871), usually attributed to Katherine Craster.
† As for Dante, so for Buddhists: it is the *sankharas* that survive us. Reincarnation is not of some abstracted essence, but of our *sankharas*, our habits – it is our repetitions which repeat until they gradually fade.

uphill movement away from the familiar. So easy to be stuck in the familiar, to be mastered by routine, to be mindlessly repeating oneself, to not be in charge. This is how it can go, and easily go. Ease is the essence of the habit machines we are.

So, how to step out of the funk? The potential for our Automatic to become stuck and gnarled, to crash and burn, is huge. But so is its potential for adaptation. We are composed of myriad parts that can respond to many calls and can be as flexible and open to the new as we will allow them to be. The Automatic can certainly disable us if it merely runs under its own guidance, merely repeats itself. So we need to be able to recognize when more is called for, when something new is called for.

And there lies the problem. Often we do not know when the new is called for because we do not call it new. Which takes us to the telling of stories and the calling of names.

PART TWO

Calls and Calling

Calls

The Owl of Minerva flies only at twilight.

G. W. F. Hegel

'I call it like I see it.' This American idiom is a kind of boast about discernment and plain speaking, about being able to cut through the fuzz of the fancy and new and to discern in it something known. It's about being able to see what things are really like. And there is the rub. *Like*.

Before the new sinks into the night of habit and routine, there is a final reckoning to be done. This is the real work of Act Three, the final act of change, what needs to happen before the curtain closes. It's a process we touched on in the discussion of dreaming in the last chapter. For the new to become old, it needs to become *like* something. We need – if we are to respond when something new occurs – to know if this new thing is really news, or if it is like something we have seen before, and if an old response will do. We need to *call* it so we can *respond*. And if it is *like*, then how much easier, how much less work; if it ceases to be news then we can draw on our well-stocked armoury of habit to deal with it, without all the fuss and bother, the clumsiness and uncertainty, the preoccupation and arousal of the last few chapters.

The habit machine needs to be able to recognize the familiar, to abstract from the mess of what-just-happened the kernel of the known that will allow it to respond with a ready answer. After all, our survival might depend on it. The quicker we call it, the quicker we can respond. *Likening* is important work. It's important when we first meet the new, in discerning what it is, and in figuring out how much of the work of learning really needs to be done. And it's important once the new is old, for then we need a story about what it *was*, what-just-happened, for we need to call it something, to *tag* it so that we can use that tag to call up our newly formed response when something like it happens again. That will make the future easier, and our survival may depend on that. Calling is important work, for it is what allows our response to happen. Biased as we are to go with the least difficult and least energetically demanding response, we are also inclined to go with the easiest call, to see the new as familiar, if at all possible. Even when it is barely there, even when something new is really called for, we'll see the familiar if we possibly can, we'll call it known and then see it as we call it.

In the thick of it, in the spellbound stage of preoccupation and thrall, we are only aware of the jangling novelty thrilling through our nerves, of the unfamiliar moves pushing our heart and mind and will into new shapes, new responses. We don't quite know what to call it then, because the meaning, the story, the name, is being worked out. That's what this stage is about, that's what all the dreams and thoughts and speeches are for during this stage, as we try to get the hang of the story we are in. On the other side of that come the after-words. With the final bedding down, with the becoming accustomed, comes a story, a fitting into place of the new into our ongoing narrative. At twilight, as the new passes below the horizon and becomes familiar, we at last figure out what it really meant. In the throes and thick of it, the meaning is fluid and uncertain; in the settling down, in the crystallizing and forming, we get its sense – we get, or make, the sense of what just happened. The owl of Minerva, of wisdom and discernment, flies only at twilight, because only as the new fades into the night of routine do we figure out what it was like; and it is the figuring out, the calling, that allows the settling into routine to happen. We need to liken, to call, so that we can move on. It is definitive of the traumatic event that we *cannot* call it, that it isn't like anything else we have ever encountered.

Likening, the calling of names, and the telling of stories, is what allows us to get on with life.

Amelia's Whisper. We are at a party. Amelia and a hundred others are at a club, one of those clubs where the tribe is very tight-knit, where we sort of know most of the people and most of the people we know are there, one set of them at least, the set that Amelia and I hold in common. It's in Brixton, in London, in an old railway arch, dark and domed with brick, lit with red and strobes, loud and cosy, wild and fine. We are at the party and I don't quite know what to make of it. I'm dipping my toes, sipping the potions, trying to get into the spirit, but I'm not quite there yet. Amelia comes with her amazing open vivid eyes, and she talks to me. She tells me, over the music, in an intimate whisper, she tells me how on that day she had been in the supermarket. That day was sometime in late September 2001, just after the fall of the towers, and she had been in the supermarket, in London, then on high alert, steeling itself for trauma, and people had been in the supermarket packing trolleys high with tins and bottled water.

'They were stockpiling,' she says, 'and they were laughing about it. People were stockpiling food and water, so frightened they were laughing.' She had become so upset at this explicit terror that she started to cry and had to leave the supermarket. 'It's everywhere,' she says, up close, all whisper, all eyes, 'everyone is feeling the same fear.'

And suddenly I get the party. We both look around, and you can see it in the wildness, hear it in the massive insistent drum and bass, the bodies swilling beer, half-naked, pounding, grinning, crazy, waving, losing themselves or trying to. As Amelia's intimate and trembling truth leaves her lips, it frames the entire spectacle, the event. She has named the event. I totally get it, I can feel the mood, the post-apocalyptic tension, the dancers at the end of time both waving and drowning, ecstatic, abandoned, fuelled by terror. The scene transforms. This is what I remember most, the scene becoming, in that moment, *coherent*. It ceased to be fragments in my perception, ceased to be fragmented bits of this and that. It more than made sense, it became what it was.

Shorthand. Later I talk to my friend Paul about this, and he talks back about tagging. Paul is a blogger (there's a tag), who records his daily stuff online to share with others, and every little article has a tag, an index mark to name and file the kind of experience the entry contains. In the community in which he blogs, tagging is as much part of the expression of the person as the article it tags, an idiosyncratic flourish that can merely identify the nature of the entry, or add a layer of humour, or underline a strength of feeling unexpressed in the body of the text. Of course any index will always be shorter than what it indexes, for the unique will have to surrender to the similar, to the like. And this of course is what Amelia did, when she told me what the event was like. She tagged it, and in tagging made it what it will, for me at least, always be. She told the story of the event. So Paul and I talk about tags, and I am excited that he has another analogy for me. I think he is going to tell me about his personal system of classification and furnish me with examples of how daily we reduce our experience to a few adjectives and nouns. Instead, he tells me, writes to me, about Daniel.

Fragment from the Book of Daniel

Daniel was like a trauma, the way all good sex is basically a kind of trauma, you know? It's an event beyond words, words come clattering back in later, trying to pick up the pieces, put you back together, tell you that it was like this or like that, like something, whereas *at the time it was like nothing but itself*. So it was leaving Daniel. He still burns. I left him burning. I'll never see him again. I walked down the road, burning, fighting off the words, empty shells clattering in to try to take the shape of the event, of Daniel. I wanted to keep them at bay for a while, to keep the fire. This experience – plural, open, raw – would soon enough be tagged and meta-tagged, would be fragmented, labelled, contained and stored away, this open burning rawness would be reduced to an anecdote, a Livejournal entry and tag. As I walked, words and images buzzed around the fresh event, trying to force it from *sensation to significance*. Words and phrases, story fragments, buzzing round in competition with image flashes and still recurring visceral sensations, and an inner voice already starting to rehearse the story it would become. All these fucking *parasites* fighting to take over *what just happened*, reduce it, fragment it, contain and store it, as *like* this or that, and I want to defy them, I swat them away as I walk away from Daniel, for he was *like nothing else*. (my italics)

Ah, the event. The feel of what just happened. The thing that changed the landscape in which it appeared. How to hang onto it? You can't, not even if you want to, and Paul's rage against the dying of the fire of the event is palpable, and that of course became another tag for him, a meta-tag; that became partly what the 'Daniel' event was about, because in the end it has to be about, it has to be like, something. We don't remember events, we remember our stories about them. Before the new is packed away and stored for good, before it becomes the conditions for the future, the new normal that future novelty will disrupt, before then there needs to be a reckoning, an accounting and recounting. The story needs to be told, the event boxed, tagged, stored. Like it or not.

This is important work. Forming your version of events. I see it at work in Lenny, this storytelling work, as his conversation recurs repeatedly to the end of a friendship. No matter where our conversation begins, it circles back to this, as he tries to name what has ended, to give it narrative and meaning. I can hear him try to fix it, not fix as in repair, no, he's trying to make it settle, form it into a story about the end of a season. This process will happen through conversation and thought for all of us; recent events will star in both, and in dreams, until their plotlines are worked out, their narrative and shape are figured and fixed for good, until they are reduced to the shorthand by which they will henceforth be represented. So, *that's* what that was about.

You can't preserve the multiplicity of the event for ever, there just isn't the space or time.* Come back from a movie or a holiday or a

---

* So enjoy it whilst it's fresh.

difficult meeting and you'll be asked, 'What was it like?', and you'll talk about it, until eventually, if enough people ask you, you'll hear yourself repeating the same anecdotes and sentences, drawing the same conclusions. So *that's* what it was like. It's how memory works. We saw before how we only get to keep the gist of things. We need to reduce the unfamiliar to the known, to abstract from the plural open raw flux a picture and a story that can be filed away in shorthand, filed away and drawn on to recognize the like again, to know how to respond in the future.

This is important work that a rare few are incapable of doing. One such was the Russian stage mnemonist Solomon Shera-shevsky. He was studied by the psychologist Alexander Luria in the 1920s. Sherashevsky had a memory disorder, a disorder that meant, paradoxically, that he had a perfect memory, which he capitalized on to make his career. Sherashevsky could remember every sensory occurrence that had ever happened, or that he had ever imagined, with unfailing accuracy. The plural open raw remained so forever. And of course this was much more of a curse than a blessing, for Sherashevsky could not get the gist of things. For him all events remained irreducibly and problematically unique:

> Sherashevsky recognized a particular fence by its 'salty taste' and 'sharp piercing sound'. Another fence would have a different quality. Their commonality, as fences, was too vague for him to compre-hend. He couldn't categorize or forget differences or think abstractly . . . He had trouble recognizing people, because a face seen at three in the afternoon seemed different than that at nine at night. The same was true of voices, which in some people, accord-ing to Sherashevsky, 'change twenty or thirty times in the course of a day. Others don't notice this, I do.'*

We need to forget the new, the unique, the plural open raw. We need to reduce because otherwise, like Sherashevsky, we would

* Michael Greenberg, *Times Literary Supplement*, 5 December 2008.

eventually get lost in the clutter of our experience, unable to decide what it meant, or what mattered, or how to respond to it.

We need to know how we feel about things. The significance and moral weight of what just happened needs to be ascertained, not just the meaning but also the *feeling*. Faced with the truly new, in the thick of it, we are as likely to be as emotionally puzzled as we are cognitively. 'I don't know what to make of it' is often synonymous with 'I don't know what I am feeling'. Television is full of those fresh from trauma, being forced by chat-show hosts to practise and fix their grief or outrage, to whittle down the emotional complexity of the event, to reduce the messy blur of what just happened to the emotional shorthand by which it will be memorialized. 'I've never been so shocked'; 'that was the worst thing that ever happened to me'; 'I've never felt so betrayed'. Everything is HEADLINED, tagged, given a label inevitably shorter and less unique than the plural open raw reaction of the time of its occurrence, which fades even as they speak. Where its occurrence, its shock, was all about the newness and the never-seen-the-like, its subsidence will be all about what it is and isn't like, about how the event fits into their continuing version of themselves and how they feel about things.

This is important work, this forming of meaning and feeling. The neuro-cognitive scientists call this process 'somatic marking'. Things that happened, things that matter, will be fixed as more than meaning, they will be fixed as patterns of feeling, bodily sensation, and as an urge to respond in the way that you did before, so that, in the future, you will know, automatically, how you feel about things like that, and what to do about them. And as such you will know who you are.

This work is crucial, for our shorthand needs to be linked to our habits, *call needs coupling with response*. With a tagging system sufficiently elaborate and elaborated, we will get the gist of the present moment, tag it immediately *and* deploy our automatic response, summon the appropriate habit. Indeed, this formulation sounds far too deliberate. The event will bypass our elaborate and deliberate mind, cut to the chase of our emotional reaction which will summon the response before we can say 'What just happened?', because we, It, will know. The best our conscious mind can do is to interfere in this process and stay the trigger finger of habit for long enough for us to figure out if this is *really* like that. But usually the mechanism is pretty smart, and we don't stop to question its decisions too much. That's just how we feel: that's just who we are and what we are like.

What Are You Like? It's not only events that we need to tag. Soon this will be over, this chapter, this book. Quite soon, when this is finished, I will have to make decisions. Not the kind of decisions which we have encountered the consequences of so far, like which friend and their trauma to use for illustration. Those decisions are just about what fragments to put next, like collage, and often one will be as good as another, and if not, I'll remove it and replace it with another; ongoing decisions about the logic of the argument, the building of sufficient weight of image and example, shoring the fragments. That I can do.

But once this is over, what exactly is finished? Sara, a friend in publishing, tells me I'll have to find my *trait unaire*, my USP, my unique selling point. I will have to form an act of identification, assume an image, take some fragment, aspect, piece of this and let it try and represent the whole, a whole I can't even adequately represent to myself or to others in an hour of conversation let alone in a title, a pitch or a blurb. Paradoxically, ironically, to figure out what my unique selling point is, I will have to figure out what else this is *like*. This is what I am deferring, this passing into the circulation of already existing products, identification, branding. This is what I am resisting, the transformation, the fixing, when I assume an image to represent me to the world. The flight at twilight. I don't want to come out.

The assumption of the armour of an alienating identity, which will mark with its rigid structure the subject's entire mental development.*

* Jacques Lacan, 'The Mirror Stage as Formative of the Function of the "I" as Revealed in Psychoanalytic Experience' in *Écrits: A Selection*, trans. Alan Sheridan (Tavistock/Routledge, 1977).

I've said before, most of the psychoanalysts put fragmentation at the heart of us, and see the 'unity' of self – the ego, the imago, the identity, the agent who represents us – as a kind of necessary compromise forced on us by the fact that others need something to tag us with, and we in turn need to decide what we are like. The French philosopher Alain Badiou makes a similar point:

> Every representation of myself is the fictional imposition of a unity upon infinite component multiples. There is no doubt that this fiction is generally held together by interest.*

As does the African-American comedian Chris Rock:

> When you meet somebody for the first time, you're not meeting them, you're meeting their representative.†

Vicky sees it at work in her friend Elsie, this identity work, this self-branding, this deciding on one's interests. They are both sixteen. Elsie is annoying Vicky more and more, maybe because she is making explicit something Vicky is doing more subtly and tentatively, something that all sixteen-year-olds are doing somehow. 'Oh My God,' says Elsie, using the 'Oh My God' you first heard on *Friends*, 'Oh. My. God. I am such a . . .'

- ➢ slut
- ➢ emo
- ➢ snob
- ➢ addict.

'Oh My God, I'm So Loud,' was her most recent, shouted in Starbucks. But forgive her – we're all it, or have been.

---

* Alain Badiou, *Ethics. An Essay on the Understanding of Evil* (1998; English trans. Verso, 2001).
† Chris Rock, *Bigger & Blacker* tour (1999).

Identity work, important work, deciding and becoming what you are like, through confession and repetition. Couples are always doing it, particularly in the early stages, and so are groups of friends, indeed, any unit trying to maintain or advertise its coherence will have to do some version of this work, will have to say something like: that's not what we like, that's not the kind of people we are, we don't approve of that sort of thing, that's not how it happens with us, we're not like that. Proclaiming the tags that will allow them to take their place in the public world of values. We're like this.

Parts and Wholes. There is a new movement in queer theory, one that questions the core value of the gay liberation movement, the importance of Coming Out. In essence, their objection is to tagging, to the use of one feature of the person, the fragment that is their sexuality, to identify the whole. For, in doing so, the now 'gay' individual becomes processed, labelled and likened to a set of people, practices and values with which they may in fact feel little affinity. And there's something rather safe about it too, the messy blur of sexuality is cleaned up for public consumption, neatly divided in two, with the straight world on one side and the gays over there – them and us. It keeps things perhaps a little too contained and simple.

But on the other hand, the lack of narrative, of containment, can be difficult to bear. I can think of two relationships where people who were once lovers ended this phase but did not come to an end, and in them both there was some painful version of 'what are we now?' played out by at least one of the pair. 'There is no us!' shouted Lenny at his ex-lover, a phrase born of the frustration at the neither-fish-nor-fowl dyad they had become, a *sui generis* intimacy, more than friends but less than lovers, a relationship without a name, without a publicly available narrative. Always one partner is less able to bear this, demanding a tag. 'He always wanted a name for us,' says his ex, 'he was always asking, "What are we, what are we doing?"' And his ex, annoyingly, would quote Keats at him, the Keats quote that he had learned from Lenny, about negative capability, the poet's true gift:

> when a man is capable of being in uncertainties, Mysteries, doubts, without any irritable reaching after fact and reason . . .*

. . . or name, or tag, or story.

But still we reach. We want names and tags, reasons and stories, about what we are and what things are like. Few can stay inside the closet, the Schrödinger's box of neither this nor that, for we want to know where and what we are, and where and what everyone else is too. This work is important. Think of how your perception would change if you learned that your new acquaintance was a lawyer, a schizophrenic, a president or a killer. Like Amelia's whisper at the club, this one small fragment, this one piece of the whole will form the frame and frame the whole, identify it and contain it. This is what tags and stories are for. We need the identity. In the sociology of health and illness, they talk about chaos narratives. When people cannot come up with a coherent story to account for their disease or their distress, they become more distressed, more diseased, because the story is a container, a place to put the fragments and make them cohere.

We need a story. For sure, there will be a loss of uniqueness, a reduction of the plural open raw to sentences, stories, tags. But, good, because what just happened needs to be put away. If it went on resonating in all its complexity, its plurality, we would get stuck there, as Sherashevsky did, and we really need to move on – to the next moment and the next. So long as we remain undecided in the face of what-just-happened, we remain preoccupied and anxious. For as long as it is undecided, it is a threat to our equanimity. We need to contain the present, and put it away. This is the enormous

* Letter reproduced in *The Complete Poetical Works and Letters of John Keats* (Houghton Mifflin, 1899).

and irresistible power of naming and storytelling – its power of *containment* allows us to let go and move on. Without it we would wander lost in a world of fragments, neither knowing who we were or what we felt, neither knowing what things were called, or how we should respond to them.

This is important work, this work of call and response, and urgent too, but in its very urgency and importance lies our weakness for seeing and doing the same as always. Which is fine, if things really are the same as always, if matters are routine, if business really is as usual. And, in the daily grind of daily living, most things are. But pan the camera out beyond the confines of the day and take in the narrative sweep of a life over time. An organism designed to automate call and response may struggle, as it ages, with the tide of chance and change; it may struggle to stay awake and responsive to reality as it freshly unfolds. An organism so good at running on Automatic may find itself reluctant to respond to any other call than its own present momentum, it may get stuck in an automotive movement that is really going nowhere, nowhere desirable, honourable, sane or new.

We are now back where we started, to asking who's in charge and who is calling the shots.

Calling

... man is compared to a house in which there is a multitude of
servants but no master and no steward. The servants have all
forgotten their duties; no one wants to do what he ought; everyone
tries to be master, if only for a moment ...

G. I. Gurdjieff*

The Servants of the Soul. Of course, usually what is in charge is
something fairly mundane and our struggles are less cinema, more
soap opera. Most of the time, we are under the dictatorship of the
what-just-happened, reacting to correct the impact that it has had
on our current well-being. Something happens which upsets the
status quo. It is then quickly tagged with what it means and how it
makes us feel, and this then acts as a call to arms, with the appropriate team of agents deployed in response to get us feeling OK again.
We live in a constant dialogue between ease and unease, mediated
by call and response. We could spend long stretches doing nothing
but that.

But we can do more. As Gurdjieff reminds us that the servants
can indeed take over the household, so the *Bhagavad-Gita* reminds
us that the servants are there to be deployed for *any* work:

'I am not doing any work,' thinks the man who is in harmony, who
sees the truth. For in seeing or hearing, smelling or touching, in

* Quoted in P. D. Ouspensky, *In Search of the Miraculous* (Harcourt, Inc., 1949).

eating or walking, or sleeping, or breathing, in talking or grasping or relaxing, and even in opening or closing his eyes, he remembers: 'It is the servants of my soul that are working.'*

There is a great emphasis in the *Bhagavad-Gita* on discerning and doing one's work and recognition that in finding a purpose – a higher calling, and the work it entails – we achieve a measure of peace and harmony. Mundanely we know and feel this when we become caught up in a project, when we go with the flow of a task where the rhythm is complex and seamless, where the what-just-happened is in active dialogue with the what-we-just-did. We all like to lose ourselves sometimes. In sex, cooking, DIY, writing, cleaning or conversation. We like those times when we give our agents and routines, the servants of our soul, something less boring to do than pleasuring and repeating themselves.

And the potential for grandeur is there. We are, after all, an army of agents who can turn their collective hand to anything, depending on what is calling the shots. We are a multiple held loosely together by a common interest, a common calling. So if the calling changes, then so does the whole, though all the elements stay the same. We are capable of many convocations. And it's hard not to talk of value here, of lower and higher callings and so to trace the camber of the slope whose summit could be something honourable.

Imagine a mountain. At the bottom of this notional slope we will place, as Dante did, the idiots of addiction, jerking to the demands of bare and naked craving. A few tiers up are those caught up in the dance of mere reaction, avoiding pain, increasing pleasure. Their movements are circular and stiff as they repetitively tend to their aversions and their appetites. There are legions of these, racked according to how much room they give themselves to make some small movement, by how much they are more than just the sum of their attempts to feel OK. At the top of this level you'll find those who, while still in the grip of reaction, can also hold a decent

---

* *Bhagavad-Gita*, 5: 8–9.

conversation, can also look outside themselves and laugh and love. You wouldn't mind spending time with some of them, and you'll see them caught up in other projects, dancing to something other than the inner idiot. By this point we are moving out of Hell and into Purgatory. Moving further up into the light and open air, we see those who are mostly moved by something other than themselves, whose army of agents are in the service of something other than the appeasement of their appetites. You can see that their movements are less predictable as they respond to the call of creation, as they try to nurture and bring into being their projects and their visions. Pleasure and pain are more incidental to them. As our camera crane ascends further, as we head to the summit, the space narrows and the populace thins. Near the top, we witness the rare and stunning spectacle of those who dance to an alien music. People transfigured by destinies and missions, transformed by passion, sustained by fidelity, careless of self, plummeting recklessly forward into life. Behold them dying for the cause, these revolutionaries, maniacs and lovers. And at the very top, there are one or two holy fools, the heroes of compassion, the incarnations of Love.

Ah, the epic finish, the grand finale.

For a minute there, I lost myself.

Upstream. There is a yearning note in some music, where the note changes not by stopping and another note following, but by sustaining itself and modulating, becoming a different version of itself. You find it in Indian devotional raga music – a sustained note on the sitar is gradually pushed up, as if something insistent is moving through it, transforming it, or as if the note itself is trying to reach up, to change or transcend itself. You find it in most voices that are in any way moving, like Billie Holiday's, where the direction is more often down than up, from major to minor. Either way it touches something in us and pulls us along with it, up or down. It raises our spirits, or wakens within us the longing for our spirits to rise. So, too, does the spectacle of real ethical goodness, of someone, despite the odds, behaving well, nobly, honourably, courageously. This also catches at something in us and tugs at it. Acts of difficult kindness, of real love and duty, can move us, make us want to move, get better. The movie-makers know this, that we are as affected by the spectacle of real ethical behaviour as we are by horror. It touches something just as visceral. It awakens in us the desire for change, to be better than ourselves.

We are fascinated by transformation, by the spectacle of someone stepping out of the dance and changing in response to a new calling. It's particularly compelling the way it is now being presented in the media. The base metal of the fat and the uncouth is transmuted into the gold of the thin and the beautiful; the lost, the shy and the lonely become superstars. In just half an hour, or half a page, with pictures, before and after. It's astonishing. Real people really changing before your very eyes. It is magical because we know it is so unlikely. We struggle to stay afloat while the televisually transformed are effortlessly swimming up the stream of entropy, shedding habits the way that snakes shed skin. They look so happy and it looked so easy. Well, that's editing, a large budget, extensive physical, technical and emotional support, expert advisers and the presence of a camera crew for you. We know that. These transformations aren't quite right or real but they make us smile anyway, as at a good magic show, because the illusion is lovely. They tickle our fancy for change.

However, past a certain point, transformation becomes rather uncanny. Back at the top of our notional summit, the extravagantly transformed, those who have boot-strapped themselves to some higher place, are a rare and unsettling spectacle, and one that the cameras are unlikely to capture in the process of becoming. They *do* awaken something in us, but often as not it is a profound anticipatory weariness or a simple bafflement that anyone could push themselves against the force of habit and the drift of chaos quite so, well, forcefully. They enter another register altogether. At the top of the higher calling's premier league of ethical celebrity, the all-time greats – Jesus, Buddha, Muhammad – are figures who have ceased to be seen as human. They have truly transformed to the extent that we cannot imagine them having been like us in the first place. Our disbelief speaks of the profoundness of the change. There is something traumatic in that degree of transformation, which few would genuinely wish for. Even as we move down the league, back to the more obviously human – hello Dalai Lama, Gandhi, Mother Theresa, Martin Luther King, Nelson Mandela – there is still in these lives an inhuman dimension, a dedication to something other than the getting and keeping of comfort. There is an *askesis*, an ethical self-discipline more formidable than the most exhausting physical training regime and, well, frankly, most of us can't be bothered. These people are touchstones or icons or inspirations, but we rarely take them as role models. We want a little more ease than that. Easier to walk the beaten path, to go with the flow, repeat ourselves, to drift and sink, to become a little worse every day.

To walk away from one's habits, from the stock calls and stock responses, is like trying to swim upstream, against the tide of ourselves. It's difficult, rarely done and it's a version of what we mean by 'getting better'. Beginning and then sustaining change is never easy, for as hard and terrible as they are, endings and beginnings are also very delicate times. Easily disturbed and derailed, easily discouraged. Just a little discouragement and you're back as you were. There is something disappointing, too, about these first steps. The clumsy and deliberate gestures that we described in Chapter 6 feel as though they will never feel right. The quickened energy, that brief glimpse of a better future and the yearning to be there, the glimpse of the Elsewhere we saw in Chapter 5, can be dispelled alarmingly quickly, the journey abandoned at the first sign of adversity, or even at the first faintly enticing distraction. Or we begin to feel the bite of the effort that this is really going to take. That's why dedication is necessary at the start of the walk away from habit, at the beginning of moving out of step with yourself. Dedication, fidelity to the fugitive impulse, to keep you going, to start things rolling, until the process develops a momentum of its own. And so we end, as we began, with dedication.

Dedication. My father and I used to go walking sometimes in the countryside that started just at the top of our road. There was one walk where, for a while, there was a view of a long straight road in front of us. It seemed we could see it dwindling away for miles. There was something thrilling in that view. It reminded me of the image in a book I had of Jack and the Beanstalk (see Figure 9). Jack, having climbed the beanstalk, stands, stranger in a strange land, at the beginning of a road. It stretches forever in front of him. He cups his hands over his eyes and looks to where it disappears into the hills on the horizon. There is such a feeling of the anxieties and excitements of beginning in that picture. The road does not lead immediately into a darkened wood, the way is straight and clear for a long time. But you know that by beginning, by putting one foot in front of the other, things will happen, unpredictable, unimaginable events and encounters. And he is about to begin.

Now, I was never a traveller. I have travelled a little, and to good effect, but the fact that I was somewhere else seemed incidental to the fact that my attention was released from routine, that a certain alertness was called for.

> But I see my mind is asleep. If it were always awake from now on, we would soon arrive at truth.*

That's what travel can do – force you to stay awake, focused. But I've met too many hardened travellers for whom travel is a habit, a way of staying asleep and avoiding the wakefulness that establishing a settled life would demand of them. It's the attention that matters. The sustained wakefulness and vigilance to the moment, to the task at hand, a degree of mindfulness that stays the trigger finger of mere repetition, call and response. That is one of the ingredients of

* Rimbaud, *A Season in Hell* (1873; New Directions, 1961).

transformation. It's why prayer and meditation are the keystones of all spiritual practices. Prayer, willed attention, is a form of sacrifice. In dedicating your focus to the present situation or an object or a person or a project, you renounce all others, including the getting and keeping of your own ease, and devote yourself to seeing what is really called for by the present moment. That is not necessarily an easy thing to do. This is what I hoped the writing of this

Figure 9. The Beginning of the Journey

book would be for me, a higher calling, a compelling project that would convoke this multiple self in some new and transfigured way. Become a sustained act of wakefulness. So I dedicated myself to this calling.

Surely, like Jack, I would meet my fairy godmother, my holy guardian angel, from whom I would receive guidance, develop courage and find treasure. No? Aren't these the rewards of the dedicated? Doesn't a sustained act of will lead to a magical transformation?

But I've been putting off this ending for months now. Stalled and circling at the end of the road, and at the prospect of a new beginning. Becoming the illustration of the possessed and mindless reactive life that is the recurring theme of this last chapter. Rather than end, or begin, or just put one foot in front of the other in wakeful, forward deliberate motion, it has been so much easier to let this man, this forty-four-year-old man, run himself on Automatic. By now he has (you could say he *is*) a fair collection of habits. A good man with a few bad habits, as a therapist once told him. And that's fine, when those habits are the little recurring refrains in an otherwise changing dance. Fine. But when habit is running the show?

Months on end, my Lord.

Only recently, the image occurred to me of the circle and the line. The circle, like the ever-decreasing diameters of Dante's Hell, which is nothing if not repetitive, standing for the ever-diminishing rounds of Automatic life. You can, as I did, watch yourself go round in circles. You can be as appalled as you like, watching yourself go on and on, like the girl from *The Exorcist*, screaming, 'Mother, make it stop!' as nevertheless her body continued its repetitive jerks. It will keep going until you or something stops it, and that takes more effort the more time you let it go on. It becomes more and more difficult to step out of the gyre, to leave the dance and begin to walk forward again, like Jack in the picture. To step out of the circle and begin to walk the line. A long, unpredictable line where you don't know what you'll meet, what will be called for. That's the enormous risk and can't-be-botheredness of this walking forward. It really is, however appalling, in many ways much more comfortable to stick with habit and let it run the show. For months.

But tonight, some combination of boredom and clarity, some little shoot of springtime strength, took me back to beginning, to beginning to walk and learning to walk forward into the end of this, this season, this project, this container, this calling.

This ends tonight. And I want to say this:

> How else can one write but of those things one doesn't know, or knows badly. It is precisely there that we imagine having something to say. We write only at the frontiers of our knowledge, at the border which separates our knowledge from our ignorance and transforms the one into the other.*

That's a kind of apology, and a kind of disclaimer, but more than that, a credo for moving forward, for walking the line, however many little circular diversions you and I might step back into on the way. For to push forward, to move away from the known, to make that one small movement, to step willingly into an Act Two of our own calling, does not come easy to us habit-machines. Nor is it always necessary, for maybe we are fine as we are. But sometimes it's good to go against your grain. When Kurt Cobain was asked why he had picked a particularly difficult song to cover, he replied: 'I want to struggle with the vocal'.

Like Deleuze, Cobain was reminding us that there is something bracing, awakening and arousing about putting habit at risk, about walking forward. If my example is anything to go by, our old routines will, left to their own devices, take over the house and slowly wreck it. But we can be more than this. If the habit-machine is in

---

* Gilles Deleuze, *Difference and Repetition* (1968; English trans. Athlone Press, 1994).

the service of a consciously chosen project, a set of values that we can stand beside and affirm, if it is responding to a thoroughly apprehended present, rather than repeating the past, then our acts are truly ours and not mere impulses.

It depends on who is calling the shots. The Automatic that is most of us needs guidance and direction. Like a film crew with a great cast and ample funding, our host of inner agents are ready to turn their hands to nearly anything. Left to their own devices, the result will be the downhill slide of a life dictated by whatever happened last, by happenstance and habit. This teeming crowd of talent that is us deserves better, a great script and strong direction. They, we, deserve a higher calling.

Ah, the rhetorical postures of something coming to an end.

Acknowledgements

This book had a long gestation, a relatively brief and painless birth and then (analogy collapses) lay dormant for about five years before becoming this public thing in your hands now. Within the book I've implicitly acknowledged – and explicitly dedicated it to – a lot of the people involved in the preparation and writing stages, but now I would like to mention some of those who have helped getting it out into the world.

The first step out of dormancy, and the first person to thank, was my dear friend Sara Holloway. She had worked in publishing for a long time, so I thought she would be a good pair of eyes to set it in front of to judge its world-worthiness. I still remember the text I got from her a few days later: 'I love your book.' From there things progressed quite quickly. Sara gave me a list of agents to approach and soon I found myself in the unanticipated position of having to choose between several. A luxury problem for sure, but nevertheless a difficult one. Subsequent events have confirmed the rightness of my choice, and so the next person to thanks is my agent, Patrick Walsh of Conville and Walsh. I still remember the email I got from him within a week of sending him the book: 'Can we meet?' We did, and I have not looked back. His dedication, charm and confidence – and that of his team – have expertly guided me through this publication process.

The season of dormancy officially ended at 10 p.m. on Friday, 11 January 2014, when I received a phone call from Patrick telling me we had secured a deal with Penguin. Of course, I still remember that, and the lunch a few days later when I met Stefan McGrath, the managing director of Penguin Press, and my editor-to-be, Laura Stickney. Immediately I knew I was in good hands, and that they not only got the book, they also got that I was a little freaked out by this rapidly accelerating ride: from zero to Penguin in months. I am immensely grateful to them for having the confidence to get so wholeheartedly behind the work of this first-time author. 'It's a bit like an arranged marriage,' said Stefan at lunch, 'we're stuck with each other now.' So far it is working out beautifully. Laura has been a delight to work with and negotiated my nerves and my ego with equal grace and helped make this a much better book. I also want to thank the publicity team at Penguin, particularly the director Rosie Glaisher and my publicist Annabel Huxley, who have shepherded me through the part of this journey that I was least prepared for.

A few more personal thanks. Tim Rapley, friend and colleague, helped me think through some of the more sociological parts of the book, and took a professional/ethnographic interest in its journey of becoming public that not only helped at the time but also generated material which will inform the next book. Colin Hamilton from Northumbria University and Lilian Edwards from Strathclyde University looked over the chapters on memory (Colin) and on persona and the law (Lilian) and contributed ideas and text which helped to shape these parts. Of course, any mistakes are mine. Finally, thanks to my two guides/counselors of recent years, Philip and Simone, who in their very different ways have helped me to find the courage to finally get this out.

Grateful acknowledgement is given to the following for permission to reproduce copyright material. Lines from 'These Boots Are Made for Walkin', by Lee Hazlewood, copyright © Universal Music Publishing Ltd. Lines from 'The Daily Things We Do', by Philip Larkin (1979), in *The Complete Poems of Philip Larkin*, copyright © Faber & Faber Ltd. Lines from 'Debit Night', by John Ashbery, from *Notes from the Air: Selected Later Poems* (1st edition), copyright © Carcanet Press Ltd. Lines from 'The Eighth Elegy', by Rainer Maria Rilke, from *Duino Elegies: with English Translations by C. F. MacIntyre*, copyright © University of California Press. Lines from *The Hogfather* (2006), Sky television adaption of Terry Pratchett's novel, copyright © Sky One British Sky Broadcasting Ltd. Lines from 'Donal Og' ('Young Daniel') by Anonymous, trans. Lady Augusta Gregory, from Seamus Heaney and Ted Hughes (eds.) *The Rattlebag*, copyright © Faber & Faber Ltd. Lines from 'Dockery and Son' (1963) by Philip Larkin, from *The Whitsun Weddings*, New Edition, copyright © Faber & Faber Ltd. *Every effort has been made to contact copyright holders. The author and publisher would be glad to amend in future editions any errors or omissions brought to their attention.*